Spoken langua
applied linguistics

D0474890

CAMBRIDGE
UNIVERSITY PRESS

PUBLISHED BY THE PRESS SYNDICATE OF THE UNIVERSITY OF CAMBRIDGE
The Pitt Building, Trumpington Street, Cambridge CB2 1RP, United Kingdom

CAMBRIDGE UNIVERSITY PRESS
The Edinburgh Building, Cambridge CB2 2RU, United Kingdom
40 West 20th Street, New York, NY 10011–4211, USA
10 Stamford Road, Oakleigh, Melbourne 3166, Australia

First published 1998   410
                        M

Typeset in 9.5/13.5pt Swift Regular [CE]

A catalogue record for this book is available from the British Library

Library of Congress Cataloging-in-Publication Data

McCarthy, Michael, 1947–
Spoken language and applied linguistics / Michael McCarthy.
    p.   cm.
Includes bibliographical references.
ISBN 0-521-59769-2 (pbk.: alk. paper). – ISBN 0-521-59213-5 (hardback: alk. paper)
1. Colloquial language.   2. Language and languages – Study and teaching.
I. Title.
P 408.M38   1998   98-39755 CIP
401'.41–dc21

Printed in the United Kingdom at the University Press, Cambridge

ISBN 0 521 59213 5 Hardback
ISBN 0 521 59769 2 Paperback

To the dead and living of old Splott, Cardiff

Contents

Acknowledgements

This book owes thanks to many colleagues and friends who have given intellectual and personal support during its production. Firstly, as always, the book would not be what it is without the productive partnership I have enjoyed over the last decade with Ronald Carter, colleague and friend. Ron has read the whole book, and offered comments and insights both formally and informally, for which I am extremely grateful. Four other colleagues in the Department of English Studies at the University of Nottingham who have been instrumental in my thinking also deserve special thanks: Rebecca Hughes, Roger Smith, Martha Jones and Julia Harrison. At Cambridge University Press, Jean Hudson, who provided the initial design for the CANCODE corpus, which this book is based on, has provided me with many insights on the data, as well as the flow of data itself. The one million words of the first phase of the CANCODE corpus would not have existed without the contributions made to it by fellow-researchers and students at Nottingham: Bethan Benwell (now at the University of Stirling), who recorded hours of small-group university tutorials and who understands spoken genres better than most, deserves especial thanks. Other colleagues and friends around the world whose comments (in formal contexts such as conferences as well as informal ones) have inspired many of the statements in this book include the late David Brazil, David Nunan, Nik Coupland, Justine Coupland, Guy Cook, Robert Cockcroft, Paul Drew, Doug Biber, Sue Conrad, Michael Lewis, Mike Baynham, Joan Cutting, Nkonko Kamwangamalu, Joanna Channell, John Sinclair, Norbert Schmitt, Mike Hoey, Merrill Swain, Mike Makosch, Jim Lantolf, Tony Fitzpatrick, Aria Merkestein, Geoff Tranter, Almut Koester, Bruce Pye, Matilde Grunhage-Monetti, Barry O'Sullivan, Jeff Stranks and Nurdan Özbek. Without the encouragement of Alison Sharpe, Commissioning Editor at CUP, and the continued, generous support of CUP, and Colin Hayes, ELT Group Director, in particular, for the CANCODE project, I would not now be writing these words. I put the finishing touches to the manuscript while enjoying a semester as Visiting Professor in Linguistics at Cornell University, USA, where colleagues in the Department of Modern Languages (especially Hongyin Tao and Linda Waugh) have offered invaluable intellectual support in the book's final stages of revision. As always, the book would probably never have happened without the personal and domestic support of my partner Jeanne McCarten. All of these people deserve a big thank you. An anonymous reviewer for CUP was very patient with earlier versions of the manuscript and offered detailed suggestions for improvement. In the final editing and preparation for publication, under the guidance of Mickey Bonin of CUP, comments and suggestions for final revisions from him, Geraldine Mark and Jane Clifford have proved invaluable. Whatever faults remain in the book must be laid entirely at my door.

The author

Michael McCarthy is Professor of Applied Linguistics in the Department of English Studies at the University of Nottingham, UK. He entered the English Language Teaching profession in 1966 and has since then taught English in Spain, The Netherlands, Great Britain, Sweden and Malaysia. He has taught at the Universities of Cambridge, Wales, Birmingham and Nottingham. He has published several books, including *Vocabulary and Language Teaching* (with Ron Carter, Longman 1988), *Vocabulary* (Oxford University Press 1990), *Discourse Analysis for Language Teachers* (Cambridge University Press 1991), *Language as Discourse* (with Ron Carter, Longman 1994), *English Vocabulary in Use* (with Felicity O'Dell, Cambridge University Press 1994), *Exploring Spoken English* (with Ron Carter, Cambridge University Press 1997), *Second Language Vocabulary* (with Norbert Schmitt, Cambridge University Press 1997), as well as many academic articles on vocabulary and on spoken discourse. He is also Series Editor of the Cambridge University Press *Word Routes/Word Selector* series of bilingual thesauruses.

1
Introduction

1.1 Genesis of this book

This book is the result of ten years of study of the spoken language and its importance to language teaching. Initially this involved transcribing and analysing brief conversational extracts, and latterly (but with the same aim always in mind) examining large numbers of conversational extracts brought together in the CANCODE (Cambridge and Nottingham Corpus of Discourse in English) corpus in the Department of English Studies at the University of Nottingham (see 1.2 below). Over those years, I have presented and published papers and written books, sometimes of my sole authorship, often with my close colleague and co-researcher Ronald Carter (and recently also with my colleague Rebecca Hughes). Those papers and books have led me more and more into questions concerning everyday spoken language as a model for language teaching, how different types of spoken language can be classified, and what status the spoken language should have as an object of study within applied linguistics in general. That is essentially what this book is about, and the CANCODE corpus has been an invaluable tool in getting answers to (some of) these questions.

1.2 Overview

The book brings together revised versions of papers published over the period 1988–1996 and some new, previously unpublished chapters, all drawing on corpus data, occasionally quantitatively, but mostly qualitatively, for it is in the latter that I see the greatest potential for gathering useful pedagogical insights from close observation of how people 'do' everyday talk. In this first chapter I outline the CANCODE corpus project, upon which most of this book is based. I have tried to contextualise it with reference to other corpus projects. The chapter also takes a historical glance at the status of spoken language in language study and the

1

teaching of languages over the centuries. There is a tendency in applied linguistics nowadays to consider anything published more than five years ago as ancient, and a historical perspective is often absent from MA course syllabuses and professional textbooks. I firmly believe that we have much to learn from our scholastic predecessors, not least in that their achievements may urge humility upon us when we are tempted to think that our 'science' has made massive steps forward. Chapter 1 then, concludes with a note on the contributions made by speech-act theory and discourse- and conversation-analysis to our improved understanding of spoken language, though with notes of caution expressed along the way.

Chapter 2 attempts to construct the outlines of a theory of spoken genre. In particular it focuses on the variation present in speech events which, nonetheless, still share a lot of common features. Chapter 2 also stresses the importance of looking for evidence that participants themselves are aware that they are engaging in the creation of genres, and that we are not just indulging in analytical fancies. We find such evidence partly in terms of the participants' orientation towards past events and upcoming ones, the need for agreement among participants as to 'where they are' in the talk and the need to bring into effect procedures whereby events assume their final shape that we as analysts can recognise. Chapter 2 uses the CANCODE corpus matrix outlined in Chapter 1 to show how extracts display similarities at the lexico-grammatical level which correspond to higher-order features of generically-oriented activity. The chapter concludes that genre will always remain a difficult notion to pin down because social activity is prone to so much variation. What is apparent is that seen as a whole, behaviour is integrated: the transactional, the interactional, the goal-orientation, the relationships among participants, and the local lexico-grammatical details all complement each other. Chapters 1 and 2 together are an attempt to sketch out a theory of spoken language that will have pedagogical relevance.

Chapter 3 raises the question of just what should and can be taught about the spoken language. I take a number of concepts from discourse analysis and conversation analysis and examine existing research to try to get answers to questions such as 'Do these features matter?', 'Are they universal?', 'Are they likely to be transferred, and if so, under what sorts of learning conditions?', 'How can syllabuses and methodologies take such features into account?'. The features examined include exchanges and adjacency pairs, discourse markers, ellipsis, openings and closings, and in each case I look for the lexical and grammatical realisations of the features and their cultural import, using CANCODE data examples to illustrate the way speakers encode the features. The chapter concludes that there is a good deal to be incorporated into teaching from the research available in the areas looked at, but that traditional, presentation-based methodologies are inadequate to the task. I propose an alternative methodology outlined by Carter and McCarthy (1995b) based on what we call 'the three I's', in contrast to the traditional 'three Ps' of presentation, practice and production.

Chapters 4 and 5 are both devoted to issues of grammar. Chapter 4 argues for a discourse-based view of grammatical choice, and uses spoken data to substantiate the claim that certain aspects of grammar are best understood when examined in context. I try to demonstrate that sometimes we need to re-think how we group items in grammatical paradigms, taking the words *it*, *this* and *that* as examples. I then move the discussion on to the treatment of the past perfect, and attempt to show how choice of that tense is discoursally motivated, rather than by some deterministic rules about time. The chapter continues in this vein, examining features that are differently distributed in spoken and written data, and a typically spoken feature that has long caused problems for grammarians, the English *get*-passive. Central to the thread of discussion in the chapter is the advocacy of the usefulness in language teaching of probabilistic statements (statements about the most likely conditions of occurrence of a form), rather than only viewing grammar as deterministic rules. I conclude that a discourse-based view of grammar, backed up by spoken data, is extremely illuminating and has direct consequences for what and how we teach in grammar classes.

Chapter 5 pre-empts two possible dangers: (a) that we may rush off and assume that everything is different in spoken grammar and that nothing we say about written language has any validity for the description and the teaching of spoken language, or (b), equally dangerously, that we should assume that descriptions of the written grammar can simply be imported wholesale into spoken grammars. Taking a discoursal framework built on the work of the late Eugene Winter, the chapter looks at how sequences of verb tense choices can 'frame' whole written texts and spoken episodes, and how these framing functions are found in both spoken and written. The data shows that the realisations of these functions are in some cases the same in spoken and written, but also that their realisations are sometimes crucially different. This evidence is used to support the arguments that contextual grammars as advocated by Winter are indeed very powerful descriptive instruments, and that spoken grammatical features cannot always be assumed to follow the same realisations as their written functional counterparts. It is also an exercise in showing the usefulness of direct comparisons between written and spoken texts.

Chapters 6 and 7 shift the focus to vocabulary, but still within the perspective of a spoken discourse-based approach. Chapter 6 begins by laying out some of the constraints inherent in multi-party interaction that are likely to influence vocabulary selection, and then examines various lexical features in spoken language extracts. The question of lexical density is discussed, and especially the sorts of vocabulary found in low-density, language-in-action episodes. These types of vocabulary present the teacher with challenges that traditional, content-based notions of vocabulary do not need to concern themselves with. From there, the chapter shifts to looking at how speakers take up one another's vocabulary choices, either to progress or to hold up the smooth development of the talk, and how the role of listener is just as important as that of main speaker in building the vocabulary of an interaction, especially in oral narratives. Wider issues of the differences between spoken and written vocabulary lists generated from corpora are then examined, and the sorts of problems frequency-counts raise for teaching are touched upon. The chapter concludes that training learners' observational powers might be just as useful as pumping them with large numbers of new words.

Chapter 7 is about idioms, a subject most language teachers can identify with as part of the stock-in-trade of vocabulary teaching, especially at higher levels of proficiency, and yet one that has rarely been dealt with from a discourse perspective, and one where available information on usage in everyday spoken language is scant. After discussing problems of definition, I offer data from spoken narratives to support the claim that idiom selection is not random, but plays a key evaluative role in storytelling. The chapter then casts its net wider, with examples from discourses where speakers are commenting on aspects of their world in general; once again, idioms have an important evaluative role to play. The data shows that speakers often 'unpack' the literal meanings buried in idioms and create extended puns and images that thread through the text. Idioms also have a role in reinforcing cultural membership. The chapter ends with a discussion of the problems of teaching idioms, and the kinds of exercises and contexts that can be exploited while remaining faithful to a discourse-oriented approach.

The last chapter of the book returns to a grammatical area that usually has its place in any language-learning syllabus: reported speech. We begin by comparing two extremes in speech-reporting: classic literature and everyday conversational storytelling. The conversational reporting looks at first glance to be rather impoverished when compared with great literature, but I attempt to show its richness and flexibility. I then look at other spoken reporting strategies, such as past continuous reporting verbs and the narrative historical present. With the quantified evidence from the CANCODE corpus, the chapter then compares what is frequent in the corpus with what is usually found in literary reporting, and shows that the corpus examples are very varied, serving a variety of strategic functions. The chapter ends with a general set of recommendations for teaching speech reporting, as well as a general conclusion on the book as a whole. (There is a glossary of terms on pages 176–81.)

1.3 The CANCODE corpus and its context

The CANCODE (Cambridge and Nottingham Corpus of Discourse in English) project was established in the Department of English Studies at the University of Nottingham, UK, with the help of a generous research grant from Cambridge University Press, the publisher of the present work and (to date) of two other works (Carter and McCarthy 1997a, and McCarthy and Carter 1997a) which draw on CANCODE material. A complete list of publications based on CANCODE is given at the end of this book. Cambridge University Press's support enabled Ronald Carter, me and our research assistant Jean Hudson to assemble an initial corpus of 1,061,274 running words of informal spoken English, completed in 1996. Further support from Cambridge University Press is, at the time of writing, enabling us (with the help of our new additional assistant, Julia Harrison) to expand the corpus to five million words.

It must seem, to a profession dazzled by ever larger language corpora, a rather puny enterprise to be working with only a million (or even five million) words. Corpora now regularly consist of hundreds of millions of words and the race to be first to hit a billion is undoubtedly one that will run in tandem with the tick of the clock towards the new millennium. Technology seems boundless and gigantic corpora can now be marshalled with an case that would have been considered pure science fiction when I entered the ELT profession in 1966. CANCODE, therefore, is numerically small by today's standards. It is also relatively modest even by the standards established some time ago by pioneers in corpus linguistics.

It would be unfair, however, to judge CANCODE's size only in relation to huge written or mixed written/spoken corpora. More important is to consider it in relation to the development of spoken corpora in general, and to the problems that make spoken corpora much more difficult to assemble than written ones. Spoken corpora are not new: anthropologists and dialectologists have long used tape-recorded data as a major source of evidence (Biber 1990), and such work continues (for example, the Northern Ireland spoken corpus described by Kirk 1992). Some of the earliest spoken investigations were carried out within the study of child language acquisition (an example of this is the child-language word-frequency analyses described in Beier, Starkweather and Miller 1967).[1] A notable early spoken corpus project of the kind that has since become quite common was the *Oral Vocabulary of the Australian Worker (OVAW)* (Schonell *et al.* 1956 gives a full account of the data and its collection). The *OVAW* corpus consisted of some 500,000 words of spoken language and is still very useful for anyone interested in idiomatic words and phrases in speech (e.g. Schonell *et al.* 1956: p. 67), a subject I pursue further in Chapter 7 of this book using CANCODE data. The *OVAW* also records the ubiquitous discourse markers found in everyday spoken language. A decade after *OVAW*, the Davis-Howes Count of Spoken English (Howes 1966) in the USA brought together half a million words of interviews with university students and hospital patients, and produced some interesting statistics for spoken usage.

Also in the 1960s a spoken-word count for Russian was published (Vakar 1966), which was small (based only on 10,000 words taken from drama texts), but which offered useful statistics about text coverage of high-frequency words. The University of Leuven Drama Corpus (approximately one million words from contemporary plays; see Engels 1988 for details) continued this tradition of using drama texts as a model for the spoken language (see also the reference to Vanrespaille 1991 in Chapter 4). Further evidence that literary (or at least written-fiction-based) corpora can also be useful for the comparative study of spoken language may be seen in the work of researchers investigating the 1.5 million-word TOSCA corpus at the University of Nijmegen (e.g. see Oostdijk's 1990 study of fictional dialogue, based on TOSCA).

Meanwhile, in Great Britain, the half-million-word spoken segment of the London-Lund corpus (itself a half of the one-million-word spoken/ written Survey of English Usage (SEU) at University College London; see Svartvik 1990), and the conversational transcripts available in Svartvik and Quirk (1980) have been instrumental in some very important investigations of the vocabulary of everyday spoken English (see McCarthy and Carter 1997a for further examples). Nowadays, as noted above, gigantic corpus projects such as the COBUILD Bank of English (see Moon 1997 for a recent description of the project) and the British National Corpus (see Crowdy 1993 and Rundell 1995a and 1995b for details of design and content) contain considerable amounts of spoken English data, including broadcast speech as well as everyday unrehearsed conversation. Broadcast data of many different types form the basis of the British English Lancaster/IBM spoken corpus (see Knowles 1990). In the USA, work by Chafe and his colleagues, initially based on the British London-Lund spoken corpus design (Chafe, Du Bois and Thompson 1991), has developed into larger enterprises such as the five-million word Longman Spoken American Corpus (see Stern 1997), which Biber and others are investigating to great effect, and which is planned to feed directly into language-learning resources.

Australian English has been subjected to corpus analysis in the Macquarie University corpus project (see Collins and Peters 1988), and by Eggins and Slade (1997), who look at everyday conversational activities such as gossiping. Also important is the ICE (International Corpus of English) project, which plans to bring together parallel corpora of one million words from 18 different countries where English is either the main language or an official language. The samples in the ICE corpus include 300 spoken texts, although these include many scripted samples, and broadcast interviews and discussions, with only 90 samples being face-to-face informal conversations (see Nelson 1996; also Fang 1995). Spoken corpora have, therefore, come of age, and many lessons have been learnt along the way. What all the projects mentioned so far have contributed to our understanding of spoken language and of corpora in general is massive. Amongst other things, we have gained a better understanding of the types of talk people engage in, instead of simply assuming that the text typologies of written language applied the same to spoken. We have gained a great deal of experience about transcription of speech (see 1.4 and 1.5 below). We have also learnt the advantages (e.g. time/cost) and disadvantages (e.g. lack of naturalness) of spoken corpora taken from broadcast or drama-text sources. Technology has enabled huge improvements in sound quality and unobtrusiveness of equipment. Last but not least, being aware of previous corpus projects helps to prevent the continual re-invention of the wheel, and builds up a body of evidence against which new corpora can be evaluated. Things have come a long way since the early recordings of dialectologists and anthropologists, but the design of spoken corpora is still often opportunistic ('get whatever data you can'). The CANCODE corpus has tried to avoid opportunism, and to follow design principles that will make its material maximally useful to teachers, pedagogically-oriented researchers and materials writers (see 1.4 below).

1.4 The CANCODE corpus and generic features

In setting up CANCODE, the research team decided to attempt to cover as many useful speech-types (useful in terms of language learners' perceived needs) as was feasible. However, the immediate problem was that no satisfactory classification of 'text types' for spoken language was available to parallel existing text typologies for written language. Chapter 2 discusses this problem within the framework of genre theory and demonstrates the theoretical stance the CANCODE team finally adopted. Here I shall outline the more practical steps that were necessary for the operationalisation of the notion of speech-types in the corpus design.

In the gathering of spoken data for corpora two approaches seem prevalent.[2] The first of these may be termed the 'demographic' approach, where a population of speakers is targeted and where that population records its spoken output over a given period of time. Biber (1993) stresses that the targeting of the population is much more important than sampling size. A well-chosen population sample would certainly seem, intuitively, to generate a qualitatively better corpus than mere opportunistic sampling or dumping of huge amounts of undifferentiated text simply to compete in the corpus 'numbers game' that is gripping the profession at the time of writing. Crowdy (1993) also argues for a demographic approach, which was used by the British National Corpus researchers. The other approach may be termed the 'genre' approach, in that it attempts to target not only a population of speakers but particular environments and contexts in which spoken language is produced. This approach does not simply rely on a pre-ordained notion of what a speech 'text' is. As Atkins et al (1992) have argued, there are various ways of defining textual boundaries in speech (e.g. the moment interlocutors come together or part, or the marking of opening and closing features linguistically). The genre approach tries to seek a balance between speaker, environment, context and recurrent features. It has the advantage that the corpus can be analysed from different perspectives (e.g. types of speakers, emergent text types, situation types, etc.). It has the disadvantage that genre is an ill-defined notion in the study of spoken language in general (see Chapter 2). In the genre approach, decisions have to be made about situational/contextual types as well as population types, and these decisions are by no means straightforward. The CANCODE project, which is based on a genre approach, confronted the problem of generic coverage by attempting to control contextual variables of different kinds in the collection of data. The data once collected could then be examined for 'episodes' (or linguistically marked speech events) that displayed similar linguistic patterning at both the global levels and the local levels. This will be exemplified below. The resultant model provides a proposed classification that brings out the commonality of spoken episodes; it does so in a way that offers the possibility of linking their contextual and social features directly with the lexico-grammatical 'nuts-and-bolts' of their step-by-step creation. The model eschews categories such as 'written-to-be-spoken' or 'rehearsed spoken', which have traditionally informed the study of variation in speech and writing (see Crystal 1995 for a good recent discussion). This is because (a) it is very difficult to know whether something is one thing or another (e.g. a radio interview, or a university tutorial) and (b) the CANCODE team decided to focus on, wherever possible, unrehearsed, non-formal talk.[3]

Five broad contexts for data collection based on the type of relationship among participants were identified (principally by the team's corpus manager, Jean Hudson):

Transactional
Professional
Pedagogical
Socialising
Intimate

Transactional relationships were defined as those where speakers display needs or imperatives and move towards satisfying those needs in a goal-oriented fashion outside of the contexts of professional, socialising or intimate relationships. A clear example would be day-to-day service encounters in shops, restaurants, etc., between servers and customers, transacting goods, information or services. *Professional* relationships are displayed in talk between professional colleagues in professional situations (e.g. informal company meetings, staff meetings, desk-to-desk talk).

Pedagogical relations are those between teachers and their students and student–student (e.g. informal tutorial conversations, pair- and group-work). *Socialising*[4] relations accord with social or cultural activities entered upon by participants but not in professional or intimate settings (e.g. a group of friends preparing a party, talking with a stranger on a train). *Socialising* is thus one of the most common categories, covering much of our day-to-day activity. *Intimate* relations pertain between family members or close friends in private, non-professional settings.

For each of these categories, three typical goal-types were posited:

> Provision of information
> Collaborative tasks
> Collaborative ideas

Provision of information is predominantly uni-directional, with one party imparting information to others. The role of information-giver may, of course, rotate among participants, but the dominant motivation for the talk is information-giving (e.g. an enquiry at a tourist information office). *Collaborative tasks* show speakers interacting with their physical environment while talking (e.g. two people packing a car prior to a journey). *Collaborative ideas* are concerned with the interactive sharing of thoughts, judgements, opinions and attitudes. Just as the context-types are broad and refer to predominant rather than exclusive traits, so too are the goal-types.

Some examples of how the categories were operationalised are given in figure 1:

Context-type	Goal-type	Example
Transactional	Information provision	Tourist information office requests for information
Professional	Information provision	Company sales conference, informal informational talks
Pedagogical	Collaborative ideas	University small-group tutorial
Socialising	Collaborative task	Relatives and friends preparing food for a party
Intimate	Collaborative ideas	Mother and daughter discuss family matters

Figure 1: Examples of operationalised categories

The five broad context-types and the three goal-types for each one yielded a matrix of 15 cells, each of which were targeted to be filled with data samples complying with the context- and goal-types. Although the initial target was to gather approximately 65,000 running words per cell, it did not prove feasible to fill each cell with the same amount of data. All kinds of data can be very sensitive and participants reluctant to release it (e.g. intimate conversation, business plans). However, wherever possible, a balance has been sought to cover the broad types within the corpus, and adjustments were, and are being, constantly made to the make-up of individual cells. The progress from one million to five million includes the target of filling some of the 'less full' cells of the matrix. If this proves difficult or impossible, it will be a useful evaluation of the corpus design, and this, in CANCODE's terms, is important. In the past, corpora have tended to become fossilised, either because the initial design is rigidly and uncompromisingly held to, or because a particular numerical target has been achieved. The corpus thus becomes a 'finished object'. The CANCODE project has in-built, ongoing evaluation of its structure and of its size, the former relating to the viability of the cellular model as it stands, the latter in relation to the recoverability of information with sufficient power of generality. This second problem includes the fact that, for many high-frequency grammatical structures, even one million words yields too much information, and sub-samples have to be extracted, while other, low-frequency words and structures (e.g. -ing clauses) suggest that larger amounts of data might be necessary. This continuous evaluation process is central to CANCODE's development, and the corpus becomes more of what Sinclair (1995) calls a 'flow of data'.[5]

The data samples assembled as the corpus builds provide possibilities for comparisons over and above the particular settings in which they were recorded. For instance, what does a 'socialising' (more public) collaborative task have in common with one conducted in an intimate setting? How does decision-making in the home (a goal-sub-type) reflect the same generic activity as decision-making in the workplace? If only partial answers can be found to such questions, then the possibility of useful genre-oriented classification translatable into typological frameworks for spoken language pedagogy would be within grasp. All along, though, it must be remembered that the *products* of the classifications exemplified in figure 1 are *samples of spoken text*; they are not themselves the speech genres. We are moving towards building a bridge between genre and text-typology rather than 'capturing' generic activity when we pluck out recurrent features that have left their traces in the spoken transcripts. It is such textual samples that are the raw data for the subsequent chapters of this book. Their recurrent features reflect, in different ways, the generic activity their participants are engaged in; Chapter 2 goes into greater detail as to how such activity is manifested in lexico-grammatical and discoursal features of the extracts that comprise the cellular structure of the corpus. As the corpus builds, there may be adjustments to make to that structure,[6] but its initial output has been promising in terms of pedagogical relevance, as the rest of this book attempts to show.

1.5 Continuing problems with spoken corpora

Despite the many successful projects undertaken to date, no-one could deny the continuing difficulties of assembling natural spoken data. Even the best recording equipment is apt to produce tapes with frustrating amounts of distracting noise (miraculously filtered out in real life by the human ear) when used anywhere outside of a soundproof recording studio. The catch is that good technical quality of sound recordings almost certainly means the recordings were made with a microphone obtrusively near the speakers, creating an unwanted degree of artificiality. The most natural, uninhibited data inevitably comes from recordings where technical quality has had to be sacrificed to unobtrusiveness of the equipment and its human operator. These problems have led some spoken language projects to opt for broadcast data, which is comparatively easy to collect. The CANCODE corpus has eschewed this temptation (though Carter and McCarthy 1997a include a local radio phone-in transcript to achieve maximum variety in their selection of spoken texts). We believe that a corpus biased towards large amounts of broadcast data would, in the main, not be the best model for the spoken language in relation to our overriding purpose. Our aim is the development of a description of spoken English that is relevant and useful to language teachers, especially in connection with the teaching of everyday listening and speaking skills in informal situations.

Transcription is also a (wickedly expensive) problem in terms of time and cost, as well as in terms of the system adopted. On average, an hour of recorded spoken data can take 20 hours to transcribe to a satisfactory degree of detail and accuracy, and, even then, there will inevitably be inaudible segments and segments undecipherable even to the original speakers (when these can be brought in as informants). So one is always dealing with an imperfect product, especially compared to the accuracy with which the latest optical text scanners can quickly gobble up vast amounts of written text and deposit them in machine-readable form into the maw of even a modestly powered desk-top computer. Good transcribers of spoken language have to be trained to the task. Even the best audio typists often simply 'miss' relevant details (highly relevant to the spoken discourse analyst) such as repetition and overlapping speaker-turns, and can be (as Watts 1989 most memorably demonstrated)[7] deaf to the presence of discourse markers and other 'little' words which become important the moment one starts to analyse the work they do in the creation of interaction.

1.6 Transcribing: the black hole on the trail to infinity

Cook (1990) speaks of the problems of transcribing real spoken data as potentially infinite, to the extent that one could, theoretically, include in transcription any amount of contextual data, from intonation and body language to what the participants were wearing, or the colour of the wallpaper in the room where they were talking. A veritable black hole lies at the end of such a quest. The CANCODE corpus has attempted to transcribe what we consider to be relevant to our research aims and has left unstated a number of phenomena which may well have played a role in the configuration of the original utterances. The principle has been a mix of perceived usefulness to language researchers and teachers, machine- and human-readability of the text, time and cost, and large dashes of common sense. Thus overlaps and interrupted utterances are marked, as are truncated words and (where feasible) the number of syllables occupied by a sub-audible segment (i.e. where the speech can be heard but not sufficiently to make sense of it) along with extralinguistic information where this helps the interpretation of the text (e.g. 'a baby is heard crying in the background'). Even with these restrictions on what ends up in the final transcription, the text as entered in the computer can look extremely messy and daunting to the reader who wishes to focus mainly on content. The following extract is (fortunately) not how things always look, but such segments do occur very frequently:

(1.1)

[Two men talking about gardening.]

<$1> Worms they're good.

<$2> Well balance of opinion on that is that er worms are generally good
    excepting <$=> er the wor= <\$=> the casting worms on lawns.

<$1> I don't think they <$O1> do any harm at all <\$O1>.

<$2> <$O1> <$=> That they on balance <\$=> on balance
        <\$O1> they do more harm than good.

<$1> I don't think I'd go to the trouble of getting rid of them.

<$4> <$G?> <$E> pause <\$E> No actually although we don't profess to be
    green we don't use pesticides.

<$3> Mm.

<$2> We don't use <$O2> fungicide either really do we <\$O2>.

<$4> <$O2> <$=> And we don't <\$=> Fungicide <\$O2> and+

<$2> Mm.

<$4> +only weed killer on the paths.

<$1> Mm.

The symbols <$1>, <$2>, etc. at the beginning of turns tells the computer
which speaker is speaking and enables researchers to get back to archived
information about individual speakers (e.g. age, gender, etc.) if required.
Symbols such as <$O1> and <\$O1> indicate the onset and end of overlaps
in competing speakers' turns (in this case the first such overlap in this
particular conversation). The 'equals' sign (=) indicates an unfinished
word or a unit truncated in some way, with <$=> and <\$=> showing
truncated clauses. <$G?> means an (uncountable) number of sub-audible
syllables. <$E> means 'extralinguistic information'. The + signs indicate
'latched on' talk (in this case <$4>'s final utterance is continuous, broken
only by <$2>'s *Mm*. A certain degree of 'normal' punctuation is included,
but with specialised meanings (e.g. a full stop means end of speaker turn
or low pitch termination of a unit within a turn).[8] (See glossary for an
explanation of terms.) Such information on the transcript makes extracts
virtually unreadable when they are being examined for their content,
and so the extracts reproduced in this book simplify the transcripts and
indicate overlaps in a more reader-friendly, visual form such that our
extract above might become:

(1.2)

[Two men talking about gardening.]

<S 01> Worms they're good.

<S 02> Well balance of opinion on that is that er worms are generally
good excepting, er the wor, the casting worms on lawns.

<S 01> I don't think they do any harm at all.

<S 02>   ⌊That they on balance, on balance they do more
harm than good.

<S 01> I don't think I'd go to the trouble of getting rid of them.

<S 04> [inaudible] ... no actually although we don't profess to be green
we don't use pesticides.

<S 03> Mm.

<S 02> We don't use fungicide either really do we.

<S 04>   ⌊And we don't, fungicide and

<S 02>   ⌊Mm.

<S 04>   ⌊only weed killer
on the paths.

<S 01> Mm.

In addition, we shall use square brackets to indicate inaudible segments,
and also to enclose back-channel utterances, that is when a listener says
something such as *mm, yeah, uhum* or suchlike simultaneously with (and
without interrupting the flow of) the speaker's talk, for example:

(1.3)

<S 05> The nicest pizza I've ever had was in Amsterdam [<S 03> oh yeah] I
had a brilliant pizza

We use three-point ellipsis (...) to indicate pauses between one and two
seconds; pauses of two seconds or longer are given in round brackets, in
seconds. Commas will be used where there is a truncated structure or re-
casting of the structure, and, for practical purposes, in any other place
where serious ambiguity might arise. These conventions are purely for
the readability of extracts in this book; for research, the original tapes
and transcripts were referred to.

1.7 The status of spoken language in applied linguistics

Although it may seem obvious that spoken language is primary and that
written language is secondary in terms of their occurrence in human

societies, written language became, over the centuries, quite under-standably, what linguists and applied linguists utilised as their baseline data. Written language was easy to observe and to codify, and the codifications themselves, in grammars and dictionaries, being written, took on a life of their own and acquired the status of 'correct' bench-marks to which any question or dispute about usage could be referred.[9] That is not to say that the spoken language was ignored in the study and description of language or within language teaching before the advent of tape-recorded corpora. In Tudor times, in Britain, for example, the *Vulgaria* (the textbooks from which grammar school pupils learnt Latin) were concerned with spoken Latin (see White 1932) and contained in their Latin teaching examples and their English translations many surprisingly colloquial utterances, such as *I was beten this morning* (i.e. beaten by the schoolmaster), and *Thou stynkest* (you stink) (White 1932: 19) and *This bredde is moulled or hore for longe keping* (this bread has gone off from being kept too long) (Horman 1519: 142). Likewise, Ben Jonson's (1640) English Grammar declared itself to be:

> For the benefit of all Strangers, out of his observation of the English Language now spoken, and in use. (front matter)

Jonson further stated that:

> Grammar is the art of true, and well speaking a language: the writing is but an accident. (*ibid.*)

Admittedly, Jonson went on to describe the English Language in Latin grammar terms, which had their origin in the study of written texts, but at least in Jonson's mind there was an important link between linguistic description, language use and speech. The sixteenth century onwards in Britain also saw a steady flow of manuals of rhetoric and eloquence in speech which lay emphasis on oratory, good pronunciation and enuncia-tion, etc. (see e.g. Sherry 1550; Peacham 1577; Holmes 1738; Herries 1773).[10] In the seventeenth and eighteenth centuries, there was, too, much scrutiny of the links between pronunciation and orthography in English (e.g. Robinson 1617; Watts 1740). The nineteenth century saw a veritable explosion of manuals describing the spoken languages of speech communities newly contacted by Europeans in locations such as New Zealand, the Orient, Africa, etc., where the absence of written texts or their inaccessibility made a practical necessity of confronting spoken tongues.[11] All of this goes to show that speech was never out of the minds of the community of scholars who described, taught and encouraged use of language(s) over the centuries, our applied linguist ancestors. It is nonetheless true that the dominance of classical models meant that the written code continued to overshadow how the language was conceived, with an underlying written bias.

In the twentieth century, some early advocates for the inclusion of spoken language within the purview of English teaching (both L1 and L2 teaching) may be found. Baker (1924) urged that mother-tongue English teaching should not just be grammar and theoretical principles of the language (and possibly essay writing), but should focus on language in its social context, as a tool for spoken communication. Baker's work was based on a survey of business men and women, and she concluded that the overwhelming language need was for spoken communication. The 1920s and 1930s also saw the rise of recorded media in the form of radio and talking cinema pictures, and this influenced the debate on the status of spoken language in education. Trueblood (1933), for instance, saw the growth of spoken mass media as a positive thing, promoting 'good' speech amongst the population. Displacements of peoples during the Second World War in Great Britain also contributed to the debate amongst mother-tongue teachers over the status of speech in education: evacuations from cities under threat from bombing to the countryside more acutely focused the differences in accent and possible communication problems among dialect groups. Within this climate, Compton spoke of the importance of training young people to speak in an 'easy, clear, reasonably exact, and friendly' way, without the influence of the 'dead hand of the elocutionary tradition' (1941: vi–vii). It was not long, with the advent of tape recorders, before voices were heard re-evaluating existing assumptions about grammatical description and advocating the collection of natural spoken data to counteract the written bias of existing grammars (e.g. Dykema 1949). Clark (1946) in a book entitled *Spoken English*, promises that grammar rules are illustrated with colloquial examples; however, the examples all seem still to have a strongly written flavour, and it was to be some time before the real influence of recording technology was felt.

From the point of view of English as a foreign language teaching, perhaps the most significant publication of the early part of the twentieth century was Palmer *et al*'s (1924) *A Grammar of Spoken English* (revised and rewritten by Kingdon in the third edition of 1969). This extraordinary book had much in it which a grammar of spoken language should ideally have, most notably its willingness to depart from single-sentence examples and to admit what we would now call (with the benefit of a terminology elaborated by discourse analysts in the last two decades) exchanges and whole utterances. Its examples often take more than one speaker into account, as in this illustration of ellipsis:

> A: It must be mended.
> B: What must? (p. 193)

or in auxiliary tagging:

> A: I must leave early.
> B: Yes, you must (p. 193)

The authors also acknowledge (*ibid*.: 283) that informal speech prefers co-ordination of clauses over embedding, and that some grammatical phenomena are the result of 'real-time' processing. The work of early pioneers such as Palmer is often forgotten nowadays amid the torrent of publications on language teaching that has rained on us since the early 1970s, but it should not be ignored, and its influence should not be underestimated.

1.8 Spoken language and communicative pedagogy

Despite the examples cited above of voices raised in favour of the spoken language, there is no gainsaying that spoken language remained the poor relation of the written in most foreign language teaching right up to the 1970s, even in those methodologies, such as the audio-lingual, that did encourage learners to speak and drill target usages. It was not that learners were not allowed to speak – the 'conversation class' and oral tests of various kinds have a long pedigree – but that the models of grammar and vocabulary that were the raw input were firmly based on the written code. This was not assisted by the dominance of Chomskyan views of language in studies of first- and second-language acquisition, views that happily sanctioned the use of invented data and that demoted real speech to the level of 'performance data' or held it to be downright corrupt (for a trenchant critique of Chomskyan-influenced applied linguistics, see Beaugrande 1997). The growing interest in speech-act theory in the 1970s and 1980s may have been hoped to change all that; indeed the communicative revolution that overtook English as a foreign language teaching has, ultimately, made it possible to talk about an applied linguistics more at ease with the study of spoken language as one of its important components. But the communicative enterprise has not been without its problems. Notional-functional approaches to language (e.g. Wilkins 1976) offered the possibility of wedding a view of language that focused on 'doing things with words' (i.e. language as social action rather than as abstract system) with the perceived need for 'real communication' in and out of the language classroom, both in writing and, more and more, in speech. One cannot help concluding, though, that mistakes were made along the way. Most notably, there was an overly simplistic tendency to equate speech-acts with particular linguistic formulae, a sort of 'phrasicon' of speech acts, or 'functions', as they were often popularly called, and there was a tendency simply to invent such formulae rather than examine real data.[12] This kind of reductionism inevitably led to generations of learners who were taught, for example, that in English, to disagree with someone, one might say *I disagree with you*, or some such formulaic utterance. Real data usually show speech-acts to be far more indirect and subtle in their unfolding. Disagreement is a good case. In the CANCODE corpus, there are only eight occasions where someone says *I disagree*, and none where *with you* follows. All eight occasions have some sort of modification which suggests a reluctance on the part of the speaker to utter such a bald statement; these include *I just disagree*, *I beg to disagree* (context: semi-formal meeting), *you see now I do disagree*, *I'm bound to disagree*, *I'd er, I'd disagree*. Where the verb-form *disagree* occurs, the contexts mostly either 'report' (or predict) disagreement with someone, or disagree with ideas and propositions, rather than people. This is just one of the kinds of problems a simplistic advocacy of speech-act theory can create with regard to raw material for language teaching. It would perhaps be reasonable to assume that other speech-acts behave in this way too, unfolding indirectly and in negotiation, with due sensitivity to interlocutors' personal face. It may also turn out that speech-act 'performative' verbs such as *disagree, complain, invite*, etc., may be more useful as a means of reporting, predicting or in some way talking *about* speech-acts, rather than performing them. Another point about speech acts that needs to be taken into account is their staging, in what Cohen (1996) refers to as 'semantic formulas', in that an act such as 'apology' may be composed of a number of phases (e.g. acknowledging responsibility, promising non-recurrence, etc.). What is more, in Cohen's view, speech acts imply sociocultural choices (concerning the appropriacy of particular acts in particular situations) as well as sociolinguistic choices (which linguistic form is the most appropriate). The point is that we can only appreciate the delicacy and subtlety of how speech acts are realised in spoken interaction by examining real data, and the early advocates of functional syllabuses and early investigations of learners' performances of speech acts signally failed to do so. None of this should surprise us, since the status of the spoken language as an object of study in the applied linguistic enterprise had yet to reach the level it deserved. Indeed, it is the feeling that things are still out of kilter with regard to our ambitions to teach 'real language', 'language for communication' and 'spoken skills' on the one hand, and our readiness (or otherwise) to accept revised descriptions of target languages based on what their speakers actually say on the other hand, which is a principal motivation of this book.

1.9 Discourse analysis, conversation analysis, and conclusion

The influence of discourse analysis and conversation analysis on language teaching and language acquisition studies has helped improve the status of real spoken data, not least in our endeavours to record and analyse the spoken output of our own learners, and Chapter 3 of this book refers to many such studies. Discourse analysts, with the useful insights they provide of language patterning above and beyond the sentence (see Cook 1989, and McCarthy 1991 for general surveys), offer frameworks for higher-order structuring of syllabuses and materials (see Aston 1988b; McCarthy and Carter 1994: ch. 5). The American traditions of conversation analysis and ethnomethodology, on the other hand, offer the possibility of fine-grain descriptions of how participants orient themselves towards mutual goals and negotiate their way forward in highly specific situations (see Psathas 1979, 1995; Atkinson and Heritage 1984; Boden and Zimmerman 1991). These insights can have direct applications in the construction of materials and activities for language teaching. Conversation analysts study 'talk in interaction'; all aspects of interaction (including the non-verbal and non-vocal) are considered relevant, and the recurrence of 'order' in talk is the crucial object of investigation (Psathas 1995: 3). Much of this sort of work, however, remains little known to many practising language teachers, and suspicions that studying the details of real spoken language, with all its stops and starts and faltering utterances is the study of illiteracy, slang and lazy speech habits abound. Even more worrying is the accusation that studying real speech is part of yet another conspiracy to impose southern British speech habits (or American speech) on a global community desirous of using English in culturally independent international contexts. Such views still abound in the language teaching profession and may be heard at any large language teaching conference (see also Prodromou 1997). This book has no such conspiracy in mind, but its author is curious to know just what 'global' or culture-free varieties of English would look like as a syllabus. Whatever work has been done on spoken British English, in corpus projects such as the Survey of English Usage, COBUILD, The British National Corpus, the ICE corpus or CANCODE, can (and ideally should) be duplicated for any dialect or sociolect of English (including 'global/international' English) and for any other language or dialect where there is a need for pedagogical modelling. The problems in deciding what can be called 'standard features' of spoken (or written) language will likely be the same whether it is British English or some other variety that is being described, as Mair (1992) has shown in relation to a corpus of 'standard' Caribbean English. The point is one has to start somewhere, and start with an open mind. Despite continuing problems, the prospects for better spoken corpora are good, and the contributions to language pedagogy and other applications thus made possible by both the quantitative and qualitative study of spoken language can only increase. This book respects the spoken language, sees it as our most important raw material in understanding language in its social context, and wishes its place within pedagogical models to be at the forefront. We will not jettison the written language; it too must remain the raw material, but we will more and more be able to compare the written and spoken in a way that will complement our understanding of both ways of communicating.

One final point that needs to be made is that it is not my position that *only* by examining corpora can language teachers come to understand how spoken language works. Corpora are useful, and are a good short-cut to seeing how language forms are used across a variety of users, but even the biggest spoken corpus pales into insignificance compared with the number of words 'processed' over the years by an adult language user. It must also be constantly remembered that computers may 'have knowledge' of what has been spoken, but cannot 'use' that knowledge. Proficient users of a language may not be so good at reflexive 'knowing', but use their knowledge whenever they speak. It is thus only when *good* observers of language combine their talents with the display and analysis of data by the computer that the optimum gains can be made. We must not, therefore, diminish the importance of experienced applied linguists' and language teachers' experience, observation and intuition (see Owen 1996 for persuasive arguments in favour of teachers' intuitions being respected). What is more, the absence of any feature from a corpus that actually does occur in use does not mean it is a 'freak', or any less worthy of study. Finally, it is my experience that 'reading' the corpus like a book or like a living drama script cannot be substituted by mere number-crunching by the computer. The right balance between quantitative and qualitative analysis of the corpus is crucial. We might illustrate this with the word *just*.

If we examine the more than 6,000 occurrences of this word in CANCODE, we see that, numerically, it overwhelmingly collocates to the 'right-hand side' with high-frequency verbs, such as *go, have, said, think, come, put, want* and *take*. These represent its 'semantic preferences' (Sinclair, personal communication). However, equally important are its 'left-hand' collocates, which reveal an unexpectedly high occurrence of modal verbs (*can, could, would, might, should*). These left-hand phenomena tell us much about the semantic 'prosody' (*ibid.*; see also Louw 1993) of *just*, in that it seems to occur in contexts of tentativeness/indirectness/face-saving (CANCODE examples include: *Could you just pass the gravy; Can you just take me through stage by stage; Could you just tell me about the department*). How this actually operates can then only really be fully appreciated by examining individual conversation segments in detail. *Just* therefore becomes a significant pragmatic particle, operating as a marker of politeness/indirectness, as well as retaining its traditional place in the language-teaching lexicon of combining with *have + past participle* to express recent events.[13] These qualitative judgements are crucial, and come only from close observation allied to the number-crunching power of the computer.[14] Being open to what the power of the computer can reveal and not approaching the data with any prejudice about how words work is part of that philosophy that Tognini-Bonelli (1996) refers to as a 'corpus-driven' philosophy. This she contrasts with a 'corpus-based' approach, where the philosophy and ideas are taken for granted beforehand, and the corpus is simply used to reinforce those ideas. The 'corpus-driven' way is the one which demands even more qualitative work, since the insights available are neither preconceived nor do they always simply leap out of the statistics. CANCODE is corpus-driven in this sense. However, we also reserve the term 'corpus-*informed*' for what we do with the insights in pedagogy, since insights alone are no guarantee of good teaching, and must be mediated in some way to create models that are meaningful and useful to language learners. This may include editing corpus extracts before using them in class, or constructing a role-play activity based on the phases of a particular spoken genre, rather than using an actual transcript as part of the activity. One final remark that needs to be made here is that we should also be aware of the dangers of taking over wholesale the metalanguage of written corpus studies when analysing spoken data. It is not for nothing that I put 'left-hand' and 'right-hand' in scare-quotes above. 'Left-hand' and 'right-hand' are page-driven metaphors, based on the written output of concordancing programs. If we are really true to spoken language, we should be talking about 'prior-' and 'post-'collocates, not left and right, since spoken language exists in time, not space. I return to this problem in section 3.2.2, in relation to grammatical terminology.

As long as we keep a cool head in the face of the exhilaration of computer power and vast arrays of text, we will not fall into the temptation of substituting cold numbers for the real people who actually produced the words.[15] I can identify best with Chafe's (1992) definition of the corpus linguist as someone attempting to understand language:

> '... by carefully observing extensive natural samples of it and then, with insight and imagination, constructing plausible understandings that encompass and explain those observations.'

That is what I shall try to live up to in the rest of this book.

Notes

1 Another example, which includes informal spoken language by adults, as well as by selected age groups of children from 6 years upwards, in a corpus of some 84,000 words, may be found in Carterette and Jones (1974).

2 I refer here to methodologies of data collection, not end use. For a discussion of the different motivations for the *use* of corpora, see Nelson (1992).

3 Inevitably, some more rehearsed types of discourse creep in here and there, for example (semi-) prepared classes and tutorials in the 'Pedagogical' category, or indeed, personal anecdotes, which may well often represent the umpteenth telling of a particular story, and therefore cannot truly be called 'unrehearsed'.

4 I am grateful for assistance with the choice of the term *socialising* for this category to Merrill Swain of OISE, University of Toronto, Canada. Merrill

persuaded me that our earlier name for the category, *sociocultural*, ran the risk of being too general and of overlapping confusingly with current work in socio-cultural theory and second language acquisition.

5 Sinclair actually has a slightly different idea in mind, that of the continuously self-updating corpus which takes advantage of an automatic inflow of new data (e.g. newspaper texts electronically imported); this is unrealistic with regard to spoken data in the present state of technology.

6 Atkins *et al* (1992) make the point that balance can only be achieved after an initial corpus has been built. One might suppose this to be as true of written corpora as it is of spoken, and one should not assume that existing text typologies for written language are a reliable reflection of the output of a speech community, most of whom rarely if ever indulge in the kinds of written *production* that inform some written corpora, even if they may have to read such material.

7 See also Stubbe and Holmes (1995) on public perceptions of discourse marker usage.

8 For information on the British National Corpus transcription methods for spoken language, see Crowdy (1994).

9 Mitchell (1957) states: 'It is certainly the common view that the written form is the only one deserving serious attention, study and cultivation.'

10 See also Hale (1903) for a summary of 16th century views of rhetoric. Courtly eloquence was also considered a selling-point for at least one language textbook for learning French '... as it is now spoken in the court of France', which included 'familiar dialogues, the niceties of the French tongue and twelve discourses.' (Boyer 1694).

11 The reader is referred to the Nineteenth Century bibliography on CD-ROM published by Chadwyck-Healey (1994), where numerous examples of language manuals based on 'exotic' (for the Westerners of that time) spoken languages may be found. This was true of Japanese, for instance (e.g. Mutsu 1894), but was also true the other way round (e.g. Coningham's 1894 course in business conversation 'Specially written for Japanese merchants dealing with foreigners.').

12 Even more fundamental problems are inherent in speech-act theory when applied across cultures, since the Western-based model of the individual act fails to take cultural and social contexts into account. See especially Rosaldo (1982) for a good critique of speech-act theory from a cross-cultural viewpoint.

13 Aijmer's (1985) study of *just* in 170,000 words of spoken language notes that it is many times more frequent in spoken rather than written language, but she too takes the matter much further than numerical proportions and interprets several different functions for the word, the most common being, in her data, an emphatic particle stressing the truth of the utterance. Sinclair's approach, involving semantic prosody, looks at a more general level of context, implying an even greater degree of qualitative analysis.

14 Another example of the need for qualitative interpretation is Tottie's (1983) discussion of the numerical fact that spoken English contains much more negation than written English, which she puts down to the pragmatics of interaction and the presence of acts such as explicit denials and rejections in the spoken.

15 Biber (1990) rightly urges that we should not be 'intimidated' by large corpora, and that smaller corpora are quite adequate for many purposes.

2

Spoken language and the notion of genre

2.1 Introduction

As stated in Chapter 1, in the design of the CANCODE corpus, it was decided to aim for adequate coverage of everyday genres that would be useful for pedagogical purposes. However, the notion of genre was not an easy one to define or to put into operation. Much good research has been done on genres in more specialised varieties of written language (most notably Swales 1990; also Christie 1986; Reid 1987; Martin 1992), and a broad definition can be gleaned from such work, which emphasises the socially-rooted nature of genres and their recognisability for participants within 'discourse communities'. In this respect, the fact that native language users can label written and spoken discourses with genre-names is clearly significant from the point of view of the recognisability of genres for participants themselves (see Walter 1988: 6); one does not have to be a linguist to recognise a 'story' or 'an argument'. Degrees of institutionality are also an important factor, and are most noticeable in highly conventionalised contexts such as academic writing, scientific and technical reports, literary genres such as the novel or the sonnet, and so on. Stubbs (1996: 12) stresses the mutually defining nature of institutions and genres (though he alternates between 'genre' and 'text-type' to refer to characteristic modes of expression): as institutions change and develop, so do the text-types that give voice to their activities. And yet the question remains as to how we recognise the relevant linguistic facts that reveal the presence of different genres, how participants orient towards them and how they show their recognition of them. These problems are particularly acute in spoken language, where, apart from well-studied genres such as service encounters (Merritt 1976; Hasan 1985; Ventola 1987; Aston 1988a; Iacobucci 1990) and narratives (Labov 1972; Jefferson 1978; Polanyi 1981; Goodwin 1984), many of the everyday forms of talk we engage in remain unclassified in generic terms. There have been a number of studies of 'register', i.e. the relationship between language features and their context of utterance (most notably Halliday 1978), much of which research focuses on levels of formality, interpersonal aspects of meaning, and spoken/written differences. Within the context of register studies, Biber's (1988) seminal work on the distinguishing features of written and spoken texts and how key language features cluster in different types of texts overlaps to some extent with the study of genre. In his later work, Biber uses the term 'register' for 'all aspects of variation in use' (Biber 1995: 9), and his research covers aspects that we shall here relate to genre. Register studies contribute greatly to an understanding of the different factors that influence linguistic choice, but do not offer a clear model of what, for example, a service encounter *is*, and how participants show their recognition of being engaged in such a generic activity.

2.2 Theories of speech genre

Perhaps the most notable early example of the type of study that will interest us in this section was Mitchell's (1957) investigation of the language of buying and selling at markets and shops in Cyrenaica. Mitchell's study was concerned with how different aspects of the context of situation (the participants, the setting, purposes, etc.) shaped the language that was used between buyers and sellers into a recognisable, patterned form of interaction. In a manner that has since seen echoes in the work of spoken genre analysts such as Hasan (1985) and Ventola (1987), Mitchell identified *stages* in service encounters he observed. Service encounters are interactions concerned with the transaction of goods, information and services, most typically exemplified by conversations in shops, restaurants, etc. The stages Mitchell identified included *salutation* → enquiry as to the object of sale → investigation of the object of sale → bargaining → conclusion. Within each stage, considerable variation is possible (for example, generated by different spatial relations between the participants – open air markets created different proxemics to those in closed markets), and whole transactions proceeded dynamically to construct texts, summed up by Mitchell in a memorable piece of imagery:

> A text is a kind of snowball, and every word or collocation in it is part of its own context, in the wider sense of this term; moreover, the snowball rolls now this way, now that.

Since Mitchell's seminal research, the notion of genre in spoken language has been explored by various other linguists, most notably Hymes (1972), who sees genre as a higher-order feature of speech events. Hymes stresses the dynamic characteristic of genres, and separates them from the speech event itself: a genre *may* coincide with a speech event, but genres can also occur within speech events, and the same genre can show variation in different speech events. Much of the subsequent debate has centred round this question of dynamism and local variation in the actual realisation of genres. Most linguists entering the debate seem to accept the (theoretical) existence of genres as recognisable norm-governed activities comprising varying degrees of institutionalised linguistic and non-linguistic behaviour. Coupland (1983) stresses this variability and offers the contrast between buying and selling stamps or newspapers and buying a holiday at a travel agent's: both are 'service encounters' but the latter is less likely to be played out as a ritual, following a template, and is likely to offer more possibilities for interactional/relational talk (i.e. talk oriented towards the establishment or maintenance of social relations) alongside the transactional talk that gets the business done. Bargiela-Chiappini and Harris (1995) make a similar point in distinguishing between the more institutionalised roles and goals in settings such as service encounters as compared with (in their case) business meetings, where activity may be more fluid and open to variation. Ylänne-McEwen (1997) has shown in great detail just how significantly the transactional and relational elements intertwine dynamically in service encounters (once again in the travel agency context); so much so that any modelling of genre would be fruitless without at least equal regard for the interactional/relational process as well as the transactional process(es) that are realised in typical encounters. Underlining this, Lindenfeld's (1990) study of small talk in urban French market places shows that relational 'small talk' is far from random, with vendors' small talk focusing mainly on utilitarian concerns, while customers' small talk tends strongly towards personal topics. Vendor and customer are both constructing and re-affirming their identities in the discourse. And, although predominantly expressed in ethnographic/conversation-analytic terms, Komter's (1991) study of job interviews also considers the small talk that usually takes place at the beginning of an interview as a legitimate phase in the unfolding interview process, echoing Mitchell's (1957) seminal study by talking of the 'phase structure' (p. 54) of the interview as a whole. Thompson (1997) in an in-depth study of university oral research presentations, also stresses the building of an appropriate relationship between speaker and audience and the co-construction of roles as being an integral part of the research presentation genre. The research presenter usually constructs him/herself as 'the modest, self-deprecating expert' (p. 334) and engages in complex facework, that is to say, protecting him/herself *and* the listeners from potential damage to mutual esteem, in order to establish and maintain that relationship. All this is important, since it suggests that models of genre that look upon relational episodes (episodes concerned with establishing and reinforcing social relations, as opposed to 'doing business') as things that merely 'crop up' on the record in an unpredictable way and disturb the normative 'flow' of the transactional elements of the genre are misleading and misguided. As we shall see below, a view of genre that gives equal attention to the relational unfolding must have significant implications for models of teaching the spoken language.

Some studies focus more on the variable sequences and mixing of activities that characterise genres. Duranti (1983) argues for a dynamic view of genre: the same genre can be performed in different ways according to the particular event, depending on who the speakers are, what their purposes are, where the genre occurs in sequence in the speech event, etc. Walter (1988: 2–3), in describing the generic characteristics of jury summations, also lays emphasis on the setting in which speech occurs as a crucial variable. Fairclough (1995: 167ff) highlights the way genres are sequenced and intermixed, using broadcast political discourse to exemplify how generic characteristics can change over time, in this case the process of what he calls the 'conversationalisation' of political discourse. The question of sequencing of elements, separating obligatory and optional elements, and, above all, how such elements are recognised amid the variation common in genre-building activity is stressed by Eggins and Slade (1997: 230–5), who also, in the way that the present book attempts to do, recognise the importance of lexico-grammatical analysis (e.g. lexical evaluation devices) as well as the analysis of elements beyond clause-level such as turn-taking or adjacency pairs.

Bakhtin's work (especially Bakhtin 1986) has been very influential in promoting an understanding of genre. Bakhtin's notion centres on the 'utterance', a somewhat abstract unit of talk which may vary in length from one speaker-turn to a whole monologue or (in written language) a whole novel, the defining feature being its termination at a point where an interlocutor may respond.[1] Bakhtin sees utterances as reflecting specific conditions and goals of different areas of human activity, which reflect those conditions and goals not only through their lexical, grammatical and phraseological configurations, but through their 'compositional structure' (1986: 60). Whilst utterances are locally configured and individual, 'each sphere in which language is used develops its own relatively stable types of these utterances' (*ibid.*), and these stable types are what constitute genres. Also central to genres for Bakhtin, as well as their relative stability, are their interpersonal aspects: 'each speech genre in each area of speech communication has its own typical conception of the addressee, and this defines it as a genre' (*ibid.*: 95). Kelly Hall (1995) reinforces the Bakhtinian perspective on interaction by exploring the interplay between the conventionalised/socio-historical meanings of the generic resources available to interactants and their practical strategies in each new situation they encounter. The importance of Bakhtin's work (and indirectly, too, that of Vygotsky; see Emerson 1983; Wertsch 1985) is that it breaks down the distinction between language as the product of the individual psyche and language as a social construct. Any theory of genre needs to include that perspective.

2.3 Goal-orientation in interaction

A picture of dynamism, fluidity, variability, mixing and negotiation emerges as the current consensus on spoken genres. This is to be expected, since conversationalists, especially in less rigidly institutionalised settings, are social animals with practical goals, and it is their goals that drive interaction, rather than some sense of obedience to generic norms. What is more, goals may not be fixed or pre-ordained, and may be emergent within the discourse (i.e. become apparent as a result of the interaction, rather than shaping it from the start), and multiple in nature (Tracy and Coupland 1990). Seeing genre in terms of participant goals is paradoxically both fruitful and problematic. If we take a goal-orientation view, we are able to integrate more satisfactorily the transactional elements of conversations and the relational/interactional elements: Iacobucci (1990), for example, shows how relational episodes in customer calls to a phone company are far from marginal or simply to be seen as 'side sequences', but are often clearly oriented towards fulfilling the transactional goals of the discourse more efficiently. What is often termed 'casual conversation' is perhaps the prime example of how useful the study of goal-orientation is. Casual conversation displays a variety of features which have led some to the view that it is too vague a notion to qualify for the label of genre, or else that it is defined by the very fact that, in terms of genre-mixing and embedding, 'anything goes'. Yet casual conversation is no less goal-driven than any other type of talk, even though the goals may be multiple, emergent and predominantly relational. In (2.1), a group of female students are chatting casually over a cup of tea on a Sunday evening. The first topic is 'Sundays', but it is clear that the overall purpose of the chat is to reinforce the camaraderie the students have built. Then there is a sudden, apparently incoherent switch in topic as one of the girls notices a piece of jewelry. Such switches are unproblematic in casual conversation, since the underlying relational goals can provide coherence, here taking the form of complimenting, admiring, approving, etc.

(2.1)

<S 03> I like Sunday nights for some reason, I don't know why.
<S 02> [laughs] cos you come home.
<S 03> I come home.
<S 02> You come home to us.
<S 01> And pig out.
<S 02> Yeah yeah.
<S 03> Sunday's a really nice day I think.
<S 02> It certainly is.
<S 03> It's a really nice relaxing day.
<S 02> It's an earring it's an earring
<S 03>　　　　　　　⌞Oh lovely oh, lovely.
<S 02> It's fallen apart a bit but
<S 03> It's quite a nice one actually, I like that I bet, is
　　　that supposed to be straight.
<S 02> Yeah.
<S 03> Oh I think it looks better like that.
<S 02> And there was another bit as well another dangly bit.
<S 03> What, attached to
<S 02>　　　　　　　　⌞The top bit
<S 03>　　　　　　　　　⌞That one
<S 02> Yeah … so it was even
<S 03>　　　　　　⌞Mobile earrings
<S 01> What, that looks better like that it looks better like.
　　　that

So, looking at relational goals can often help us understand casual conversation better than simply pursuing notions such as 'topic' or 'business in hand'. On the other side of the coin, the problem with studying participant goals is how one actually determines what the goals are, since these will often not be explicitly stated by participants, and the evidence for the analyst is usually indirect, and available only in the shape of phenomena such as 'formulations', and other similar kinds of linguistic evidence we shall consider below. Formulations are paraphrases of previous talk or summaries of positions reached in the ongoing talk, whereby participants articulate their view of the directions and goals of the unfolding discourse (Heritage and Watson 1979), which the analyst can use as direct evidence for statements about the way the discourse is progressing.

Goal-orientation is part and parcel of a view of genre that ties it closely to action. Dolz and Schneuwly (1996) see the link between genre and social action as a defining characteristic, and the ability to use the generic resources to achieve goals as inseparable from the ability to act in the immediate social situation. As always, however, such concepts are elusive in real data, and the analyst is working with imperfect records of what actually happened. Nonetheless, attempting to see things from the participants' viewpoint and how they articulate their own understandings at least avoids the worst excesses of the imposition of an order by the analyst, using rhetorical frameworks that may not reflect in any way the reality of the conversational encounter for those involved in it.

2.4 Genre as social compact

Here I shall take the line that genre is a useful concept that captures the recurrent, differing social compacts (i.e. co-operative sets of behaviour) that participants enter upon in the unfolding discourse process, whether writing or speaking. Sociologists provide frameworks whereby such social practices can be seen to create and reflect or are constrained by social structure. Sociolinguists and ethnographers in their turn observe how participants orient themselves towards necessary actions such as establishing roles and identities, protecting face, achieving goals, and so on. The genre analyst stands somewhere between these and actual texts; it is a series of textual extracts of recurrent events which are the genre analyst's hard evidence. The texts are not the genres in themselves, they are simply patterned traces of social activities. It is the task of the genre analyst to construct the bridge between texts and socially constituted activity so that texts become meaningful and can yield clues (probably no more) to their original, real-time processes of unfolding. To this end, the genre analyst may work with a variety of types of evidence, some more immanently linguistic than others. In this way, different types of 'generic activity' become the focus, rather than a static notion of 'genres'.[2]

But we must be sure that we can adduce at least some evidence that generic activity has a socio-psychological reality for language users and that we are not just creating an edifice for the satisfaction of analysts. Amongst the many linguistic traces of genre-oriented behaviour which may be found in texts are features that may be classified along four dimensions, which do suggest that generic activity has a real basis in language use. In addition to 'formulations', already mentioned above, I shall refer to these under the headings of 'expectations', 'recollections' and 'instantiations'.

Expectations

Speakers may signal expectations regarding the kind of generic activity that is to be negotiated prior to or in the course of realising social compacts. This corresponds more or less to what Kelly Hall (1995) refers to as 'expectations of the use of the [generic] resources', and is prospective. Most obviously one finds this in spoken narratives in the form of bids to embark upon story discourse:

(2.2)
[Speaker is talking about recent earthquakes in Greece.]

<S 01> About seven people died outside Athens, more down in Corinth **but this one guy, [laughs] this is true**, there was a guy down down in Mega and that town got you know it got really badly hit

Here, complex expectational signalling occurs in the transition from 'reported fact' to 'true story', including the topic-shift marker *but*, and the narrative-specific use of *this* instead of *a* (see Wald 1983), which opens up the expectation that a story is about to happen (with the usual suspension of casual turn-taking routines, a particular kind of listener-ship, etc.). Also there is laughter (despite the tragic context, this is going to be a funny anecdote), and a claim to truth, all of which express an expectation of the kind of activity that will unfold. There is, of course, no guarantee, in spoken interaction, that that is what will unfold. But not only narratives and institutionally-sequenced activities such as service encounters show evidence of participant expectations: the following is the opening talk between two people who are about to prepare a punch-bowl for a family party:

(2.3)

<S 01> **Right.**
<S 02> **Right** ... **so where.**
<S 01> **Oh we're going to need** more than that [**laughs**].
<S 02> **More** orange juice.

Here we have again quite complex expressions of expectations. The discourse-marker *right* sets up the expectation that a new phase of activity is about to commence, the *so* suggests order and considered action, *we're going to need more* signals an expectation of further actions which will be collaborative, not authoritarian, the *oh* and the laughter introduce an expectation of more relational/interactional elements of affect and social enjoyment. <S 02> converges with the expectation set up, echoing <S 01>'s use of *more*. This can be seen as a kind of communicative accommodation, as Giles *et al* (1991) define it, the 'strategy of adapting to each other's communicative behaviours'. We can sense generic activity emerging in the form of convergence on the level of actions and social relations, particular alignments of the participants, and an emerging compact (they are deciding as they go along how things will proceed; they are not pre-determined) that anticipates the activity that will follow. The text we are left with as analysts at the end of the activity (when the punch-bowl is full) may well be a 'language-in-action' generic type (i.e. an interaction where the language is generated directly by the actions of the participants; see section 6.2), but at its incipient stage it is simply working its way towards the product we as analysts call language-in-action, by setting up expectations along different social parameters that make the emergence of a language-in-action text most likely.

Recollections

Recollections refer to participants' past experiences of social activities and are manifest in the 'voices' (in the Bakhtinian sense)[3] from other discourses that echo in our discourses. These may be ritualised expressions that overtly mark activity as recurrent and patterned (e.g. *Did I tell you the one about ...?* indicating repeated joke-telling encounters, or *Okay as usual we're going to start by talking about* … as an opener to an informal meeting), or more oblique references to related or relevant other discourses. In (2.4) a group of students are chatting informally during a university small-group tutorial at a point where the tutor has left the room to allow the students to get on with some group-work uninhibited by his presence:

(2.4)

<S 01> It's really embarrassing, he always comes back into the room
when nobody's talking! [laughter]

This marking of the context as recurrent, and (in this case) unsatisfactorily so, manifests at least some desire to orient towards an ideal pattern of behaviour known and familiar to the participants (perhaps from other tutorials with different tutors): to the students, the tutorial is seen as an occasion when *they* should do the talking. That tutorial group-work should be a collaborative activity accompanied by discussion is recognised in the participants' amusement and/or discomfort (the laughter) at what they see as their past failures to play their proper roles. Their recollections are foregrounded here and clearly constrain their orientation towards the current activity. In (2.5), recorded at a hairdresser's, the activity that begins with the customer sitting in the cutting chair evokes previous occurrences, and the hairdresser acknowledges her own repeated 'voice':

(2.5)

[<S 01> hairdresser <S 02> customer]

<S 01> Now, are you all right?
<S 02> I'm fine thanks and you?
<S 01> I'm fine thank you, yes [<S 02> [laughs]] **are we cutting it as
normal or anything different or?**
<S 02> Erm **any suggestions,** or [laughs]? **I always ask you that**
<S 01> Without touching the back.
<S 02>   ⌊Ya.
<S 01> **I mean you could** go very wispy into the neck and sort of have a
wedge.
<S 02> Yeah.
<S 01> Keep that back wedge, keep that very into the neck like sort of
wedge.

Here it is as if the participants are trying to break free from their past pattern of behaviour. The use of *we* to the customer invokes informality and signals the regularity and echoic nature of things, but both parties then freely enter a more negotiative phase that results in a different discourse (we suppose) from the normal one, and new possibilities for convergence (that is to say the 'meeting of minds' that assists the discourse in efficiently achieveing its goals) are opened up.

Formulations

Formulations comment on the current, ongoing activity in terms of its present progress, with speakers periodically summing up where they think the discourse is. They are different from recollections, in that recollections refer to past, related discourses, linking current activity with previous experience. (2.6) carries on from (2.5), with the hairdresser and customer continuing to talk about what is to be done to the customer's hair:

(2.6)

<S 01> Would you like height?
<S 02> I do like height yes it has gone a bit sort of flat on the, yeah.
<S 01> That is the only thing.
<S 02> Yeah.
<S 01> I mean the top heavy here, but I know you like the height.
<S 02> You can do it as normal.
<S 01> Do you want it cut over your ears?
<S 02> You did that last time and I, it was alright but I wasn't too struck you know.
<S 01> **So basically you want it cut shorter?**
<S 02> **Yes.**

The hairdresser sums up the gist as she perceives it and offers it as a formulation of the current activity. The customer is, of course, free to reformulate the assessment. Such formulations enable participants to take the conversation in collaboration from one staging post to another.

Instantiations

The first hairdresser extract, (2.5), simultaneously allows us to talk about instantiations, the fourth and most frequent type of evidence crucial to understanding how genres unfold, for, in recognising the possibly socially stultifying nature of the repeated discourse, the hairdresser and customer activate a procedure for instantiating a new set of goals and it is such instantiations that give generic activities the fluidity and dynamism that make them often seem unamenable to classification. Instantiations are goal-oriented, both in the sense that they enable transactional elements to proceed more efficiently (for example, signalling a change of mind in ordering food in a restaurant, politely or otherwise cutting someone short to produce closure, etc.), and in that they may be interactionally-oriented (e.g. complimenting/joking), or both simultaneously (as the hairdresser extract would seem to be, creating both a better social bond and agreeing the business to be carried out). In (2.7), recorded in a bookshop, note how the customer instantiates the closure of the encounter, which takes several turns before it is accomplished and the assistant converges. The extract begins at a point where the assistant is explaining that the book the customer wants is not at present available but will be soon:

(2.7)
[<S 02> assistant <S 01> customer]

<S 02> It's on a stock list so we should have it back in the space [<S 01> mm [inaudible]] we don't have it here now.
<S 01> **I'll probably call here again, there's no particular**
<S 02>   ˪Sure, it's
going on here Handy's [inaudible] [<S 01> mm] space on here instead of
<S 01> Erm.
(8 secs)
<S 01> **Well I'll call back then**
<S 02>   ˪I'm sorry about that
<S 01>   ˪**see whether it's**
<S 02>   ˪I'll
make sure, it will take to, going through again but it erm probably will take a couple of days it'll be back [<S 01> **yes**] in stock again [<S 01> **yes**].
<S 01> **Thanks very much indeed.**
<S 02> **Thank you.**
<S 01> **Thank you.**

Expectations, recollections, formulations and instantiations are not always discrete entities, nor would we expect them to be, but they do offer a suggestive classification of different orientations towards generic activity. Such orientations are ever-present, but only manifest themselves overtly at particular points in the discourse when the goals require it. Thus what we have termed expectations might typically, but not necessarily, surface during openings, whilst instantiations would include decisions about topic change, closure, etc., and operationalising topic shift, pre-closure, etc. But, whereas it seems possible to talk about participants' more global orientation towards generic activity, considerable problems still remain in attributing generic significance to the numerous particular, selected language forms that comprise speech events. For anyone in search of a useful pedagogical model of genre, at some point the observation of form-functional correlations, whether locally (i.e. lexico-grammatically; see below), or also, ideally, on a more global scale (where we can observe regular patterns of events such as openings and closings, topic change, etc.), becomes a matter of great interest, and it is a problem that genre theorists have only supplied partial answers to. Below we shall consider some evidence for the generic significance of local, lexico-grammatical features present in texts of different types in the CANCODE corpus.

2.5 Integrating higher- and lower-order features

Comparisons of speech texts from different settings and with different participants often yield lexico-grammatical similarities that enable us to observe generic patterning wherein the lower-order features of lexis and grammar correspond to higher-order features of goal-type and context-type in the CANCODE matrix (see section 1.4). Equally, differences in distribution of lexico-grammatical features across texts may be significant of different context-types as well as goal-types. Biber and Finegan (1989) show this clearly with differences between written and spoken texts which can be in many respects similar, but in crucial respects different. For example, in their corpus, personal letters share features with many non-conversational spoken genres, but are distinguished by a greater number of 'affect markers' (e.g. *I feel*; see Biber 1988: 131–3 for further discussion). Let us compare some CANCODE extracts to illustrate this type of variation. (2.8) continues the punch-bowl filling task which opened in (2.3) above. More speakers now participate, a mixture of close family relations and more distant ones, all assembled for a family party. The problem under discussion is how to cool the punch down quickly.

(2.8)

<S 01> If you put this in the freezer
<S 02>   ⌞Yes
<S 01>   ⌞That'll cool it down quicker won't
        it.
<S 02> Yes and it won't freeze
<S 01>   ⌞No no
<S 02>   ⌞Cos of the alcohol anyway so.
(4 secs)
<S 03> Oh yeah there should be room in the top here.
<S 01> Mm yeah that'll cool it down.
<S 04>   ⌞Erm there's erm two of them.
<S 01> That'll cool it down very quickly.
<S 02> Orange ... oh.
<S 05> Too much orange in there is there Tone.
<S 02> No there wasn't enough orange.
<S 05> Well the extra bit you've got there.

The goal-type is a collaborative task (see section 1.4) and the context is socialising (i.e. not intimate at this moment, even though some of the participants, being close family members, may sometimes behave intimately). We might safely say that there is a high degree of shared knowledge, both in terms of the goal and in the fact that the physical setting is immediate and visible. The atmosphere is relaxed and informal. Speech is not constant, and silences, intolerable in other contexts (e.g. the four seconds indicated), are acceptable while action is ongoing. These features are reflected at the lexico-grammatical level. Immediacy of context and the close relationship between the words used and the task being carried out (what Ure 1971 calls 'language-in-action') is reflected in a high number of deictic items (*this, the, here, there*, etc.) that point to things in the immediate environment, discourse markers (*oh, well*), and a low number of full lexical words (since things do not need to be named). These lexical words are sometimes repeated (*cool, orange*), so that the lexical density of the text (a measure that counts the number of contentful, lexical items as a percentage of all the words in the text) is only around 22% (see section 6.2 for a further example and discussion), which is very low (the average density for all texts, written and spoken together, usually comes out at round 40% for full content items). Contractions of subject and verb abound, and there is also a possible ellipsis of initial *there is* in *Too much orange in there is there Tone* (though this could equally well be simply considered as a feature of flexible word-order in highly informal speech).

If we shift the context to an intimate one (brother and sister, at home, alone, packing things for sister to go away to university), we see some of the same features again, with some accentuated:

(2.9)
[<S 01> sister <S 02> brother]

<S 01> Mm can we try and get this stuff downstairs.
<S 02> Well you take that, you give yourself a er hernia ... so is this this
    styling brush going in or, it won't go in will it.
<S 01> Which one ... I'm gonna use it.
<S 02 Oh right so you want it left up here.
<S 01 Yeah.
(14 secs)
<S 01> Cos I got er things like plates and.
<S 02> I'll leave the stereo somewhere where you can't find it okay.
<S 01> I'm not going without that.
(4 secs)
<S 01> Helen's just gonna go right.
<S 02> Don't they look after it, it was all, it was all dusty when I got it
    back off holiday, looks cleaner again, only cleaned it before I came
    back from university.
<S 01> I'm wearing this.
<S 02> Oh yeah I was gonna take them down actually.

The degree of shared knowledge is high here in terms of the immediate physical setting, but lower in terms of the goal, i.e. precisely which items must be packed, which the sister must decide. Unsurprisingly, the lexical density is higher (28.5%), corresponding to the wider range of items in the environment, from which important selections have to be made by the sister, but it is still low, well below Ure's 40% general average for all texts. Two of the lexical items are vague, general ones (*stuff, things*), appropriate to an intimate and relaxed relationship. There is still a high degree of deixis (*this, that, the, down,* etc.), action-oriented discourse markers (*oh right, oh yeah*), and subject ellipsis in *(It) looks cleaner again* and *(I) only cleaned it,* as well as subject- verb contractions in quantity. There is a directness that is unproblematic in the intimate relationship (in the sound recording the *you's are stressed,* as: well *YOU take that, YOU give yourself a hernia*). Long silences are also unproblematic (e.g. 14 seconds). (2.8) and (2.9) thus do seem to have much in common, enabling us to talk of generic commonality in which activity, convergence towards transactional and relational goals, along with the differences in the relationships pertaining among participants, can be seen reflected in local linguistic choice. The further example of 'language-in-action' given in section 6.2 only serves to underline this view.

If we shift to a different goal-sub-type within the general heading of 'collaborative tasks' (see section 1.4), decision-making for future action (i.e. not the simultaneous tie between language and action of the previous two extracts), we see a different pattern of features which again varies internally depending on relation-type. In (2.10), a married couple are at home, planning their next holiday in the presence of two close family relatives who are house-guests; the relationship is intimate.

(2.10)
[<S 01> the husband <S 02> the wife <S 03> female house guest]

<S 01> Mm that's interesting [<S 01> what] there's two places offering
    deals at the same hotel let's compare them.
(6 secs)
<S 02> Bit dear.
<S 03> Yeah one's by boat and one's by plane.
<S 01> Oh I see.
(7 secs)
<S 01> It's even the same library shot they've got of the hotel.
<S 02> Why don't you have a look and see if we should take the car or go
    on the train have look at *The Rough Guide* and see.
<S 01>   ⌊I think we should go by
    train.
<S 02> Do you think, take the car to Felixstowe and go over on the boat.
<S 01> Yeah we haven't got to worry about parking then and finding our
    way back.

<S 02> Well have a look at *The Rough Guide* and see what it says about train travel.

<S 01> I don't want to at the moment I'm too tired.

<S 02> Oh come on do it.

<S 03> I'll do it I will plan your holiday [laughter].

<S 01> You two managers get together and leave me and Dave to have sleeps.

<S 03> Alright where's *The Rough Guide* ... erm.

<S 01> This is the same have you got two the same or something oh you're there.

<S 03> Where's *The Rough Guide* then.

<S 02> It's in that bag you're sitting on it.

<S 03> You great elephant.

<S 01> I couldn't feel it cos my bottom is so enormous [laughter].

<S 02> Yeah we'll just leave the car behind and go on the bus, go on the trains.

<S 01> I reckon that's what we should do [<S 02> yeah] the only problem that we've got then is carrying luggage.

<S 02> Yeah I won't take any.

<S 03> Just take a ruckie.

<S 02> Just take one, just take a Sainsbury's bag.

<S 01> Well this is what we usually do I haven't got a rucksack.

<S 02> Well at least take, we've got the cool bag so we'll take that and just so we can keep, it's only small so we can take things in that and we can get the train down to Brugge and then cos it's only a wee bit south then take the train back up and go into Delft and up to Amsterdam and there's somewhere else nice on the way go up to Amsterdam and then just get it back again is Delft in Holland or Belgium?

<S 03> Delft Holland.

<S 01> Holland.

(5 secs)

<S 02> And it says in my book the train's quite cheap.

<S 01> The only problem I suppose if we do go by train is the hassle of finding the right buses and coaches and.

<S 02> Nah cos the train stations'll be in the cities won't they it'll be fine.

Here, at the higher-order level, the goal is a series of decisions. These are dealt with on a problem-by-problem basis, each problem converging to a solution accepted by the participants and enabling decisions to be made. Hoey (1983) describes 'problem-solution' patterns in written discourse in terms of a regular sequence of discourse segments moving from the situating of a problem, to responses to it, to evaluations of those responses, and thence to a solution. Much the same is apparent in problem-solving in spoken discourses. In this extract, shared knowledge is high in terms of the overall goals but low in terms of <S 01>'s possession of travel brochures, which only he can see at this point. The atmosphere is relaxed and informal. Silences are acceptable, it would seem, only when the brochures are being consulted (a language-in-action phase); talk is otherwise continuous. The lexical density is 35.5%, reflecting the higher number of necessary lexical references to places and activities beyond the immediate situation. Deictic references to the immediate environment are only high in number towards the end of the extract, where the speakers are trying to find *The Rough Guide* travel book (*this, there, that*), which is another mini-language-in-action episode. *The* is frequent, referring to shared knowledge in the speakers' world (*the car, the boat, The Rough Guide*, etc.). Suggestions by individuals are an important part of the goal-orientation, and are realised both in formulaic and more indirect ways (*Mm that's interesting ... let's ...*; *Why don't you ...*; *I think we should ...*; *Do you think ...*, and imperative verb forms). The formulation at the end of the extract projects convergence (*Yeah we'll just ...*; *I reckon that's what we should do*).

In comparison, let us look at another decision-making collaborative task extract, this time in a publisher's group meeting. The context-type is professional, but informal. The speakers have a number of publication plans for books on the table and have to decide key dates and actions to ensure their efficient publication. Once again, problem-solution episodes make up the higher-order framework. Shared knowledge is high in terms of the goals (such meetings are a regular event), but low in terms of each individual's expertise and current perspective on the problems. The extract (2.11) begins as the group have been discussing whether to reprint a particular title and have made a number of decisions:

(2.11)

<S 02> That first six month's going to be a killer ... not to worry erm any other questions.

<S 01> No that's all.

<S 02> Well I've got one [<S 01> yes] and that's about the readers [<S 01>

yes] can you just fill me in again [<S 01> mm] just very quickly
[<S 01> mm] how many and when are they likely to hit me.

<S 01> How many books [<S 02> yeah] how many titles.

<S 02> Was it sixty did you say.

<S 01> Erm we were talking about, well the adult series will be six levels
and ... er thirty initially.

<S 02> Right and six months after that another thirty [<S 01> yeah] and
that's likely to hit me in a year.

(4 secs)

<S 01> Erm.

(3 secs)

<S 01> Yes ... year to eighteen months.

<S 02> Right that, and to what degree I mean that means that they'll
come into production thirty titles will come into production or er
that that will be the beginning of looking at an identity and pre-
planning.

<S 01> No I suspect they will actually be going into production in about
say about summer next year.

<S 02> Right.

<S 01>   ⌊It's what I would aim for.

<S 02> Right well then what we need to do is erm er sit down together
and have a planning meeting [<S 01> mm] I think again [<S 01> mm]
just go over it I know you've already spoken to me about it but er I'd
like to just go over it again and think what the issues are and see
erm ... I'm pretty confident about the extents which I gave you but
I'd like to have a look at the production issues involved and who's
going to actually do the setting.

<S 01> Mm.

Silence is again tolerated when participants attend to the physical
environment (in this case the papers in front of them), but otherwise,
talk is continuous. Turns are longer than in the other extracts we have
been considering in this section. Lexical density is 35.7%, again reflecting
the necessary lexical references to entities beyond the immediate environment, but still firmly on the 'spoken' side of the overall textual
average. Although not officially chaired, the meeting is steered in phases
by individuals (e.g. <S 02> in the opening turns). Metalanguage concerning meetings and decision processes is apparent in formulations
(again the opening turns, also *That will be the beginning of looking at an*

identity and pre-planning; What we need to do is erm er sit down together and have a planning meeting I think again just go over it). Discourse markers indicate decision phases and topic shifts (*right, well*). Spatial deixis (items such as *here, over there*) is non-apparent. Participants signal their satisfaction with (or worries over) the ongoing interaction (*not to worry*), and suggestions are signalled collaboratively (*It's what I would aim for; Well then what we need to do is …*). Politeness and indirectness are used (*Can you just fill me in again just very quickly; Erm we were talking about …; No I suspect …*).

We have compared four extracts and seen that they fall naturally into two pairs on the basis of not only activity type but in terms of their lexico-grammatical features. They do, of course, vary within the two pairs, but we can say that more unites them than divides them on the parameters considered, despite their different settings and relation types. We could broadly indicate the generic similarities thus:

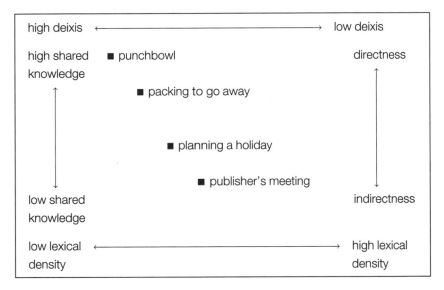

Figure 2: Generic patterning of four extracts (2.8, 2.9, 2.10, 2.11)

Figure 2 is, to say the least, an idealised version of what are quite complex differences, but it is intended to show how spoken texts may be usefully positioned with regard to their similarities along just a few dimensions. Other dimensions could also be brought into play. Plotting texts in this fashion enables us better to capture the variation present in texts which share similarities in generic-level activities, and enables us to make at least some links between higher-order concerns and the basic lexico-grammatical choices which speakers make in line with their goals and relationships in particular settings. The gradability of generic features thus displayed is in line with Wikberg's (1992) advocacy of the recognition of gradience and variability in the classification of written genres, which are often subject to over-simplified text typologies. As Biber and Finegan (1991) advocate, genre study should include both a characterisation of typical texts as well as a characterisation of the range of variation. Within the narrow scope of this section, I have suggested some directions in which a genre-based methodology may go in the search for an adequate framework of description for spoken genres.

2.6 Conclusion

In this chapter I have attempted to draw a tentative theory of spoken genre in light of the variation which is acknowledged to be present in speech events which seem, nonetheless, to share common features. I have tried to account for participants' awareness of generic activity partly in terms of their orientation towards past events, upcoming ones, the need for formulation of ongoing activity and the need to instantiate those procedures whereby events take on shapes and characteristics that enable linguists to categorise them into different genres. I have used the CANCODE corpus matrix to demonstrate how extracts controlled for variables such as goal-type and context-type can be seen to display similarities at the lexico-grammatical level which fit in with the higher-order features of generically-oriented activity. Genre will always remain a slippery notion precisely because human activity is open to so much variation, driven by the common-sense purposes of interactants and the need to build and maintain human relations. In all the extracts used in this chapter, relational work is high on the agenda for participants, and it is only rarely separable from the transactional business at hand, however institutionalised that business may be. What is apparent is that at all levels, behaviour is integrated: the transactional, the interactional, the goal-orientation, the relationships among participants, the local lexico-grammatical selections, and that all we can hope to do as analysts is occasionally to tease out those different exigencies and put them under the spotlight. This chapter and Chapter 1 have attempted to lay the foundations for a pedagogically-driven theory of spoken language in applied linguistics. That theory may be said so far to be founded on the following principles:

- Spoken language pedagogy cannot simply just proceed from the same assumptions as written language pedagogy with regard to language use. The historical dominance of the written language in applied linguistics has militated against good understanding of the spoken language.
- Spoken language has its own grammar and lexicon, which, although coinciding in most cases with the written language, differ in crucial areas that correspond to the goals and relations of interactants in particular settings.
- We can only begin to describe the special lexico-grammar of talk by looking at real data.
- The best data for a pedagogical theory of spoken language is everyday, informal talk.
- The text-typologies often used in the description of written language should not be simply transferred to spoken language. We must first research what the differences are in different types of spoken events and come to understand spoken genres.
- Central to a theory of spoken genre are participant goals and relationships.
- A corpus of spoken language for pedagogical purposes will be designed with goal- and context-variation in mind, and will include goals and contexts relevant to language learners (e.g. pedagogical relationships, service transaction goals). These design features will be more important than mere size of the corpus.
- The corpus needs qualitative as well as quantitative analysis to be pedagogically useful.
- Observation of spoken language use by participants in real encounters of various kinds is the first step in building language syllabuses and teaching materials.

Against this background, the next chapter will ask and try to offer answers to more detailed and practical questions about language pedagogy.

Notes

1 See Hasan (1992) for a critique of the ambivalence of some of Bakhtin's categories. Hasan is right to criticise Bakhtin's work as being difficult to operationalise. However, as long as one does not regard Bakhtin's ideas as a model or instrument of analysis, but rather as a thought-provoking set of

theories, their value in assisting our understanding of and our ability to construct the nature of the spoken language remains intact.

2 Young (1990: 75ff), in her study of written and spoken academic language, refers to the 'generic situation' that influences selections of field, tenor and mode (in the sense of those terms as laid out by Halliday 1978), rather than to 'genres' as such. Young is attempting to make a separation between the linguistic 'code' (where field, tenor and mode are represented by lexicogrammatical selections) and language as 'behaviour', which is a social/contextual level, where the generic situation is located.

3 Bakhtin (1986: 89) talks of the multiple voicing of discourse: 'Our speech ... is filled with others' words'; all language, for Bakhtin contains echoes of previous discourses: any speaker 'is not after all the first speaker, the one who disturbs the eternal silence of the universe' (*ibid.*: 69), and each utterance is 'filled with echoes and reverberations of other utterances' (*ibid.*: 91).

3

What should we teach about the spoken language?[1]

3.1 Introduction

Chapter 1 outlined how the status of the spoken language in applied linguistics has developed over the centuries and how it has grown in importance in recent decades with corpus projects coming to the forefront. Chapter 2 looked at a number of studies that point towards a model for spoken genres. Nowadays, a vast amount of descriptive literature is available on spoken language, for English and for other widely-used languages. Sociolinguists, discourse analysts and conversation analysts, coming at spoken language from their several perspectives, all offer the interested language teacher something to get excited about, and often present findings that seem to be (or which seem as though they ought to be) relevant to second or foreign language teaching. Chapter 2 abounds in such references. Further studies of this kind are reviewed and discussed in McCarthy (1991), McCarthy and Carter (1994), Schiffrin (1994), and Stenström (1994). These studies are many and varied in their general characteristics, ranging from major attempts to model the spoken language in terms of structure (e.g. Sinclair and Coulthard 1975), prescriptions of socio-cultural norms to which conversational participants orient themselves, such as turn-taking (e.g. Sacks *et al* 1974), prescriptions of generic features that define whole spoken episodes such as narratives (e.g. Labov 1972), descriptions of complex surface manifestations such as discourse-marking (e.g. Schiffrin 1987), and a host of other concerns. We have seen, in Chapter 2, how these and other resources combine to characterise the genres we are familiar with as language-users; on the practical level, we need to examine each type of linguistic resource in detail, in order to be able to relate them to our higher-order concerns such as goal-orientation and relationships. In later chapters, we shall examine lexico-grammatical resources of particular kinds; in this chapter we concentrate more on discourse-level features. For this reason, it may be helpful from the outset in this chapter to divide the somewhat amorphic world of spoken language studies into very broad types, and to discuss each type in terms of its possible implications for teaching. By 'teaching' here I mean intervention in the learning/acquisition process in the classroom and designed input in the form of syllabuses, materials and methods. The broad classification which follows is essentially synthetic and pedagogy-driven, since this chapter is concerned with examining the spoken language from the point of view of creating what Widdowson (1980) calls 'relevant models' of language description.

3.2 The spoken language: key descriptive areas

3.2.1 Structural features

Three structural units fundamental to all spoken interaction emerge from a wide range of studies in discourse and conversational analysis: *the transaction*, *the exchange* and *the adjacency pair*.[2]

The transaction

The term *transaction* is here used broadly in the sense that Sinclair and Coulthard (1975) use it, to label stretches of talk identified by certain types of activity at their boundaries. For example, in the classroom, teachers will typically divide the business of a lesson up by marking the transitions to new phases with some sort of conventional marker (*right*, *okay*, *now*,[3] *so*, etc.) characteristically uttered with falling intonation and often followed by a pause or 'silent stress'. Around these markers, metalinguistic activity may also take place, for example in a phone-call: '*Okay*, *well*, that was the main thing I was ringing about, *but* there was one other thing' (attested). The transaction, like the paragraph in written language, has no pre-defined length, and is only recognisable by its boundaries.

It is hard to imagine talk proceeding efficiently without participants signalling in some way or other and recognising such boundaries, and the transaction, as a structure, is probably a discourse universal. What we can say as language teachers, however, and this statement will apply equally to a number of other features, is that the transaction as a unit of discourse *may* present us with a problem on two distinct levels. On the first, there may be a problem of awareness, among both teachers and learners, that transaction signalling is an important part of behaving linguistically in the target language (for example, there is evidence that in certain types of more formal talk, lack of metalinguistic signalling can affect comprehensibility; see Williams 1992). On the second level, the problem is principally a lexical one: how does the target language realise such marking (compare English *well* with Spanish *bueno* and *pues*, French *bien*, and Swedish *nå*)? Are the L2 literal lexical equivalents for items like *good!* and *now then!* also those used for marking purposes?[4] Bilingual dictionaries are notoriously poor sources for such cross-linguistic information, and the teacher may best be able to attack both the awareness problem and the lexical problem via observations of real data, a point to which we shall return. But even if the awareness problems and the lexical problems can be resolved, there still remain the problems of generating classroom activities that offer the learner opportunities for transaction-marking in naturalistic settings, which the teacher-fronted classroom is unlikely to be able to do. In the teacher-fronted classroom it is usually the teacher, and the teacher alone, who marks the transactions. I have elsewhere presented limited data to show that task-based contexts where students carry out group activities can yield natural use of boundary marking by participants when the teacher is no longer dominant (McCarthy 1991: 131), but such manifestations of ideal and natural discourse are not guaranteed, and the many factors bearing upon task success will have to be taken into account (see Skehan 1996).

I have focused on the question of the transaction and its 'teachability' because, in many ways, it sums up the questions we may ask of all the discourse features which are examined in turn below, and these are:

1 Are discourse features automatically transferred from L1 behaviour to L2?
2 Can such transfer occur effectively without lexico-grammatical input (in other words, are things like markers usually just 'picked up' along the way or do they need to be taught)?
3 Is teacher/learner awareness of the spoken language sufficient to pre-empt and address the possible problems raised by questions 1 and 2?
4 Is communication in L2 *without* the performance of features such as transaction-marking adequate, satisfactory and satisfying for learners?

A related question, one that Scarcella (1983) takes up, is whether there are developmental factors at play in the learner's ability to be discoursally competent in the target language. Scarcella is concerned with whether features such as conversational strategies increase with general language proficiency and whether some strategic areas are likely to be acquired before others, offering a qualified yes to both of these questions. The same questions could be asked about structural features such as transaction-marking, and it is likely that a qualified yes is the answer there, too, though little hard evidence exists.

Questions 1 and 2 above are linked to each other. Most features of linguistic behaviour do, sooner or later, carry over from one language to another, given sufficient exposure and motivation, and considerable amounts of language are just 'picked up' within and without the classroom, as all experienced language teachers know. But it would be an odd pedagogy that refused to teach, say, the past tense, or the vocabulary of food and drink because these would be 'picked up anyway' sooner or later. What is important is to identify those features which are natural in L1 performance and desirable in the learner's L2 performance, to offer short-cuts to the necessary lexico-grammatical knowledge to realise such features, and, above all, to enable the appropriate contextual environments to be created in the classroom and in the teaching materials so that it may be observed whether or not such behaviour is in fact transferred and is part of the learner's repertoire. Question 3 under-lies the motivation of this entire book. I do not believe that a teacher who is unaware and a bad observer of the spoken language can really give the kind of input necessary to raise the learner's awareness of the key, defining features of talk. I do firmly believe that learners trained to be good observers of data have taken an important step towards facilitating uptake of those very features, however long-term or delayed the actual output of such features may be in terms of actual use. Question 4 above surfaces again later when we consider discourse-marking in general.

The exchange

Similar problems to those raised for transactions apply to the notion of the exchange, although there are specific features that make it worth discussing separately from the transaction. The exchange is the minimal structural unit of interaction, consisting of an initiation and a response (for example, a question and its answer, or a greeting and a return greeting). But this minimal condition is typically elaborated in casual conversation to include a third function, the follow-up, and is in fact often realised in quite complex configurations (see Hoey 1991b). A canonical example of the structure Initiation-Response-Follow-up (IRF) is this CANCODE extract:[5]

(3.1)
[<S 01> is asking her great-niece about a forthcoming trip to London.]

<S 01> What part of London would you be actually in?   I
<S 02> Well I would be going from Paddington to Victoria.   R
<S 01> I see yes.   F

However, more complex sequences (for example, where checks are felt necessary) can sometimes mean that the follow-up is delayed, though still present:

(3.2)
<S 01> What time is it?   I
<S 02> Twenty to six.   R
<S 01> Is that all?   R/I2
<S 02> Yeah.   R2
<S 01> Oh I thought it was later.   F

Learner repertoires often range from only performing the Response function (especially in early stages or in the traditional, teacher-fronted classroom, where the teacher commands both *I* and *F* slots), to Initiating but still not making any follow-up. This latter behaviour is sometimes noticeable in classroom pair-work where the teacher is often hovering and monitoring performance (but see Kehe and Kehe 1989 for how the teacher may respond constructively to such difficulties). The follow-up very frequently has a relational/interactional function, where social, cultural and affective meanings are encoded in relation to responses, in addition to acknowledging the response and its information, and where key conversational processes such as convergence are effected. It is thus a crucial structural element in our global, generic framework, where relational features are given the same priority as transactional ones, as we advocated in Chapter 2. Making it part of the learner's repertoire is therefore very important. The reactions encoded in the follow-up are often formulaic, and can be viewed as a lexical problem across languages (compare the British English reactives *Really!, Oh, right, That's nice!, You don't say!, I guessed as much!* and *How interesting/awful!* with their realisations in other languages and/or other varieties of English). But as before, solving the lexical problem alone may not be sufficient to foster natural interaction complete with the follow-up function. Contextual conditions for its natural occurrence must also be assured, and where these are non-existent, the learner will never have the proper opportunities to practise this basic, core function of the spoken language. The awareness problem in this case is usually related to learner expectations that it will be the teacher who follows up, normally by evaluating the linguistic quality of the learner's response (whether a response to a teacher-initiation or to an initiation by a fellow-student in pair- or group-work). The learner needs to be made aware that follow-up is not just for teachers, and not just for evaluating correct or incorrect performance. Textbooks with dialogues that do not have follow-ups certainly do not help in this task, and where natural data is inaccessible or unavailable, the next best thing may be the editing of textbook dialogues to ensure the inclusion of at least some follow-ups. To be a good editor, though, presupposes an appropriate awareness of when and where and how follow-ups are used. Careful observation and/or access to a corpus gives a great advantage in this respect.

The adjacency pair

The adjacency pair is a unit associated with American conversation analysis (e.g. Schegloff and Sacks 1973), usually conducted from an ethnomethodological standpoint, typically concerned with how participants behave in interaction in terms of alignment (i.e. how they position themselves socially in relation to their interlocutor(s)), achieving goals, negotiating outcomes, etc. Speakers naturally orientate themselves to bring together in the discourse utterances that mutually condition one another, such that the sequence in (3.3) is considered to be in line with participants' expectations:

(3.3)
[at a dinner-table, <S 02> is the guest]:

<S 01> D'you want some olive oil Dennis?
<S 02> Mm ta.

In (3.4), later in the same conversation, a remark by <S 05> is responded to by his wife, <S 04>, but the response is problematic:

s that can cause conversational tensions between 'silence-
ourse styles such as that found in American English, and
ere silence is permissible thinking-time and face-protecting,
anese (Noguchi 1987; Lebra 1987). A second problem is related
le forms of interruption across cultures, for example the
for direct interruption with markers such as *ma* (*but*) in
pared with the indirect use of *well* and/or agreement contrasts
(Testa 1988). The third problem is that of differing styles of
nel' (the noises and verbalisations made by listeners to show
ding, continued interest, etc.) (Yngve 1970). Spanish speakers
nowledge incoming talk with what translates to English as a
un-like 'Yes-yes-yes!', and which frequently indicates im-
or irritation with the speaker in British English. There seems
re, to be a mix of lexical and cultural problems which need
g in the classroom. And yet turn-taking (and especially interrup-
he area in English language teaching where there is no shortage
advice. Course-books frequently offer conventional phrases for
ting, such as *Sorry to interrupt* and *Can I just say something?*. Useful
uch phrases may be, they are no substitute for close observation
When one does this using data from informal conversational
(and even in some semi-formal contexts) one finds, in the case of
that an interruption often simply occurs and is then followed or
broken off by the interruption marker, as in (3.7) and (3.8):

interrupts a conversation in a corridor between two women.]

with Carol and he doesn't even realise
⌊Helen, **sorry to interrupt**, erm did
u manage to ring Patrick?
ed)

interrupts a colleague during a semi-formal discussion.]

well it would have to go to a later meeting
⌊I don't ... for this document,
orry to interrupt, but I don't think you can ignore the importance
f [etc.]
ted)

(3.4)

<S 05> The nicest pizza I've ever had was in Amsterdam [<S 03> Oh yeah]
 I had a brilliant pizza.
<S 04>   ⌊In Cyprus.

The incoming information has not prompted convergence, but is openly
challenged, and it will require work on the part of the speakers to resolve
the possible hold-up in the talk. The first part of the adjacency pair
predicts the occurrence of a second part, and the second part is seen to
fulfil that prediction in some way. In the case of (3.4), we might expect a
response showing interest and encouraging <S 05> to go on and describe
the wonderful pizza. Instead the unpredicted happens: the information is
contradicted. The adjacency pair, in its concern with local decisions by
speakers, does overlap with the notion of exchange; the difference is that
the exchange is primarily seen as a structural unit building up into
higher order units, while adjacency is concerned more with local convergence between participants. Another way of putting it is that discourse
analysts working with the exchange are much more interested in the
presence of the pattern as a trace in the text for the analyst's purposes,
while conversation analysts who work with adjacency are trying to understand local, individual choices from the participants' viewpoint.

There is no evidence to suggest that learners do not orientate themselves to create appropriate adjacency, however imperfectly they may
actually realise it, and thus adjacency, as a global notion, is interesting
but may not be an essential component of a relevant linguistic model for
pedagogy, and probably does not need to be 'taught'. However, once
again, a number of adjacency pairs are highly formulaic and can be
treated as an aspect of the lexico-grammatical content of the syllabus.
One may not need to be taught to 'be adjacent', but one may well benefit
from learning a number of ready-made formulae (what Nattinger and
DeCarrico 1992 and Lewis 1993: 94 refer to as 'lexical phrases' and
'institutionalised expressions', respectively) which will enable fluent,
natural and culturally and pragmatically appropriate adjacency pairs to
be realised. Examples that readily spring to mind are reactions of
condolence, congratulation-sequences, seasonal greetings, telephone
opening conventions, phatic exchanges, etc. In a related way, there is the
problem of 'dispreferred' second parts of adjacency pairs (Pomerantz
1984), that is to say responses that do not fit in with expectations, as in
the wife's challenge over the pizza in (3.4). For example, how does one

disagree with an assertion (see the discussion in section 1.8 on 'dis-agreeing') or refuse an invitation without causing offence or making the receiver feel threatened? What tends to happen in native-speaker speech is considerable elaboration of the second pair-part (the second part of the adjacency pair) to include reasons for the divergence, and often a preface to the actual 'dispreferred' utterance. These conditions, of course, apply to generally co-operative discourse; people will always exercise their right to be conflictual and rude when they choose to be, or at least fairly direct, as <S 04> feels she can be to her husband in example (3.4). Two further corpus examples illustrate typical co-operative behaviour, the second more direct than the first:

(3.5)
[A young daughter, <S 01>, is being helpful and offering to make everyone toast. Most family members accept two slices. She then addresses her father.]

<S 01> Dad, one piece or two?
<S 02> **One'll do for me**, Jen, if you
<S 01>   ⌊Right, okay.
<S 02> Cos I've gotta go in the bath in a minute, love.

(3.6)
[<S 01> addresses his sister-in-law, <S 02>, and tells her he never realised she made her own Swiss rolls.]

<S 01> And I've never realised that you've made it, I thought this was
          probably, I probably thought it was bought.
<S 02> Oh, you're joking! **It's our speciality of the house!**

The dispreferred utterances are here indicated in bold. Clearly, speakers generally wish to avoid over-blunt refusals, divergences and contradictions, and, once again, considerable lexical effort is expended in elaborating the dispreferred response. In (3.5), there is a risk that the daughter will interpret her father's choice of only one piece of toast as a snub to her efforts to help in the kitchen. We have what looks like an aborted polite conditional and a reason from the father. In (3.6) we have a conventional informal preface of disbelief that softens the confirmation that the first speaker was saying something wildly wrong. Here discourse and culture overlap, and notions of politeness, threats to face (Brown and

Levinson 1987) and acceptable beh
the surface, for example, customs
refusal of food, cultural expectation
or shop-bought, etc. Once again, the
can effectively 'teach' L2 culture vi
whether language and cultural awa
where the goal is to observe, discuss
interaction rather than to 'learn' o
several arguments for advocating suc
models of language and culture have
culture is simply 'there' in language (
more towards interactional models, wh
situation-dependent and as something
(Blommaert 1991). The other argumen
probably gain better awareness from e
encounters with real data rather than ha
(re-)presented by teachers (see Jackson 1
own language analyses and a good discuss

3.2.2 Interactional features

Under this heading we include those are
speakers manage the interaction in less obv
sense of regular patterned occurrences of r
proceed effectively towards their goals w
equilibrium. Amongst many such featur
marking and information-staging are centra
tions as to their 'teachability' as did the more
in section 3.2.1.

Turn-taking

Turn-taking, although a universal feature, ma
cultural plane. Indeed, one might argue that
English language teaching materials have erred
seeing the issue as primarily a lexical one. Th
quently to arise. One is that some cultures s
silences between turns, for example as is of
Europeans during conversations in Finnish. Anot

rule-conflic
filling' disc
cultures wh
such as Jap
to accepta
preference
Italian con
in English
'back-chan
understan
often ack
machine-
patience
again, he
addressin
tion) is o
of lexica
interrup
though
of data.
settings
English.
is itself

(3.7)
[<S 02>

<S 01>
<S 02>
          yo
(attest

(3.8)
[<S 02

<S 01
<S 02

(atte

In (3.8) the interruption has in fact already taken place *before* the marker is used. Once again, it is the combination of lexical items and culturally acceptable behaviour which should be of interest to the teacher and learner, and, as before, observation and awareness of what happens in real data must be added to the act of providing the lexical resources. The lexical resources alone are simply insufficient without culturally sensitive insights from direct observation. In terms of our over-arching genre-model, interruption may be more permissible in some genres than others. Overlap and interruption in language-in-action collaborative tasks among intimates may be seen as practical and goal-facilitating; in discussion and argument genres in professional or socialising settings, it may be seen as aggressive or downright rude.

Discourse marking

Discourse marking has already been referred to in connection with transaction-boundary marking, but discourse markers are widely used to signal many different functions in conversation (e.g. *well*, mentioned above as a marker of disagreement or divergence) (see Schiffrin 1987; Fraser 1990). All languages seem to have a finite set of lexical items (single-word and phrasal) to signal functions such as shared knowledge (e.g. English *you know*), proclaimed knowledge (English *you see*), topic shifting (English *but* and *so*), pre-closings and returns to interrupted topics (English *anyway*), boundary marking, and many other interactive and structural functions. What is more, hardly any stretch of informal conversation is without markers: extract (3.9) is by no means untypical of natural conversational data:

(3.9)
[<S 01> is explaining a consumer report scheme her mother got roped into.]

<S 01> She gets a pound or something, **you know**, a month, **but** it was something that, I remember I was a kid, **and, well, sort of**, about sixteen seventeen or something, **and** this woman came to the door *and* erm I agreed to it [laughs] **and** my mother kept, **you know**, my mother did it **and** she kept it on, **you know**, for about the last twenty years doing this.

Watts (1989) has shown just how unconscious native speakers can be of their own use of discourse markers, and markers do seem to display an automaticity characteristic of the more routine aspects of speech. This may be one of the reasons why they are so often absent from concocted dialogues in language text-books, and indeed from many dictionaries. Research evidence also suggests that where spoken discourse *lacks* a normal distribution of markers, it can create problems of comprehension as well as sounding unnatural (Tyler, Jeffries and Davies 1988).

There seems to be no obvious reason why the set of discourse markers for any language should not be part of the most basic lexical input in the syllabus and materials, for they are indeed very useful items and, lexically, usually quite simple and straightforward and often familiar to learners from their basic semantic meanings (e.g. *good* may already be known as the opposite of *bad*). Of all the features considered in this chapter, discourse markers, on the face of it, lend themselves most easily to a presentational methodology.[6] However, a note of caution must be added in that much work remains to be done in actually establishing how and when native speakers use markers. Aston (1995), for example, has shown that English *thank you* has an important phase-marking function in service encounters over and above its meaning of 'expressing gratitude'. It may thus be premature to teach the set of markers as lexical formulae. As always, though, one would hope that raising awareness of their widespread role in spoken language through discussion and exemplification might proceed in tandem with learning them as items, and observation of natural data, as much as word-learning, is again desirable wherever feasible. Furthermore, the fact that a presentational methodology might work for inputting discourse markers is no guarantee that they can be successfully produced in pair- or group-work, and it may be better simply to allow production to be delayed until suitable natural opportunities arise.

Information staging

Information staging brings us to some interesting observations on the grammatical level, as opposed to the lexically- and culturally-oriented interpretations offered above for some of the other discourse phenomena. The canonical word-order for the clause in English of Subject-Verb-Object-Adverbial is frequently manipulated in informal speech to produce a variety of re-arrangements of the information encoded. These re-arrangements enable foregrounding of entities, signalling of topically-prominent items and interactive features such as tags and tails (see glossary). As well as front-placed objects for foregrounding or contrast, we find items placed before the core clause elements and after them. Two examples follow. (3.10) shows how a pre-posed item copied in the main clause can supply useful information to anchor a topic in the listener's consciousness (see Geluykens 1992 for further examples; see also Carter and McCarthy 1995b). (3.11) shows a typical interactive function, the end-copying of items singled out for evaluation (see Aijmer 1989; McCarthy and Carter 1997b):

(3.10)

<S 01> Well, Karen, where I'm living, **a friend of mine, she**'s got her railcard and I was telling her ...

(3.11)

<S 01> It's very nice **that road up through Skipton to the Dales.**

All evidence suggests that word-order phenomena (including cleft structures) and information-structuring of this kind exist in many languages (e.g. for French, see Lambrecht 1988; Italian, Duranti and Ochs 1979; Swedish and Yiddish, Källgren and Prince 1989; Japanese, Ono and Suzuki 1992; Spanish, Guitart 1989). It is interesting to ponder whether features of this kind are automatically carried over from L1 to L2 (e.g. see Trevise 1986), and precise grammatical realisations may vary across languages. The grammatical inventories of language teaching syllabuses often ignore these phenomena, as do concocted text-book dialogues. This would certainly seem to suggest a revision of the grammatical categories which need to be addressed if a course is adequately to cover conversational phenomena. A significant level of linguistic encoding of relational functions is lost if the learner has neither the opportunity, nor the grammatical apparatus, nor the confidence to transfer such features from L1, to realise the kinds of functions we have illustrated. A revision of the grammatical component of the syllabus in this way will probably mean far greater emphasis on front- and end-placing in the clause and manipulability of the core elements than tends to happen at present. Such an admission of previously ignored grammatical phenomena is not without its problems, though, not least of which is that syllabuses above all, and teaching materials in the main, tend overwhelmingly to be written, and one is faced with the conundrum of raising awareness of spoken forms through written-down examples and exercises. Another related problem is the power of the written sentence to affect our view of the nature of the grammatical information. It is no mere chance that linguists who do tackle phenomena such as topicalising and 'tails' speak of them in a metalanguage that is 'page-driven', referring to 'left-dislocated' elements (e.g. see Geluykens, 1992 on English, Blasco 1995 on French, Rivero 1980 on Spanish) or 'right' dislocation (e.g. Fretheim 1995; Valiouli 1991). Clearly, spoken language has neither 'left' nor 'right'; if anything, it has 'before' and 'next'.[7] Equally, metaphors of 'dislocation' have a tendency to suggest that something is wrong or 'out of place', rather than perfectly normal, acceptable and significant in conversational terms. This does suggest that spoken grammar methodology must lean heavily towards audiotaped support or at the very least adequate contextualisation to enable teachers and learners to reconstruct the original utterances. It also suggests that the spoken language pedagogy which emerges from our overall genre-based concerns needs a carefully forged metalanguage which the language teaching profession does not yet share.

3.2.3 Generic features

The notion of genre in spoken language as described in Chapter 2 tries to capture the sense that participants have of involvement in particular language events, which unfold in predictable and institutionalised ways and move, stage by stage, towards a recognisable completion. Much work exists in the characterisation of written genres (see Swales 1990), while in the spoken language, the notion of genre has tended to be poorly described (see Chapter 2). Obvious examples of well-circumscribed genres are church sermons, wedding speeches, jokes, lectures, service en-counters and stories. It is possible to define the elements or phases which are usually present and to recognise these in their linguistic realisations in different contexts (McCarthy and Carter 1994: 24ff).[8] Genres are typically more sharply defined at their openings and closings, for obvious reasons, since speakers and listeners need to know just what sort of language event they are involved in. Chapter 2 presented evidence for speakers' awareness of the expectations of upcoming activity and how their recollections of previous experiences influenced their view of the unfolding genre. Thus a joke may be conventionally signalled by some marker such as *Have you heard the one about ...?*, while a true-life journalistic report of a terrorist bomb outrage would never be expected to begin in this way. Genres are subject to embedding: for example, narrative anecdotes may occur during a university lecture, and casual conversational episodes may occur during a service encounter. Genres, too, as we have argued all along, depend as much on relational elements as they do on purely transactional ones; the building and maintenance of relationships simply cannot be separated from other business at hand.

Two principle problem areas seem to occur with regard to genres: firstly, openings and closings are usually highly conventionalised and secondly, learners may be more able to realise some elements better than others. Oral anecdotes are a good example of this second problem, and I have suggested elsewhere (McCarthy 1991: 137–142), with support from data, that lower-level learners may often have great difficulty in realising what Labov (1972) would call the 'evaluation' function in narrative, that is to say those lexical embellishments (e.g. intensifiers, hyperbole) and grammatical configurations (e.g. *I might easily have been killed*; *if only I hadn't been so stupid!*) which give the story interest and 'tellability'. In Labov's model, evaluative elements are just as important as the bare bones of the narrative structure, which are 'abstract' (flagging the story or giving a kind of 'headline'), 'orientation' (telling the listener who, where, when, etc.), 'complicating events' (the unusual, funny, scary, etc. events that make the story a story), 'resolution' (how the events worked out), and 'coda' (rounding off the story and bridging back to the present moment). The challenge to provide adequate evaluation often applies to listeners as well as tellers, for listeners, in natural settings, usually contribute evaluation in some form, and the storytelling is rarely a one-sided monologue, as Duranti (1991) has demonstrated with Italian data. Helping learners to master evaluative techniques (e.g. expressing surprise, horror, empathy, disgust, etc.) helps them to build better relationships with their narrating interlocutors and to present a better self-image as narrator. In the classroom, learners can be encouraged to re-tell the same story, adding better evaluation each time (a not unnatural activity, since in real life stories are usually told and re-told, with embellishments built up over time). Re-telling of stories is a departure from the usual 'one shot only' constraint of the typical oral classroom.

Openings and closings, I have suggested, are more likely to be formulaic, but there are often interesting cultural differences, as, for instance, between Greek and British English telephone calls (Sifianou 1989) , Dutch and American English ones (Houtkoop-Steenstra 1991), or Chinese and English opening greetings in conversation (Hong 1985). Edmondson, House, Kasper and Stemmer (1984) contrast content- and interpersonal-orientation (i.e. the way language is sensitive to the interlocutor rather than just to the content of the message) for conversational openings and closings in German and English, as Jaworski (1990) does for native speakers and American learners of Polish. We return, as always, to the need for observation, awareness and sensitivity in confronting the characteristic creation of genres in an L2, rather than any notion that such intercultural phenomena can simply be 'taught' in a presentational sense. Fortunately, more and more research is being conducted to produce accurate descriptions of genres across cultures, and knowledge of cultural similarities and differences can only be of positive assistance in language teaching and learning. The potential of the CANCODE corpus for classifying texts along generic lines (see Chapters 1 and 2) renders it a particularly useful tool for work towards the creation of such pedagogical frameworks.

3.2.4 Contextual constraints

Since spoken language is more likely to be immediately context-bound than written language, we find a separate set of concerns which emerge from the way speakers encode contextual features. Situational ellipsis is a good example of a typical spoken-language context-driven feature (Carter and McCarthy 1995). In English, where entities can be retrieved from the immediate situation, normally expected items of structure may be omitted, as in these extracts:

(3.12)
[<S 01> is assembling things for her friend before they go out.]

<S 01> Handbag is it, what else then?

(3.13)
[<S 01> is commenting on the listener's participation in a consumer survey, which brought the listener the unexpected benefit of a new telephone line, at the expense of the survey organisation.]

<S 01> Put the phone in as well for you, did they?

(3.14)
[<S 01> is commenting in a friendly, joky way on the listener's use of an item in <S 01>'s flat.]

<S 01> Think it's your house or something?

In (3.12) *your* (handbag) is ellipted, in (3.13) we have a typical spoken English structure of initial subject-dropping (*they*) which is later realised in a tag, and in (3.14) we have the auxiliary verb and subject omitted (*do you*). All the ellipted items are obvious in the context. This type of ellipsis gets surprisingly scant attention in currently popular British pedagogical grammars (one notable exception being Swan 1980/1995), whereas CANCODE figures suggest one occurrence of this type of ellipsis per 300 words (approximately) of casual conversation (excluding narrative segments, where situational ellipsis is rare). Scarcella and Brunak (1981) note an absence of this kind of ellipsis in their non-native-speaker data, and it may well require direct intervention by the teacher to create awareness of its existence and its contexts of use, as well as a set of guidelines for structural restrictions (e.g., in the case of the examples above, characteristically first and second person, often with verbs of mental process, etc.). Much more research is needed in this area, and better descriptions of all the types of ellipsis that commonly occur in conversation would be a great step forward. In the meantime, teachers and learners have to rely on their own inductive abilities to derive rules and guidelines, with as much help from real data as is possible.

Another context-bound feature of talk is its variable lexical density, as the examples in section 2.5 and further examples in section 6.2 attempt to demonstrate. Extremely context-bound types, such as 'language-in-action' sequences, where language is generated by some task being undertaken at the time (e.g. cooking, shifting furniture), may display very low lexical density (i.e. a high proportion of function-words as opposed to full vocabulary items; see section 2.5 for some examples of variability across different genres). (3.15) shows sequences from data of a family cooking food in their kitchen:

(3.15)
<S 01> What are you going to do with that?
<S 02> Oh, it'll go in in a minute. I can taste it as I go along and then add the same amounts again.
(7 secs)
<S 02> Yeah, I'll just give that a stir and see where we are first.
(6 secs)
<S 03> If you put this in the freezer, that'll cool it down quicker, won't it?
<S 01> Yes, and it won't freeze.

Notably, such sequences are usually high in demonstratives, pronouns, and deictic words in general, and lower in content lexis. Such raw data, by definition, can be difficult to interpret without considerable contextual information, and, for this reason, concocted text-book dialogues rarely occur in such a heavily context-bound form. However, I would argue that interesting (and entertaining) work can be done in the classroom with tantalising data of this kind precisely to raise awareness of the fundamental importance of items such as deictics in oral communication. Learners can be asked to imagine what might be going on, and to offer lexical items as possible referents. Also worth noting in this context is that deictic items do not necessarily translate one-to-one across languages (e.g. demonstratives between English and French, or the tripartite demonstrative system of Spanish) and they may need to be focused upon in their natural contexts of occurrence. Language-in-action texts are usually good vehicles for demonstrative usage.

3.3 Bringing the arguments together: pedagogical modelling

Much of what I have said in the latter part of this chapter seems to have veered away from the discourse/conversational-analytical and genre-based concerns of the present book towards lexical and grammatical preoccupations and cross-cultural comparisons, but it would be a mistake to separate the three areas. We do need to have recourse to discourse analysis and conversational analysis and we do need an overarching genre-oriented framework to establish how and when lexico-grammatical forms occur. As I have tried to demonstrate, discourse structures and generic patterns of interaction so often crucially depend on strings of particular lexico-grammatical choices for their realisation. In the final analysis, discourse is realised and made possible through the network of lexico-grammar that responds to contexts and to the needs, goals and relationships of participants, as subsequent chapters will continue to argue. Moreover, this chapter has not addressed a further level of encoding which has been shown increasingly to be discourse-sensitive, that is to say intonation, and real data again force us to re-assess sentence-grammar models of intonation and models which relegate intonation to imponderables such as 'attitude' and 'emotions'. Bradford (1988) has shown how a combination of awareness-raising and more traditional exercises can bring a discourse-sensitive approach to intonation into the classroom, basing her work on Brazil's (1985) model.

Thus materials can incorporate facts about the spoken language while still offering practical exercises that give learners a feeling of 'doing and learning'. Equally, there is no reason why a syllabus as a whole should not have as its primary headings discourse- and genre-based categories (for an example see McCarthy and Carter 1994: ch. 5), even though its actual items may be lexico-grammatically organised. A syllabus is not a methodology, but, rather, reflects a view of language and priorities for teaching.

This chapter asks the question: what should we teach about the spoken language? The answer is, clearly, quite a lot, but how and mediated by what, are different questions. I have argued that a good deal of what concerns discourse- and genre-analysts is culturally motivated, and that cultural awareness is the key to avoiding inappropriate transfer of discourse features across languages and to fostering appropriate transfer. But I have also argued that such transfer is unlikely to occur (a) if the lexico-grammatical repertoire is inadequate to the task, (b) if the teaching materials and syllabus ignore or underplay those very features of lexico-grammar that give the spoken language its naturalistic flavour, and (c) if classroom management and methodology militate against the learner ever being presented with natural opportunities to realise the kinds of discourse functions we have looked at.

Follow-ups in exchanges, transaction boundaries and interruptions, to name but a few features, cannot simply be taught via the traditional 'Three Ps' methodology (Presentation-Practice-Production). How does one 'practise' narrative evaluation? How does one 'present' transaction boundaries? How does one 'produce' discourse markers naturally? An alternative methodology to supplement the 'Three Ps' may provide the answer, one based on the convenient mnemonic of the 'Three Is' (Illustration-Interaction-Induction). Illustration means looking at real data where possible, or at the very least texts carefully concocted on the basis of observations of real data. Interaction means talk among learners and teachers *about* language (carried out in L1 if necessary), sharing and forming views, breaking down cultural barriers and stereotypes, etc., in an environment where discourse awareness activities are brought to the fore (e.g. activities which focus on particular discourse patterns of L1, or comparisons between L1 and the target language). Induction means drawing conclusions about the way in which L2 realises its discourse patterns and genres and the meanings encoded in particular instances of lexico-grammar. If this is done in tandem with a syllabus where the lexico-grammatical and intonational components are discourse sensitive and not merely sentence-based abstractions, then teaching *about* the spoken language may have an unexpectedly powerful pay-off in the more rapid acquisition of fluency and naturalistic conversational skills. Such a claim would not be out of line with the general drift of argument of second-language acquisition researchers who in recent years have attempted to show that 'noticing' phenomena in L2 is a crucial step towards effective acquisition. But it is what the target for 'noticing' is that matters most, and if the input is impoverished, there will not be much worth noticing.

Notes

1 This chapter is a revised version with expanded references of a paper published in the *Australian Review of Applied Linguistics* (1995) 17 (2): 104–20.
2 House (1985) comments on the universality of the exchange and the adjacency pair, but suggests that there may be cross-linguistic differences in the degree of routinisation occurring in them.
3 On the use of *now* as a discourse marker, see Aijmer (1988).
4 Work on the translatability of discourse markers across languages includes Fraser and Malamud-Makowski (1996) (English and Spanish), and Fischer and Drescher (1996) (English/German/French).
5 Antaki, Díaz and Collins (1996) look upon the third part of the exchange as a confirmation or refutation of the interlocutor's contribution in the second part.
6 Contrastive studies of discourse markers and lists of markers in different languages that can be used as a basis for lexical input are particularly useful in the pedagogical context. For an excellent example, see Fraser and Malamud-Makowski's (1996) study of English and Spanish discourse markers. See also the papers in Jaszczolt and Turner (1996) on English and Spanish and English and Japanese discourse strategies, including marker usage.
7 I acknowledge too, in section 1.9 of this book, that corpus linguists have also inherited the 'left/right' metaphors of the written page, and that spoken corpora force us to revise corpus-analytical terminology as well as grammatical terms.
8 This is not to say that genres are always true to their stereotypes, and generic episodes adjust themselves to the exigencies of real-time interaction and the need to move towards goals, as Chapter 2 has attempted to demonstrate (see also Benwell 1996).

4

When does sentence grammar become discourse grammar?[1]

4.1 Introduction

The first three chapters have been concerned with fairly broad questions. In this chapter, we begin to look at the lower-order choices that speakers make in the discourse process and the creation of genres. In this chapter and the next, we shall consider grammatical choices within a discourse framework; there then follow two chapters which look at lexical features in spoken discourse.

The term 'discourse grammar' is frequently heard nowadays and what it means is not always clear. In this chapter I shall try to define and exemplify what I mean by the term, and to put it forward as an essential element in a discourse-based applied linguistics. I shall also attempt to show that applying discourse-grammatical criteria to the spoken language is not just an optional extra, but a necessary tool for an adequate analysis and explication of real spoken data. The arguments in this chapter owe a great deal to the ongoing work on spoken language conducted with my colleagues Ronald Carter and Rebecca Hughes, at the University of Nottingham, in the CANCODE project (see Chapter 1; also see Carter, Hughes and McCarthy 1995 for a further discussion of some of the issues raised in this chapter). Here I shall set out a list of criteria for analysing grammatical choice as an aspect of discourse rather than as a phenomenon confined to the bounds of the clause or sentence. The corpus examples will, I hope, demonstrate that the kinds of choices contained within them depend on contextual features which cannot be ignored and without which descriptive statements about such features are inadequate.

4.2 Paradigms and actual choice

In his work on intonation, the late David Brazil spoke of 'existential paradigms', that is to say, sets of actual choices open to speakers at any given place within a discourse (Brazil 1985: 41). Brazil was concerned with how lexical items, although often apparently belonging to large, open sets, occur in real discourse in a manner constrained by context such that thinking of their occurrence as a choice from a wide range of possible alternatives is unhelpful. In real situations, the selection of an item may be from only a small range of plausible alternatives or indeed may not represent a real choice at all (as with the *of* in the compound item *Queen of Hearts*). In McCarthy (1988; 1992) I attempted to build on Brazil's work by examining how speakers create kinds of local synonymy, antonymy and hyponymy that represent paradigms valid only for those particular discourses in which the relations are realised, and which may be different from the words grouped as synonyms, antonyms or hyponyms in a dictionary or thesaurus. Something similar occurs with grammatical items: the traditional paradigms of choice of items in grammatical sets may be replaced by paradigms of actual choices in real discourses.[2] One such striking example is the relationship between the pronoun *it* and the demonstratives *this* and *that*, which come together on many occasions to form a new paradigm of three members (instead of the two-member demonstrative set with their plurals). This paradigm offers a significant choice to a speaker or writer who wishes to refer to entities in the text or in the immediate situation. Viewing the actual choice as a different paradigm is a very clear example of when 'grammar' (understood in the traditional sense as the rules that underlie structural configurations and choices from closed sets) becomes 'grammar-in-discourse', that is to say phenomena only fully explicable with reference to contextual features and speakers'/writers' choices of form.

In McCarthy (1994) I used written newspaper and magazine data to show how *it*, *this* and *that* perform similar, yet distinguishable functions in the organisation of focus and topicality in texts. I argued that (1) *it* signalled continued, ongoing topics, (2) *this* signalled new or significant focus, and (3) *that* signalled a variety of distancing or marginalising functions (e.g. other-attribution, emotional distance, rejection of propositions or ideas, downgrading or de-focusing, reference across topics, etc.). Though these three choices were exemplified in written extracts in the 1994 paper, the same can be done with spoken passages. The following data extracts illustrate the three types of signalling:

(4.1)
It as simple topic continuation[3]:
[A customer <S 01> asks an assistant <S 02> for help in a bookshop.]

<S 01> I wonder erm if you could help me.
<S 02> Yeah.
<S 01> I'm looking for two books, one's a book on organization *Schools as organizations* by Charles Handy [<S 02> oh yes] Can you tell me where it might be.
<S 02> Yes there would be one or two places we've got it on stock [<S 01> yes] it might be on the business section because all his books are generally at the business section.

(4.2)
This as focus on a new or important topic[4]:
[<S 03> is recounting the first time he heard the phrase *pin money*, when he went to get a library ticket from a British Council office overseas.]

<S 03> I worked there just a very short time erm it was when I was doing my PhD I went out there to do some research and erm I always remember there was a Director there at that time he was called Macnamara and I went along there to get to get him to sign for a library ticket so that I could use the university library or the public library or something and he said erm erm I always remember this I'd never heard this phrase before he said how would you like to earn some pin money and I was sort of, young fellah I didn't know what **this** meant [laughs]

(4.3)
That as distancing[5]:
[A university tutor is talking about Jane Austen.]

<S 01> She's looking at people who pretend for instance to have good manners and the essence of good manners is concern for other people and she can see that within that society many many people have outwardly excellent manners but **that** is something of veneer it's shallow it's pretence, appearance

In (4.2) and (4.3), the speakers could have just continued their topics with *it* instead of *this* or *that*, but they choose instead to focus or distance the discourse entities referred to. The choices available operate at a level beyond that of the clause or sentence and are to do with signalling the speaker's stance towards the message. When grammatical choices operate in this way, 'grammar becomes discourse', that is to say, grammatical phenomena require discoursal explanations.

But why should we bother to seek a discoursal context for pedagogy if the traditional explanations of items such as pronouns and demonstratives stand us in good stead for most teaching needs? The question is a common-sense one, but has its answer in the fact that the traditional explanations often cannot capture adequately the selection procedures the learner will need to engage with in constructing larger segments of text (which we surely hope our learners will do in 'writing skills' or 'speaking skills' programmes). Traditional, sentence-based grammar teaching methods (a) tend to focus on only spatio-temporal meanings of the demonstratives, and (b) do not bring together for illustrative purposes the pronoun *it* and the demonstratives, typically keeping them in separate compartments, despite the evidence of data that they frequently exist as viable alternatives in real discourse. 'Re-arranging the paradigms' is not just re-arranging the furniture to liven up the living-room; its purpose is more faithfully to represent actual language use. This (It? That?) should always be the prime motivation for treating grammar as discourse.

4.3 Rules that do not say enough

Pedagogical grammarians simplify the grammatical facts and provide rules of thumb about second language grammar that work for most learners in most situations, and we shall always continue to do that. However, simplification that fails to generate appropriate grammar may be counter-productive. One such simplified rule might be 'the English past perfect is used when an event happens in a past time *before* another past time'. This enables the learner of English to construct well-formed sentences such as *I spoke to Brian Thorne yesterday for the first time. I had actually met him once before, many years ago.* However, the same two sentences would clearly be as well-formed if the second were in past simple, although with a different emphasis. We have, then, a rule that explains a grammatical choice that is certainly well-formed, but which does not offer sufficiently rigorous guidelines to generate the choice in many other types of situations where it is equally appropriate. When this problem arises, there is no substitute for looking at choices that speakers and writers have made in real contexts and examining the contextual features that would seem to have determined one choice or another.

Contextual awareness then underpins choice, and grammar becomes discourse once more. Such an approach does not exclude simple, clear guidelines where these can be formulated. In the case of the past perfect, for example, a significant number of occurrences of the tense form are found in indirect speech reports, such as:

(4.4)
[<S 01> is talking about an accident.]

<S 01> And I chipped a bone at the end of, on the end of my elbow, I
    didn't know it was broken it was two weeks before I went to the
    hospital it just seemed to get worse and worse.
<S 02> Right.
<S 01> And then when I went finally went **they said that I'd chipped this**
    bone.

(4.5)
[<S 01> is recounting a story about a tramp who deliberately got into trouble by creating traffic accidents just to get himself a bed in the police cells for the night; she tells how he caused a collision with her car but escaped unhurt.]

<S 02> So it was a bit of a miracle he wasn't hurt wasn't it.
<S 01>   ᒪApparently it
    was his party no it was his party-piece because the police **told me**
    that he'd done it very often this 'cos it got him a bed for the night
    you know it got him in hospital.

Observation of real data that results in a simple rule or guideline is extremely helpful, but sometimes the occurrences are more complex and need closer scrutiny. In the case of the past perfect, the most interesting instances are those where there is little formal evidence (such as the presence of a reporting verb) to explicate the choice, and one is forced to fall back on contextual features only. In (4.6) below, several past perfect forms occur, none of which could be said to be conditioned by any structural or lexical constraints.[6]

(4.6)
[Two young women are talking about mutual friends from their days together at Brunel University, in the south of England. They were driving

along a motorway when the recording was made, with <S 02> driving, which accounts for her minimal contributions to the talk!]

<S 01> I got on better with Glynbob I think and John Bish let me and Trudie sleep in his bed last time we went up to Brunel or the one time when we stayed in Old Windsor with them cos erm **Ben had given us his room** cos **he'd gone away for the weekend** and erm it was me and Trudie just in Ben's room and John Doughty had a double bed so he, John Bish had a double bed so he offered us his double bed between us and then slept in Ben's room cos **Ben and PQ had gone away** for the weekend but they tried to get, **they'd gone away** and tried to get back like to catch me and Trudie before we left [<S 02> Yeah] and they just missed us by half an hour they were really pissed off because apparently **they'd been driving** really fast like trying to get back but erm I mean we didn't know they were trying to get back we didn't leave until like very late we went to the Little Chef for breakfast on the Sunday cos it was only over the road from where they were living and Andy Symons the bar manager like came back with us and stayed the night at Glynbob's house as well so he came to Little Chef with us in the morning as well.
<S 02> Oh God.
<S 02> There was like loads of us in the Little Chef . . . and we got there and we had to wait like ages for them to do the food and stuff and we were going oh we don't mind we don't mind . . . I remember going to the Little Chef after the Valedictory and erm we took the minibus down and Cooksie drove cos **he'd been driving all night** and he drove the minibus down and it was in the morning it was after like the ball and PQ still had some wine left . . .

What these examples have in common is that they give a reason or justification for the events that are recounted. They are not the main events themselves, they are rather something the speaker feels to be a necessary background to what happened. Note the prevalence of *cos* (and in one case *apparently*). This use of *cos/because* to justify or explain events has been commented on by Ford (1994) as a feature of conversation,[7] and it does seem to co-occur with the past perfect in a noticable number of cases (76 times in the one million word CANCODE sample). Another clear case of backgrounding is (4.7):

(4.7)

[<S 01> is telling a story about getting drunk when he was a young man. *Bass* is a make of beer popular in Britain. *The crew* is his way of referring to his gang of friends/colleagues.]

<S 01> During the war they lowered the specific gravity of the beer.
<S 02> Aha.
<S 03> Yeah they did.
<S 01> And er round about 1947 or so it was back to normal and **I'd gone out** it was after some exam results for the bank and, celebrating with the crew and unbeknownst to me they'd got the new deadly old Bass on you see and they finished up draping me over a hedge.

Examining the discourse conditions under which these past perfects occur enables us to posit a broad macro-function for the tense form at a level beyond the sentence, in terms of how clauses recounting events relate to one another, some being backgrounded, others being foregrounded as main events.[8] In other words, a discourse grammar focuses on the kinds of preoccupations that speakers routinely deal with in speech, that is, how can I best organise my message to make it clear, coherent, relevant, appropriately organised, etc? This accords with radical proposals to re-think the way we construct grammars such as Brazil's (1995) 'grammar of speech', where he pertinently sums up the position with regard to grammar and the language user:

> In other words, we do not necessarily have to assume that the consideration of such abstract notions as 'sentences' enters into the user's scheme of things at all. (p. 15)

By the same token, even though they necessarily may have a more conscious emphasis on grammatical form, it should not be assumed that foreign-language learners do not need or want to pay the same attention to choices reflecting organisation, staging and coherence of the overall message. However, the hypothesis that past perfect coincides frequently with explanations and justifications reflects a probabilistic view of grammar, and one which says no more than 'this is a fact of occurrence in a number of cases sufficiently large to warrant pedagogical attention and to provide a useful, probabilistic guideline'. It is distinct from deterministic grammatical statements, which are open to confirmation or falsification through structural tests of well-formedness. Many statements about grammar as discourse will be probabilistic, but that does not make them any the less useful pedagogically. Such statements may be open to modification, but if they can be shown to be reliable across different contexts, then they stand as good examples of grammar becoming discourse, and can often suggest explanations of grammatical choices that the conventional, more deterministic rules explain only very inadequately.[9] Grammar becomes discourse when the conventional, sentence-based rules simply do not say enough to enable the learner to make appropriate grammatical choices in the way native speakers do to organise and 'stage' their messages, and where choice can only be explained in context.

4.4 Spoken and written grammar

Grammar must become discourse in order to answer questions about differences between spoken and written language, for it is only by observing actual discourses that we can properly describe the distribution of forms in the spoken and written mode. Much grammar is, of course, shared by both modes, and it would be an exaggeration to suggest that huge differences exist in distribution for every grammatical feature. The crucial point is that we should never *assume* that if a grammar has been constructed for written texts, it is equally valid for spoken texts. Some forms seem to occur much more frequently in one mode or the other, and some forms are used with different shades of meaning in the two modes. Since almost all grammars in the past have based their descriptions on written norms (and even those which have used spoken data, such as Quirk *et al* 1985, have often neglected common features of spoken grammar; see Carter and McCarthy 1995b for examples), it thus becomes important to look at what really happens in the spoken language to detect significant differences. Carter and McCarthy (1995b) and McCarthy and Carter (1997a), using the CANCODE corpus, identify a selection of key areas where differences occur. These include the prevalence of certain types of ellipsis in spoken language (e.g. of subject pronouns, auxiliary verbs, articles, initial elements of fixed expressions), different formal types of speech reporting in spoken and written (see Chapter 8 of this book for a full account), and the occurrence of pre- and post-posed items (*topics* and *tails*) in conversation. These last phenomena deserve closer scrutiny and discussion. Examples (4.8) to

(4.11) represent structural configurations almost exclusively associated with informal speech:

(4.8)

<S 01> **That woman who's a verger at church, her husband, his parents** own that butcher's shop.

(4.9)

<S 01> **Paul** in this job that he's got now when he goes into the office he's never quite sure where he's going to be sent.

(4.10)

[Two friends deciding what to eat in a restaurant.]

<S 01> **I'm** going to have Mississippi Mud Pie **I am.**
<S 02> I'm going to have profiteroles. **I can't** resist them **I can't** ... just too moreish.

(4.11)

[Students chatting in doctor's surgery waiting-room.]

<S 01> You got a cold too?
<S 02> Can't seem to shake it off ... everyone's going down like flies.
<S 01> Trouble is **can** leave you feeling weak for so long **it can flu.**

(4.8) and (4.9) utilise a slot before the 'clause proper' (in the traditional sense) begins. Such phenomena have been variously termed 'left dislocations', 'themes', and 'topics' (see e.g. Aijmer 1989; Geluykens 1989 for English, French and Italian; Geluykens 1992 for English; Blasco 1995 for French; Rivero 1980 for Spanish). This 'topic slot' or 'head' (McCarthy and Carter 1997b) plays an important role in how the speaker orientates the listener, it is an act of consideration to the listener, for example in (4.8) taking him/her from a convenient anchor already familiar to some entity that is new and which is to be the topic of the upcoming clause. As such it is a quintessentially spoken feature, reflecting the demands of face-to-face interaction and the real-time synthesis of talk. Its mirror-image counterpart, the 'right-displaced/dislocated' (see Ashby 1988, 1994 on French; Heilenman and McDonald 1993 on French; Fretheim 1995 on Norwegian) or 'tail' slot (Aijmer 1989) corresponds regularly with contexts which are evaluative, as it does in (4.10) and (4.11); it signals more than the mere core clause without a 'right-hand' dislocation, and the overlay is heavily interpersonal. The prevalence of quotation marks around the unfamiliar terminology in these last few sentences is not only because the structures themselves are rarely dealt with by grammarians but above all because much of the terminology itself is locked in a written, sentence-based perspective on language. Spoken language has no 'left' or 'right' in the way that characters on a page do, and topics and tails pass without note and so naturally that it seems odd to suggest that anything is 'dislocated' at all (see also section 3.2.2). The metaphors of written text should not be transferred uncritically when grammar confronts spoken discourse, and the fact that spoken language is produced in time rather than space, for a here-and-now listener rather than a temporally displaced reader, becomes paramount in explaining grammatical phenomena. Discourse drives grammar, not the reverse.

Another example which underlines the power of context over grammar, and not vice-versa, is the distribution in spoken and written texts of the structure *be to* with a future meaning. Many teachers will recognise themselves (as I have done myself in the past) teaching sentences such as *You are to be at the airport at eight-thirty*, where the *be to* denotes a firm and unshiftable fact about the future. Yet in reality, this structure is so rare in everyday spoken language that it would, in my opinion, have no significant place in a speaking-skills grammar course. In one million words of CANCODE data, only four examples of future *be to* occur, one in a university small tutorial group, and three (one of which is repeated and co-ordinated) in semi-formal meetings as (4.12) and (4.13) illustrate:

(4.12)
[Tutor speaking in university tutorial on *Pride and Prejudice*.]

<S 01> And there's also of course the famous first sentence of *Pride and Prejudice* from which this section has received its name It is a truth universally acknowledged that a single man in possession of a good fortune must be in want of a wife. That this statement is meant to have ironic qualification is shown both by the orotundity of the diction and by contrast with what is said in the following sentence that **the concern is to be** not for the universe but with the neighbourhood not with the totality of mankind but with the surrounding families. Em that's all it says about that bit.

(4.13)
[business meeting]

<S 01> Oh no oh right well no but it's taken two months to do that.
<S 02>   ⌊**Rob is to look at it
and Ann Pascoe to look at it and formal comments to be
collated and sent back to David.**
<S 03>   ⌊And one month for that.
<S 02> Yeah.
<S 03> I think that's safest.

The reason for the rarity of this feature is quite clear: *be to* in its future
meaning is a distancing form, suggesting external and impersonal
authority of some kind that may appear pompous or face-threatening in
face-to-face talk, where speakers overwhelmingly prefer to realise the
same meanings with 'softer' expressions such as *supposed to* or *going to*.
Hardly surprising, then, that we only find it in a meeting and a tutorial,
where 'authority' and 'distancing' characterise the genres. In many
written contexts, on the other hand, authoritative statements may be
put forward without face threat, especially in journalistic reporting
registers (for examples of *be to* in newspaper reports announcing
decisions, events, changes, etc., see McCarthy and Carter 1994: 126; also
Chapter 5 of this book) or in texts denoting regulations, obligations, etc.
Grammar becoming discourse here means, once again, seeing grammatical choice and structural configuration in talk as motivated by interpersonal factors, not just ideational or transactional ones. Distinguishing
the key aspects of written and spoken contexts is crucial to the observation and understanding of their widely differing distributions of forms
and meanings and to the prioritising of those forms and meanings in
teaching.

4.5 Units of description in grammar and discourse

Several linguists have noted the relative absence in spoken data of forms
common in written texts which are often seen as core features of
grammar and central to grammatical description. Anyone who looks at
large amounts of informal spoken data, for example, cannot fail to be
struck by the absence of well-formed 'sentences' with main and subordinate clauses. Instead we often find turns that are just phrases, incom-
plete clauses, clauses that look like subordinate clauses but which seem

not to be attached to any main clause, etc. Hockett (1986) makes the point that, while analysts have long ignored such phenomena, 'speakers and hearers do not ignore them – they carry a sizeable share of the communicative load'. Therefore, the fact that well-formed sentences are not the norm urges a re-assessment of the usefulness of notions such as 'main' and 'subordinate' clauses. (4.14) amply illustrates the problem of 'subordinate' clauses:

(4.14)
[Two students are talking about what people are going to wear to a forthcoming ball.]

<S 01> I really am I'm so pissed off that everyone's erm everyone's going
    to be wearing erm
<S 02> Cocktail dresses.
<S 01> I don't, I really don't see the point the whole point of a ball is that
    you wear like a proper dress
<S 02> Wear a ball dress I know I mean my dress is huge.
<S 01> So is Nicola definitely going to, erm is Nick definite
<S 02>   ⌊Well she she
    says she is but if she sees everybody else wearing a cocktail dress
    she's bound to fork out the money she's got loads of money.
<S 01> Cos mum said to me you know that she would buy me like a a
    little black dress but the thing is then I wouldn't feel right you
    know.
<S 02> Well I mean you wear a
<S 01>   ⌊She, but you know she means like something from like erm
    Miss Selfridge or something.
<S 02> Yes if, I mean you wear a little black dress just to, you know
<S 01> Clubbing or something.
<S 02> To a party.
<S 01> Yeah exactly.

The first 'sentence' seems to be spoken by two speakers, with <S 02> providing the object of <S 01>'s verb *wearing*. In the next pair of utterances, <S 02> repeats <S 01>'s direct object in a slightly reworded form (<S 01> ... *wear like a proper dress* <S 02> *Wear a ball dress*). In the final utterances of the extract, both speakers 'complete' the same clause, but with different constituents (*Clubbing or something/To a party*). How do we analyse 'other-completed clauses/sentences'? How do we analyse 'other-repeated grammar'? Are <S 02>'s utterances here part of <S 01>'s 'sentences', or units of their own? Where both complete the clause, are the two different constituents of equal status in its structure? A grammar-in-discourse approach sees structure as a collaborative/negotiative process rather than as a deterministic product. Within the relevant factors of a description it includes real-time contextual features such as turn-taking, repetition and joint construction by more than one party.[10]

There are some items in (4.14) which do not seem to be main clauses:

that everyone's erm everyone's going to be wearing cocktail dresses
that you wear like a proper dress
(she says) *she is*
if she sees everybody else wearing a cocktail dress
(mum said to me) *that she would buy me like a a little black dress*

The first two are complement-clauses (thus not subordinate in the true sense), which are frequent in conversational language. Two are reported clauses within speech reports (also frequent; see Chapter 8), which are arguably 'main clauses' transferred from other discourses. Only one seems to be a conventional conditional subordinate clause with *if*. The clause *Cos mum said to me you know that she would buy me like a a little black dress* would seem superficially to be a candidate for subordination, but (a) it is separated from its 'main' clause by an intervening turn, and (b) it seems simply to *add* background information rather than place any restriction or contingency on the main portion. It means 'this is the reason I'm asking about Nicola' and does not exercise any causal conditioning on the main clause. It seems more reasonable, therefore, to treat the *cos* clause as non-subordinate, but discoursally as providing background/supporting information. Something similar operates with certain types of *if* clauses, as in these three further examples from the same conversation:

(4.15)
<S 01> Oh there's orange juice in the fridge as well **if you want a drink**
... erm no **if we have this and go back to your house.**

(4.16)
<S 01> Yeah help yourself ... there's scissors in the drawer **if you need to cut it open.**

The first and third *if*-clauses are best considered, from a discourse point of view, as non-subordinate explicating units, making explicit the speaker's reasons for uttering the main clause. The second example (*if we have this and go back to your house*) seems to operate as a polite suggestion without any element of conditionality. In a discoursal sense it is clearly 'main' information and resembles the kind of 'topicalisation' referred to in section 4.4 above (see also Haiman 1978 for a discussion of conditionals as 'topics').

This kind of problem of classification has led some linguists to propose abandoning the notion of 'subordination' altogether when it comes to describing and explaining spoken grammar (e.g. Blanche-Benveniste 1982; Schleppegrell 1992) and to advocate substituting the clause as a more viable basic unit for spoken language than the sentence (Miller 1995). Another good reason for advocating this is that some sentence-configurations, for example non-finite clauses / prepositional clauses plus main clause (such as *On leaving the building she noticed a black car*), which are found in formal written language, are extremely rare in conversation. Blanche-Benveniste (1995) gives examples for spoken French, and much the same applies to spoken English (e.g. see Esser 1981 on the absence of embedded clauses). Grammar becomes discourse when conventional sentence-based units of description fail to account for the facts, suggesting an alternative descriptive model based more on units of information and interpersonal considerations generated within real contexts.

4.6 Grammatical puzzles

By no means has all of the grammar of a language such as English yet been satisfactorily described and explained, and, where areas are fuzzy or indeterminate or apparently unsusceptible to rule-creating, seeing grammar as discourse can often help. Let us take the case of *get*-passives in English (as in *His bicycle got stolen*). These have been studied for a long time, though mostly on the basis of concocted sentences, with the notable exception of Collins (1996), which this present look at the phenomenon parallels, but with the intention of drawing wider implications, which Collins does not.[11] Linguists have considered the interchangeability (or otherwise) of *get*- and *be*-passives, or the place of *get* and *be* on a 'passive gradient' (Svartvik 1966), and the typical absence of explicit human agents in *get*-passive sentences (see especially Hatcher 1949, also

Stein 1979; Granger 1983; Gnutzmann 1991; Collins 1996). The debate has also homed in on the potential of *get* for focusing simultaneously on actions and their end results (see Stein 1979; Vanrespaille 1991). Other considerations that have come into play are whether *get*-passives correspond to contexts where (usually ill) fortune plays a role in the event (*He got killed*, *It got burnt*, etc.), the historical development of the *get*-passive in relation to other meanings of *get* (Givón and Yang 1994), and different distributions across different varieties of English (Collins 1996). And yet there is a general feeling that *get*-passives have continued to elude satisfactory description.[12] Once again, the way forward seems to be to look at real data, to consider grammar as discourse and to bring to the fore that discourse involves speakers and listeners, not just messages.

The CANCODE corpus contains 139 clear *get*-passives, from which a very consistent (but not exclusive) pattern emerges.[13] Of the 139 examples, 124 refer in some way or another to an 'adversative' context (i.e. a state of affairs that is signalled by the conversational participants as manifestly undesirable, or at the very least, problematic); these include verb phrases such as:

> *got flung about in the car*
> *got killed*
> *got locked in/out*
> *got lumbered*
> *didn't get paid*
> *got picked on*
> *got sued*
> *got burgled*
> *get intimidated*
> *get criticized*
> *get beaten*

Of the 139 examples, 130 have no agent explicitly stated (i.e. 93%, which sits well with Collins' 1996 figure of 92%). Among the examples which do have stated agents are:

> *most things got written up by scribes*
> *the whole bus got stripped by the Italian police*
> *and got sued by the owners*
> *she's going to get eaten by the wolf*
> *you get intimidated by the staff on the labour ward*

These agents are somewhat impersonal or, in the case of the wolf, non-human. The absence of agency or the presence of impersonal, non-specific agency fits in with what linguists have previously noted (e.g. Granger 1983: 194).

But in a number of the 'adverse' cases, we are faced with circumstances that are not *inherently* adverse or undesirable, for example:

(4.17)
[A customer in a village shop has just realised that the shopkeeper has remembered a neighbour's fish order but forgotten her order of fish for her cat. She addresses the neighbour humorously.]

<S 01> So **you got remembered** and our cat got forgotten.

(4.18)
[Students talking about upcoming hectic social timetable.]

<S 01> **I've got invited to the school ball** as well.
<S 02> Are you.
<S 03> Don't really fancy it.

(4.19)
[Students discussing job prospects.]

<S 01> Do you know **how much lawyers get paid for an hour** the best
       ones
<S 02>   ⌊I don't I don't care.
<S 01> Six hundred pound an hour.
<S 02> I don't care.

It is the *speaker's stance* towards the situation that signals it as undesirable or problematic rather than the situation in itself (see Chappell 1980; see also Sussex 1982 for a critique of over-simplifying the adversative/beneficial dichotomy). In (4.17), although the situation is clearly beneficial for the neighbour whose fish order was not forgotten, the speaker sees it as part of her own general misfortune. In one of the relatively few occasions where the context is clearly beneficial rather than adversative, we can still see the speaker overlay that can be effected by the *get*-passive, in this case suggesting a downplaying of self-praise when reporting success:

(4.20)

[The speakers are talking about <S 02>'s past successes as a tennis player.]

<S 01> And were those like junior matches or tournaments or county matches.

<S 02> Er both county and er, well I played county championships and lost in the finals the first year and er **I got picked for the county** for that and then so I I played county matches pretty much the same time.

<S 01> Right, good.

The key to understanding the *get*-passive is that it reflects the stance of the speaker rather than the content of the message. It is yet another case where examining sentences and jettisoning the people who produce them is inadequate. The *get*-passive might indeed be a linguistic puzzle, but it is considerably demystified the moment we look upon it as something the speaker overlays onto events to reflect his/her stance towards those events. Some linguists have recognised this, most notably Lakoff (1971) and Stein (1979), but the benefit of examining real spoken data is that intuitions on that score can be supported by facts.[14]

We can say that the *get*-passive coincides overwhelmingly with adverse or problematic circumstances (89% of occurrences) but that these are adverse/problematic *as judged by the speaker*. *Get* also coincides overwhelmingly with the absence of an explicit agent (93% of occurrences), suggesting that emphasis is on the person or thing experiencing the process encoded in the verb phrase, rather than its cause or agent.

These two descriptive statements are directly useful for teaching, as are many of the actual contexts and examples found in the corpus. In this case, and, one suspects many others, the linguistic puzzle can best be illuminated by treating grammar as discourse rather than merely as a feature of the internal structure of sentences. But the kinds of statements we have ended up making about the *get*-passive are different from statements of structural prescription (e.g. that the passive is formed with the past participle, not the base-form of the verb); we can therefore distinguish once again between deterministic grammar and probabilistic grammar, the latter being statements of what is the most likely context of use. Grammar-as-discourse leans more often towards probabilistic grammars, and sees probabilistic statements as no less useful for language learners than deterministic ones.

4.7 Conclusion

Whether one looks at individual grammatical items such as pronouns or demonstratives, or whether one considers wider structural phenomena such as topics and tails, subordination, tense choice, etc., in spoken discourse, grammar is often most adequately explained by referring to contextual features and, above all, by taking into account interpersonal aspects of face-to-face interaction. I have argued that a grammar-as-discourse approach includes:

- The appropriate re-arranging of existing paradigms in line with real choices in discourse.
- The re-examination of conventional, deterministic rules in the light of real contexts and probabilistic correlations between forms and contexts.
- The re-assessment of traditional units of description to reflect what kinds of units are actually (differentially) manifested in spoken and written discourse.
- The unwillingness to accept linguistic puzzles as insoluble mysteries without subjecting them to scrutiny in actual occurrence.

The more one pursues these lines, of course, the more one realises that grammar can become discourse whenever the (applied) linguist wants it to and that the two are not separate levels of language that brush shoulders only when awkward problems need solving. Grammar only really exists in discourse, and it is best viewed as the regular traces left behind by myriad conversational encounters where the exigencies of person-to-person communication are paramount, always taking precedence over mere 'content'. In the words of Hopper and Thompson (1993), grammar is 'sedimented conversational practices'. This whole book takes the view that grammar should ideally be seen, in Fox and Thompson's (1990) words:

> ... as necessarily including the entire interactional dimension of
> the communicative situation in which conversationalists
> constitute the people and things they want to talk about.

Grammar-as-discourse thus confronts the negotiation of social identities, in which formal choices are fully implicated. For the applied linguist interested in language teaching applications, a grammar-as-discourse approach is certainly challenging. Some aspects of that challenge may be unrealistic at times (for example, in a spoken language awareness lesson, just how does one bring out 'the entire interactional dimension of the communicative situation' if one does not have access to natural data in the classroom?). However, it has its unexpected rewards too in the new light that is often shed on age-old and apparently intractable grammatical problems. It also offers a way of bridging the unfortunate gap that frequently exists between the 'grammar' class and the 'speaking skills' class, too often perceived by teachers and learners alike as different worlds that have no agreed meeting place.

Notes

1 This paper is based on a presentation with the same title given by the author and Rebecca Hughes at the TESOL Convention, Long Beach, California, 1995. It repeats arguments put forward there, but uses different data sets for exemplification. A different and more extended version of the paper may be found in Hughes and McCarthy (1998).

2 The idea of re-grouping items based on their discoursal properties rather than just their formal characteristics is echoed in Hoffmann's (1989) grouping of words such as *I, you, here* and *now* as 'means of referring to elements of the situation of utterance ... they form a field of their own that is in opposition to traditional categorisation (pronoun or adverb)'. Similarly, Crymes (1968: 64–70) brings together *do so, do it, do this* and *do that* as a discoursal set of substitutes and examines their usage.

3 *It* in this example refers to a thing (a book), but, as can *this* and *that*, may also refer to events, facts, propositions, etc. (see Peterson 1982; Ehlich 1989; McCarthy 1994).

4 There is also, of course, the 'new *this*' common in informal spoken narratives where *this* is in opposition to the indefinite article (e.g. 'Then **this** policeman suddenly appears and everybody runs'). See Wald (1983) for examples and a discussion.

5 There is another sense of *that* which occurs in spoken discourse and sometimes in popular journalism, which refers to entities as given, known but not topical, exemplified in the opening segment of a story told by an elderly, disabled ex-member of the British Women's Air Force who had the 'honour' (in her eyes) of being invited onto the flight deck during a holiday flight. The story opens with a characteristic 'new *this*' (see note 4):

<S 01> Well, I don't know how I got **this** honour really. I had all the badges, you know, I used to be in the air force, and I'd spoken to two or three people, but when we got on the plane, they took me on first, because they had to lift me on, you know, with **that** lift, and the pilot was sat in one of the seats. There was nobody on the plane but me, and, I don't know, I

must have said, either said something funny about flying, or he'd said
something, noticed my badges, I don't know which it was ...

That lift here seems to mean 'one of the typical lifts they have on aircraft for
getting disabled passengers on and off, which I can assume you know about'
(reinforced by the shared knowledge marker *you know*).

6 The kind of constraint I refer to here is that exercised by words like *before*,
already or *just*, which often provide compulsory contexts for the use of past
perfect. For example:

(1)

[<S 01> is recounting how he found it difficult to be off work on sick leave.]

<S 01> Cos then at the time all I wanted to do was get back to work and being
    stuck in the, you know in for six months [<S 02> mm] you know I just I
    just couldn't believe that they could leave anybody, I mean wasn't it
    better to have me back at work instead of paying me sick pay

<S 02> Yes

<S 01> Em and because **I'd always worked and I'd never ever been off work
    before you know I just couldn't handle it**

(2) Here there are a number of past perfects but the italicised one is
    constrained by *already*, while the ones before it are not:

[<S 01> is talking about Christmas.]

<S 01> Well yeah I mean Christmas was really good for us this time. I
    mean **we'd done** a lot of pre-planning for it **hadn't we** Mary
    you know **we'd er**

<S 02>   ⌊**Saved**

<S 01>   ⌊**saved** money for the, obviously to to cut the costs
    down towards, er **we'd saved** you know a fair a fair bit for presents and
    we'd already saved a hell of a lot of money for the food

<S 02> Mm

7 See also McTear (1980) on the pragmatics of *because*.

8 On foregrounding and backgrounding in general through grammatical
aspect, see Hopper (1979).

9 The coincidence of past perfect with contexts of explaining/justifying events
seems to be true of many cases in written texts too (Hughes, personal
communication).

10 Harris (1990) argues for the integration of strictly linguistic and such non-
linguistic features of communication, though Fleming's (1995) critique of
Harris's position rightly points up some of the difficulties of integrating
temporality (e.g. the real-time constraints of speech) into linguistic description. Harris's perspective is clearly one which supports viewing grammar as
discourse.

11 Vanrespaille (1991) is another exception, in that her study of the *get*-passive is
corpus-based. Although her corpus includes spoken material from the Survey
of English Usage, she does not indicate precisely what proportion of her

approximately 700 instances of the *get*-passive are natural spoken. However, from her tables of results, it would seem that a large number of her examples come from (written) drama texts.

12 Chappell (1980) refers to 'tantalizingly unresolved questions' about the *get*-passive.

13 The figure of 139 occurrences in one million words is two-and-a-half times as frequent as Granger's (1983) figure of nine occurrences in her spoken corpus of 160,000 words. Our figure matches only slightly better with Collins' (1996) figure of 96 per million. His data are taken from the London-Lund and ICE corpora, which, I would argue, are less representative of everyday informal conversational genres than the CANCODE corpus. What is more, the 65 occurrences of core *get*-passives in a mixed written corpus of one million words (created for spoken/written comparisons with CANCODE) does not either accord completely with Collins' figure of 43 per million for written, though both corpora coincide in suggesting that *get*-passives are twice as frequent in spoken as in written.

14 Lakoff uses concocted sentences. Stein uses a corpus, but it is written (novels and plays).

5

Some patterns of co-occurrence of verb-forms in spoken and in written English

5.1 Introduction

In this chapter we continue to focus on grammar, and take further the discussion of written and spoken parallels and differences embarked upon in section 4.4. Here we redress the temptation to conclude that *everything* is different between spoken and written grammars, and show that features of patterning at the discourse level are often shared by the two modes of communication. However, the fact that the chapter also shows patterns that are *not shared* between the two modes is very important indeed, for it underscores one of the central arguments of this book, that we cannot assume that grammars modelled on written language can simply be imported wholesale into the description of spoken language. Spoken grammar must always be elaborated in its own terms, using spoken data. If, at the end of the exercise, spoken and written are shown to have many features in common, then this is a convenience to be thankful for, and not something that can be prejudged without careful research. Our task is to identify precisely those areas that are shared and those which are not.

Amongst the linguists who have always argued for discoursal interpretations of lexico-grammatical phenomena, the late Eugene Winter stands out, and his most enduring achievement has without doubt been the demonstration of the way the several levels of linguistic form work in harmony to create the text. Elements of form, whether lexical or grammatical, share a potential in contributing to the process of interpretation of the larger form: the coherent, cohesive and patterned artefact that is the text (Winter 1982). For our purposes, we could add the words 'or genre' to the last sentence. In Winter's conceptual framework the grammar of any individual clause or sentence is involved in creating higher-order patterns. Grammar and context work in synergy, and any proper study of text involves a close scrutiny of the patterning of grammatical forms. Winter's work is normally associated with written text analysis, but in this chapter I shall try to show that the principles of textual-grammatical patterning apply equally to spoken discourses. The spoken textual product is no less a record of the harmonious collaboration of grammatical form with other levels of form than is the written text. I shall attempt to demonstrate that the kinds of grammatical patterns found in certain types of written texts (narratives and reports) have their functional counterparts in spoken discourse and that the business of signalling the macro-level development of the discourse is of the same importance and given similar prominence in the spoken as in the written. But where there are differences between spoken and written, these will be noted as important. I shall, in particular, hope to develop Winter's notion of 'situation' utterance and its 'sequence' in subsequent utterances. 'Situation' and 'sequence' are two concepts which Winter, working with written sentences, sees as fundamental in the interpretation of sequences of clauses in text (Winter 1982: 2).

The written examples in this chapter are taken from British popular journalistic sources, in the tradition of Winter's own work (*ibid.*), along with some literary examples. Spoken examples are taken from the CANCODE corpus. Written and spoken examples taken side by side offer the researcher a number of possible avenues of exploration and questions to answer, including:

1 What sorts of recurring grammatical patterns can be observed over clause-boundaries in the written and in the spoken mode?
2 How determined are the patterns? Is the ordering of grammatical elements within them relatively fixed or flexible?
3 What are the functions of such patterns within the text or utterance sequence?
4 Do patterns found in one mode occur in the other with the same realisations?
5 Where patterns occur in one mode but do not seem to occur in the other, is there evidence that the same functional patterns exist but with different formal realisations in each mode?

Not all of these questions can be addressed or answered in this short chapter, but where particularly interesting evidence presents itself, relevant issues from (1) to (5) will be taken up in turn.

5.2 A clear case of parallel: the narrative 'situation-event' pattern

Within the field of grammar-and-discourse studies of written texts, published work already exists on correlations between grammatical features and text-types and macro-functions (i.e. functions beyond the level of sentence, such as paragraph organisation, reference across sentences, etc.). An appropriate example to begin with is Zydatiss' (1986) paper on so-called 'hot news' texts such as are often found in newspapers and on news broadcasts. A hot news text typically has an attention-grabbing headline and/or first sentence, operating rather in the way of an 'abstract' (to use Labov's (1972) term for the narrative-initial utterance(s)) with which a teller gives a broad outline of what the upcoming story is about and why it might be worth listening to (on the other elements of Labov's model, see section 3.2.3). In clause-analytical terms (see Hoey 1983: 138ff), the abstract has a parallel in the 'preview' segment of a 'preview-detail' textual pattern; it answers the question: *What, roughly, is this text going to be about? What is its main point?* and prompts the question *What are the details?'*. On a more general level, it corresponds to Winter's (1982) notion of 'situation'.

In the hot news texts examined by Zydatiss (*ibid.*), the 'abstract/ preview' sentence of the text typically occurs with present perfect tense on the main verb(s). Subsequent sentences then typically have past simple form. Two British newspaper examples follow, with relevant main-clause verb forms in bold type:

(5.1)

SAM DIES AT 109

The oldest man in Britain **has died** aged 109 – six weeks after taking the title.

Sam Crabbe, a former sugar broker, from Cadgwith, Cornwall, **did not give up** smoking until he was 98 and **enjoyed** a nightly tot of whisky. He **was taken** ill just hours before his death.

Sprightly Sam **became** Britain's longest living man when 112-year-old Welshman John Evans died last month.

(*Daily Mirror*, 26.7.1990: 8)

(5.2)

INVASION OF THE CRAWLIES

Poisonous black widow spiders **have invaded** Britain by plane.

They **stowed away** in crates of ammunition flown from America
to RAF Welford, Berks.
A US airman at the base near Newbury **captured** one of the
spiders in a jar after it crawled out of a crate.

(Daily Mirror, 27.7.1990: 19)

This pattern of present perfect followed by past simple is quite common
in short reports in British popular newspapers. It is immediately noticeable that the pattern is not easily reversed or re-ordered. In British
English (though perhaps less so in American) the first sentences with past
simple would sound odd:

*The oldest man in Britain **died** aged 109 – six weeks after taking
the title.
*Poisonous black widow spiders **invaded** Britain by plane.

Although there is no inherent restriction on the use of past simple
without a temporal marker indicating separation from the now-present,
the only way we could rescue the anomalous versions of the opening
sentences is by inclusion of such a marker:

The oldest man in Britain **died yesterday** aged 109 – six weeks
after taking the title.
Poisonous black widow spiders **invaded** Britain by plane when a
cargo of bananas arrived from South America **last week**.

The original versions, with present perfect and no marker, dislocate the
temporal reference of the main event and signal it as an event 'relevant
to now'. In the case of (5.1) the actual time of Sam Crabbe's death is not
revealed until the end of the text, and even then only by indirect
reference to a separate event (the death of John Evans). Not only are the
initial present perfect forms unreplaceable, but the whole sequence of
tenses cannot be reversed. We could interpret the pattern as the fronted
present perfect supplying a higher-order temporal frame (at the level of
the text), within which the individual events are realised in their normal
(unmarked) narrative/report tense: viz the past simple. The present
perfect, with its ability to signal 'now-relevance' for events in the past,
signals the now-relevance of the text itself, of all that is to follow. Each
detail or additional fact (or events and their orientations in narrative
terms) simply unfolds within the usual narrative conventions governing
chronological and non-chronological interpretation. The tense-aspect

choices, therefore, fulfil important textual and interpersonal functions rather than purely temporal-ideational ones in the developing text. In Winter's terms, the power of the initial sentence to establish an over-arching 'situation' plays a major role in the interpretation of the relationship between it and subsequent clauses. Further support for this view comes from (5.1)'s headline: as we move up to an even higher order in the text (the general statement, for which the whole text provides the particulars), we conventionally shift to another tense, the so-called historical present (Sam *dies*), this form itself conventionally restricted to the headline position.

In spoken discourse, we find a close parallel, though without the separate option of a present tense 'headline'. The narrative or report preview/abstract often occurs in present perfect and the subsequent details are told in past simple. The 'newsworthiness' element is still present in the preview/abstract, and its function seems to be to signal that (a) the report has now-relevance, and (b) the established situation extends over subsequent clauses until transaction-termination is sig-nalled (or negotiated among conversational participants). Some CANCODE examples follow, with relevant items in bold:

(5.3)
[<S 01> is a young female, aged 24, whose father is a railway employee. While she was a student she enjoyed free and reduced-cost rail travel. Now that she herself is employed, she has lost her privilege travel. She reports this to the other speakers.]

<S 01> I**'ve started paying** now
<S 02>   ⌊[inaudible]
<S 01>   ⌊As soon as I started working I **lost** it, I'm
  no longer dependent on dad and mum.
<S 03>   ⌊You're only you only get that
  when you're a student Mary.
<S 01> It **was** while I was dependent on dad [<S 03> yeah] as soon as I'm
  earning [<S 02> well] I**'ve had my lot.**

(5.4)
[<S 01> is recounting how she and her partner have experimented with pasta-making. <S 02> and <S 03>, who are also partners, report their experience doing the same.]

<S 01> We **did** this, erm, quite a lot of ravioli, didn't we, but it **was** fiddly, very fiddly, I imagine this is

<S 02> Yeah we've **done** that yeah

<S 03> We've **done** that … we **started off** trying to use ravioli moulds and then soon **discovered** that actually they're more trouble than they're worth so we just

<S 02> We **cut them out.**

(5.5)

[<S 01> is encouraging <S 02> to make her choice from a restaurant menu. He suggests scampi; she rejects it.]

<S 01> You don't want scampi, no, oh you're calorie watching are you.

<S 02> Yeah I've **been** I've **been going** to the weight-watchers but wait till you hear this I **went** on, first time and I'd lost three and a half pound [<S 01> yeah] and I **went** last week and I'd lost half a pound so I **went** down to the fish shop and **got** fish and chips I **was** so disgusted [<S 01> laughs] but I've **been** all right since.

Examples (5.3) and (5.5) are interesting as instances of symmetry in the tense-aspect framework, beginning with present perfect, going on in past simple and then coming back again to end with present perfect. (5.5) is also a complete narrative. The tense-aspect pattern fits well with the Labovian (1972) notion of narrative initial *abstract* (the story 'headline') and narrative-final *coda*, the coda being a 'bridge' from story-time back to conversation-time. Both present perfect clauses may therefore be seen to function at a macro-level, framing the text and establishing contextual relevance. In (5.4), <S 01> is using typical narrative past tense to recount what she and her partner did. <S 02> takes up the topic and flags it as a new conversational focus, raising it to a more important status in the conversation by his use of present perfect *we've done*, in contrast to <S 01>'s *we did*. The most important question for all our examples (5.1) to (5.5) is not *'When did these events happen?'* but *'How do these utterances relate to one another as a report/narrative and how should the receiver interpret the clauses that realise them in their context of utterance?'*[1]

Narratives and reports of this kind are a good place to begin the exemplification of the main argument of the present chapter, not only because of the topic-initial phenomena which are parallelled in the written and the spoken, but also because discourse analysts have long been preoccupied with the correlations, consistent over large amounts of data, between particular narrative functions and tense-aspect shifts. Narrative analysts (of which Fleischman (1990) is the foremost example) have examined the coincidence of so-called 'historical present' tense (i.e. the use of present tense to report past events) and crucial shifts in the narrative, e.g. to peaks and climaxes, from orientation to complicating events, or, in the case of Johnstone (1987), to indicate shifting participant roles in speech-reporting segments (for more on tense in speech reporting, see Chapter 8). In both spoken and written mode, tense-aspect choices seem to play a significant role in creating the conditions for interpretation of the relationships among sequences of clauses, and patterns of such sequences have become conventionalised for narratives within our culture.

5.3 *Used to* and *would*: another narrative pattern

We shall stay with narrative for this section in order to highlight another fairly common pattern in spoken data, one which has not escaped the attention of pedagogical grammarians (e.g. Alexander 1988: 235). This pattern is found in sequences where speakers are reminiscing or are reporting typical or recurrent events in the past. Once again we may observe a preview or abstract clause establishing the general situation (with *used to*), followed by subsequent detail or extending clauses using *would*. Four examples follow. The two uses of past simple *was* in (5.7) will be commented on below:

(5.6)
[<S 01> is recounting a story about a friend of hers who wanted to learn to bake cakes.]

<S 01> She wanted to bake them herself and she never really knew how
and her gran always **used to bake** cakes and she'**d go** and watch

(5.7)
[<S 01> is recounting how he and his wife, <S 02>, were involved in a market-research exercise where the research organisation tapped into an electronic machine on which he and his wife recorded their weekly purchases. This was done automatically through the telephone line, usually at night.]

<S 01> Cos it **used to ring** about three o'clock in the morning, you **used to go** down and answer it and there *was* no-one there.
<S 02> And that **was** the computer.
<S 01> You**'d hear** beep beep beep beep.

(5.8)
[Later in the same conversation; <S 03> is <S 02>'s uncle.]

<S 02> They **used to** you know **ring up** early hours of the morning, well you **would**, the phone **wouldn't ring** they**'d ring** that computer.
<S 01> And they**'d read** it.
<S 03> Yeah.
<S 01> And it**'d go** through the phone.

(5.9)
[<S 01> tells a ghost story round the dinner table.]

<S 01> When I lived in Aberdeen years ago erm we were in a cottage in the country my then wife and I you know and erm the people that lived there before **used to see** apparitions.
<S 02> Oh.
<S 03> Did they.
<S 01> Yeah ten o'clock on a Friday night regularly they **would hear** somebody and they**'d be sitting** in the living-room watching telly and at ten o'clock every Friday they**'d hear** someone walking up the stairs.
<S 03> Yeah.
<S 01> They**'d go** out there and there**'d be** nobody there you know.

The whole *used to* + *would* sequence may function as the 'orientation' (again in Labov's (1972) terms), i.e. background concerning time, place, situation, etc., for a narrative of a particular, one-off event or set of events, as in (5.5), and in (5.10):

(5.10)
[<S 01> is reminiscing about his first work experiences; Canton is a district in the city of Cardiff, UK.]

<S 01> And er I got a job with an Irish milkman and he had er a pony and cart [<S 02> yeah] and his stables was in the lane at the back

of Albert Street in Canton where I [<S 02> yeah] lived [<S 02> yeah
yeah yeah] and I **used to drive** this horse and cart and deliver his
milk ... the only snag was he was rather er fond of the booze
[<S 02> yeah] and of course as he got paid his money it **would
go** across the bar

<S 02>   ⌊Across the bar yeah yeah
<S 01>   ⌊And one Saturday I, as a matter of fact I'll tell
you my wage was twelve and sixpence a week and I was up at half
past four in the mornings with his milk as you know [<S 01 my
goodness yeah yeah] and on one Saturday he never had the money to
pay me ...

Again we may note a problem with reversibility in this pattern. *Used to*
contains within it the meaning of 'not true any more' (a point made by
Downing and Locke 1992: 364), and can stand without a time adjunct.
Used to can refer to states as well as habitual events in the past (Swan
1995: 633),[2] and thus is the ideal candidate for the 'scene-setting'
function in narrative, where stories often commence with a 'that was the
state of things then' framework. *Would*, on the other hand, needs to be
anchored temporally, usually by the co-presence of a time expression
(Quirk et al 1985: 228–9), with wording such as:

When we were involved in the survey the phone *would ring* at three o'clock
in the morning.

Quirk *et al* (1985: 228–9) note this restriction but, surprisingly, considering that their grammar does use spoken sources, confuse the issue
by suggesting that past habitual *would* is more formal than *used to*. Our
spoken data show both forms occurring in the same, highly informal
discourses, with functions which seem to have nothing to do with
formal/informal distinctions. *Used to* clearly has the potential to situate
the discourse in a way that *would* alone does not. This seems particularly
true of (5.10), where *used to* occurs in the story-orientation, followed by
more detailed elaboration. Such an observation underlines the above-
clause function of the initial verb and, once again, enables us to shift the
emphasis away from a purely temporal-ideational interpretation to a
'staging' function with textual and interpersonal implications.

It would appear uncontroversial to suppose that the *used to* + *would*
sequence should appear in the written mode too, and we do find it in
literary narrative, as these examples from Sean O'Faoláin's novel *Bird
Alone* show:

(5.11)

[The author is describing a man called Christy Tinsley. Note that the occurrence of *used* without *to* is an acceptable Hiberno-English form.]

> He came out of gaol that May ... we **used meet** from time to time and go wandering out the fields or around the city. Always he **would be chewing** the boiled sweets that he loved ...
>
> (Oxford University Press edition, 1985: 284)

(5.12)

[The author is describing how he fought against the desire to see a female with whom he enjoyed a fraught relationship.]

> I **used try** to interpose other things between us; wandering and drinking with my grander, and he hinting his sympathy and trying to plot for me; I **would** even **turn to** praying when the asp hurt cruelly. (*ibid.*: 163)

But worth noting here also is another pattern that occurs in literary text and for which some corresponding examples occur in our spoken corpus. The pattern is *used to* followed by simple past tense form, as in these examples from Joseph Conrad's *Under Western Eyes;* the form *greeted* has a habitual meaning in the context of the story:

(5.13)

[The author is describing two ladies.]

> I **used to meet** them walking in the public garden near the university. They **greeted** me with their usual friendliness but I could not help noticing their taciturnity.
>
> (Higdon and Bender, 1983: 105.23)

(5.14)

> Some of them **used to charge** Ziemianitch with knowing something of this absence. He **denied** it with exasperation;
>
> (*ibid.*: 272.16)

In spoken example (5.7) above, there was some evidence for this same pattern, with two past simple occurrences (*was/was*) between *used to* and *would*. Both patterns (*used to + would* and *used to + past simple*) are also found in example (5.15):

(5.15)

[<S 01> is talking about a female cat the family once owned.]

<S 01> But er em Mrs Baker **used to look after** her and [<S 02> mm] and
so on but when, as soon as I **arrived** home [<S 02> yeah] and it, I **put
put** the car away in the garage you know [<S 02> mm] and er and
when I was walking halfway down from the garage to the house see
erm she **used to** [<S 02 mm mm] **run up** there you know yes up up
there she**'d run up** and make sure they're [<S 02> mm] like that and
she**'d walk** down with me to the house like you know [<S 02> yes]
[<S 03> mm] [<S 02> ah] I **used to give** her a little bit of something to
eat and [<S 02> yeah] and then er if er if I had a letter, take up a
letter up to er to post [<S 02> mm] and I**'d say** to her, see show her
the letter 'Coming up the post now?' see.

Used to still seems to have its situating function and the subsequent past
simple verb forms must still be interpreted as repeated events, as with
those preceded by *would*. But we note one difference here which is
relevant: the past simple forms occur in subordinate clauses introduced
by *when / as soon as*, not main clauses as in (5.7), (5.13) and (5.14). The
pattern *used to + past simple* in main clauses is rare in the spoken corpus
compared with the much higher frequency of *used to + would*. The
difference may simply be one of conventionality, or there may also be
something characteristically literary in the choice of the more implicit
expression of habitualness that past simple in the main clause conveys.

5.4 Narrating the future: further problems concerning parallel functions

In section 4.4, we looked at the *be to* construction with future meaning,
and noted its extremely low frequency in informal spoken data. Here we
shall consider its frequent use in journalism and what parallels there
might be in the spoken mode for the functions it performs in the
written. McCarthy and Carter (1994: 126, 129) draw attention to the
grammatical pattern common in British popular newspaper reports of
future events, where a preview-detail text pattern, parallel to the 'hot-
news', past-events text, claims the reader's interest and attention in a
headline or text-initial sentence(s) employing the *be to* form for the main,
'hot-news' future event(s). Subsequent sentences, expanding on the
preview, employ the *will* future. *Be to*, just like our other examples so far,

seems to be conventionally used in this kind of journalistic report to establish general situation and newsworthiness. As with the present perfect, *be to* anchors the event in a context of present relevance but projects into the future. Two examples of this are (5.16) and (5.17):

(5.16)
ELECTRICITY CHIEFS TO AXE 5,000

> Five thousand jobs **are to be axed** by electricity generating firm National Power, it was announced yesterday.
> Smaller power stations **will close** but bosses pledged no compulsory redundancies over the next five years.
> (*Daily Mirror*, 27.7.1990: 2)

(5.17)
'KING' ARTHUR'S BATTLEGROUND TO BE WIPED OFF THE FACE OF THE EARTH

> The battleground where Arthur Scargill and 7,000 miners took on the government **is to be razed**.
> Orgreave coking plant – scene of Britain's worst industrial violence – **will be bulldozed** and **turned into** a landscaped wood.
> (*Daily Mirror*, 27.7.1990: 6)

Any informal, conversational report of the same events would almost certainly eschew the *be to* form. Indeed, in one million words of the CANCODE corpus, *be to* future simply never occurs in ordinary casual conversation. Where it does occur is in formal and semi-formal contexts such as business meetings, where three of the four occurrences in CANCODE are to be found:

(5.18)
[British National Health Service business meeting]

<S 01> You've probably heard that er a lot of the recommendations that are coming out of central government now about complaints handling are precisely about the the jargon word empowering the staff [<S 02> mm] to be able to deal with things at the front line like that ... they've got a big task on their hands if this **is to be** in place by April nineteen-ninety-six

(5.19)
[Publisher's business meeting]

<S 01> Right yeah sorry I thought you were I mean for turning it round
[<S 02> no no no no] and getting it
<S 02>   ⌊Oh no oh right well no but it's
taken two months to do that.
<S 03>   ⌊Rob **is to look** at it and Ann Pascoe **to look** at it and
formal comments **to be collated** and **sent** back to David.

(5.20)
[Publisher's business meeting, as (5.19)]

<S 01> Then there's a couple of things written in pencil there in the
schedule for the estimate for, can't remember what they are.
<S 02> Which one's that.
<S 01>   ⌊Which I **am to check** to confirm them.

Quirk *et al*'s major grammar makes no reference to any restrictions on
the occurrence of *be to* nor suggests any parallel informal spoken form
(1985: 217), which is the kind of problem that is likely to arise if the
spoken language is not rigorously examined on its own terms. Celce-
Murcia (1991), however, offers a possible spoken parallel in the occurrence of *be going to* (initial) plus *will* (subsequent) sequences when
speakers are reporting future events. In other words, we have, once
again, the suggestion of an over-arching tense-aspect framework which
establishes situation and signals newsworthiness and/or relevance, extending over a series of following clauses. In the CANCODE corpus, there
is some limited evidence for this pattern. Examples (5.21) and (5.22) offer
some support for the argument but also raise further interesting
questions that need to be addressed:

(5.21)
[The three speakers are part of a group of eight people celebrating New
Year. It is coming up to midnight and they discuss the problem of
knowing exactly when it is 12 o'clock.]

<S 01> What **are we going to get** the actual chimes from Red have we got
something that **will tell** us exactly.
<S 02> Anything on TV.
<S 03> Well my watch says it's coming up anyway.
<S 02> There'll **be** something on TV.

so raise interesting questions about the correlation of
e and adjacency pairs and exchanges.

remarks

contextual grammar supports the view that co-occur-
nd sequence of grammatical forms has fundamental
he interpretation of consecutive clauses in written texts.
ied to do in this chapter is to demonstrate that such
r in spoken data too, and that there is every reason to
milar (even if not always the same) functions are being
he macro-level by the particular juxtaposition of tense-
and the regularity of the ordering of particular elements,
e may be differences in realisation in the spoken and
all the patterns we have noted in this chapter seem to
on is the creation of a situation anchored to the moment
followed by details or events which are governed by that
amework. The situations and their sequence sentences/
erate within different temporal frameworks, whether past
d represent textual units, both in the written and the

extualised grammatical statements are of great relevance to
chers for the following reasons:

st in more clearly distinguishing notoriously problematic
r learners (e.g. *going to* versus *will*).
e the study of grammar in texts more truly related to how
mar builds text itself, rather than just picking out examples
spect usage in texts for atomistic, local interpretation.
be used to highlight fundamental, generalisable meanings of
nd aspects in a way that lists or rules, sub-rules (i.e. sub-
of rules, as are often found in big grammars) and 'exceptions'
l to do.
rrespond to everyday functions that learners are likely to want
se in their use of the target language, such as narrating,
g, talking about the future.
n assist us in distinguishing what is different between spoken
itten grammars, and what features they share. Throughout, I
rgued that we cannot simply assume where the differences or

(5.22)
[<S 02> is making punch for a party. <S 01> is watching him add each ingredient.]

<S 01> [laughs] what you **going to do** with that.
<S 02> Oh it**'ll go** in in a minute I can taste it as I go along and then add the same amounts again.

On the face of it, the pattern of *be going to + will* occurs in examples (5.21) and (5.22). In (5.21), the over-arching situation is 'establishing the correct time', and the predictions about the television provide the 'sequence' (Winter, 1982: 2). But to be more precise, the sequence is also a 'problem-solution' sequence (see Hoey 1983; see section 2.5 for a brief summary of the components of a typical 'problem-solution' pattern), and as such must be distinguished from the preview-detail reports of the newspaper examples (5.16) and (5.17). This may not invalidate the potential for *be going to* and *will* to co-operate at the macro-level; it simply suggests that it would be too simplistic to pair the spoken sequence functionally with our written examples using *be to* and *will*. *Be going to + will* as a framework for problem-solution sequences may well be a common pattern in spoken language, and is intuitively appealing. Hoey (1983: 76–7) has already noted the correlation of *present-perfect + present tense* sequences for the 'response' segments of problem-solution reports (i.e. those which look back at problems now solved); a similar correlation might be posited for *be going to + will* with current problems and their projected solutions, at least in informal spoken mode. However, more contrastive spoken and written data would be needed to validate the claim.

Additionally, *be going to + will* are used in the spoken mode for 'announcements', with *going to* signalling newsworthy items of information. (5.23) and (5.24) below illustrate such contexts:

(5.23)
[<S 01> is a health-service worker informing <S 02> about a new 'patient's handbook' that they are producing.]

<S 01> I'm sort of chairing the working group em [laughs] a document that that it's official name **is going to end up** being something like Patient Handbook [<S 02> yeah] but at the moment it it's lovingly known as the alternative Gideon [<S 02> laughs] you**'ll find** it on the locker next to the bed or something yeah [<S 02> laughs] that, well

that's right yeah I mean that's literally where we want it to be it's **going to be** in every clinic

(5.24)

[Speakers are discussing a currency devaluation.]

<S 01> It's the import bill**'s going to rise** usually it**'ll double** overnight cos exports**'ll be** half the price they are now [<S 02> uh huh] so they**'ll have to export** a lot more to get the same amount of money in [<S 02> mhm] so their costs have risen but their revenue's fallen

In the New Year's party example (5.21) above, the speakers co-operatively negotiated the problem of establishing exactly when it would be midnight by discussing current possibilities for action, and this raises the interesting point that grammatical patterns in the spoken mode may be created by more than one participant. Patterns do not only extend across clauses; we should not be surprised to find them across turn-boundaries too. The punch-bowl text (5.22) further underlines the present orientation of *be going to* (<S 01>'s question *What you going to do with that?* could be paraphrased as '*What is your current determination for action?*'), in contrast to the point-in-the-future reference of *will*. (5.23) and (5.24) appeared to have a 'headlining' function. (5.21) to (5.24) together would seem to justify claiming a situating potential for *be going to*, even if not in exact parallel to *be to* future. Indeed, Quirk *et al.* (1985: 214) talk of the semantics of *be going to* as indicating 'future fulfilment of the present', thereby suggesting a 'now-relevance', not unlike that posited for present perfect tense.[3] Moreover, they tantalisingly claim that *be going to* tends not to be repeated in a text referring pervasively to the future' (*ibid.*: 218), giving a (concocted?) example of a spoken weather-forecast sequence with initial *be going to* plus sequential *wills*. While this may be so in weather forecasts, repeated *be going to* is by no means impossible, as example (5.23) shows:

(5.25)

[Two young women are getting dressed to go out for an evening on the town.]

<S 01> What are you **going to wear** then.

<S 02> I'm just **going to put** my jeans **on** and a black top I**'m not going to think** about it Sha don't let me think about it I**'m going to be** really boring.

It is possible to interpr[...]
otherwise might be a *be[...]*
interpretation would re[...]
determinism, in the kind[...]
is certainly little disagree[...]
the *be going to* versus *will*[...]
orientation into the futu[...]
1970; Aijmer 1984a; Haeg[...]
389–90).

5.5 Bringing the argumen[...]

When we look back over t[...]
patterns, a common thread e[...]
ances, as we have called th[...]
whose semantics have somethi[...]
to, we have argued, implicitly c[...]
it apart from *would*. This link[...]
general phenomenon at the [...]
under investigation may be di[...]
'sequencing' potential, and the[...]
brought together under these gen[...]

Situating	Seque[...]
present perfect	past si[...]
used to	would[...]
used to	past sim[...]
be to	will (wri[...]
be going to	will

The patterns do not have any determ[...]
with just one or two sequencing verb[...]
longer stretches of discourse. They are i[...]
of the potential for describing convers[...]
sense of functional units of varying leng[...]
sentence and the whole conversation ([...]
some of which may be identifiable by[...]
markers, some by intonational criteria. So[...]

have looked at al[...]
grammatical choi[...]

5.6 Concluding[...]

Winter's work o[...]
rence, pattern [...]
significance in t[...]
What I have t[...]
sequences occu[...]
suppose that s[...]
performed at [...]
aspect choices [...]
but that ther[...]
written. What[...]
have in comm[...]
of utterance, [...]
situational fi[...]
utterances op[...]
or future, a[...]
spoken mod[...]
Such cont[...]
language te[...]

- They assi[...]
  choices fo[...]
- They mak[...]
  the gram[...]
  of tense/a[...]
- They can[...]
  tenses a[...]
  division[...]
  often fa[...]
- They co[...]
  to real[...]
  reporti[...]
- They c[...]
  and w[...]
  have a[...]

overlaps will be, or, even worse, assume that written-based descriptions can be transferred wholesale to the spoken mode.

- They can assist us in cross-linguistic comparisons. English is not unique with regard to the kinds of functions we have discussed for some of the verb forms. For example, other languages with future *be going to* equivalents seem to use them with a 'present-rooted' function: see Haegeman (1983) for a comparison between the English, French and Dutch cognate forms; also on French see Wales (1983); on Spanish, Bauhr (1992). It may be possible to tap discoursal knowledge of the learner's L1 as a foundation for discussion of similar phenomena in the target language.

This chapter has dealt with grammar in the written and spoken language, pointing out parallels and differences between the two modes of communication by observing grammatical phenomena operating at the level of discourse. The next chapter will shift the focus, but not the approach, to questions concerning vocabulary.

Notes

1 Hopper (1979) shows how the choice between perfective and imperfective aspect in Russian signals the relation between 'new' narrative events and already established ones (i.e. a discourse-level function), and I should certainly not want to suggest that the kinds of discourse-level patterning in verb tense/aspect choice discussed in this chapter are a speciality of English (see also section 5.6).

2 This may be seen as part of a more general overlapping between the expression of states and habits found in the English verb-phrase (see Brinton 1987).

3 Joos (1964: 139ff) sees *be going to* as a mirror image of the present perfect, in that both emanate from the present. Fleischman (1983) reiterates this, seeing *be going to* as the 'prospective' mirror-image of the present perfect's 'retrospective' viewpoint.

6

Vocabulary and the spoken language[1]

6.1 Introduction

In this chapter, we shift the focus from grammar to lexis, for if the central thesis of the book is to be adequately supported, then not only grammatical choices should be the subject of our investigation of the ways in which discourse- and genre-constraints underlie the choices at the formal, lexico-grammatical level. Our central concern with the way discourse-level phenomena such as goals and relationships motivate generic activity must have its reflection in lexical choice.

Work on the patterning of lexis in written text, such as the studies of lexical cohesion associated with Halliday and Hasan (Halliday and Hasan, 1976; Hasan 1984) and the study of the significance of multiple ties between words by Hoey (1991a), have been in sharp contrast to the rather scant amount of research into the kinds of vocabulary patterns that occur in everyday spoken language. The absence of a proper body of studies of vocabulary represents a serious drawback for anyone wishing to pursue the central argument of this book: that applied linguistics and language teaching stand to benefit greatly from discourse-based language descriptions and attention to real spoken data. Grammatical structure interpreted from a discourse viewpoint does not seem to have suffered the same lack of attention, as Chapters 4 and 5 of this book have attempted to demonstrate. It is thus a pity that vocabulary should be so often seen as beyond the purview of discourse analysts. I have attempted to fill this lacuna to a limited extent and have carried out small-scale research into patterns of lexical reiteration and relexicalisation in conversation (see McCarthy, 1988; McCarthy, 1991: ch. 3; McCarthy, 1992a; McCarthy and Carter, 1994: ch. 3). Other researchers have looked at lexical repetition (e.g. Persson 1974, who uses spoken and written data; Schenkein 1980; Blanche-Benveniste 1993; Tannen 1989; and most notably, Bublitz 1989), and at formality in vocabulary choice in spoken language (Scotton 1985; Powell 1992), but their efforts represent only a relatively small body of literature in comparison with that now available on the role of grammar in spoken interaction (see, for example, Ochs *et al.* 1996 and the copious references given therein). In this chapter we shall consider a number of general features of vocabulary in informal spoken language and point to areas of significant interest to applied linguists and language teachers concerned with achieving a clearer understanding of the character of spoken language and the creation of pedagogically relevant models.

When looking at vocabulary in conversational language (as opposed to single-authored written text), certain key points have to be borne in mind:

1 Speakers operate under the constraints of 'real-time' planning; careful composition and selection of words is the exception rather than the rule.
2 More than one speaker normally contributes to the vocabulary which occurs.
3 Roles vary in conversation; speakers may not be participating as equals, and one or more speakers may dominate vocabulary selection (see Thomas 1984).
4 Roles may shift as the conversation progresses; this may be reflected in vocabulary choice.
5 Topic – what is being talked *about* – is neither pre-determined nor singularly defined, but shifts and develops, often without sharp boundaries between topics. Vocabulary choice reflects such shifts and contributes to connectivity and 'shading' between topics (i.e. moving from one topic to another without a sudden jump, making connections between topics, etc.).
6 Speakers have no automatic rights to have their topics addressed, but have to negotiate them.
7 Spoken language is usually more implicit (Chafe, 1982) and situation-dependent. The lexical density of spoken texts may differ considerably from that of written texts on the same topics (Ure, 1971; Stubbs, 1986).
8 Conversation contains a large amount of vocabulary whose function is mainly 'relational' or 'interactional' (i.e. in the service of establishing and reinforcing social relations), rather than 'transactional' (i.e. functioning principally in the transmitting of information, goods or services). Issues such as convergence and communicative accommodation between speakers (see section 2.4) are thus relevant to the study of lexical patterning. (See glossary for definitions of terms.)

9 Conversation contains a significant number of prefabricated lexical expressions which facilitate fluency and which are often idiomatic in structure and meaning (see section 3.2.1; Chapter 7).

With these factors in mind, I propose here to look at a number of pieces of natural conversational data and some features of their vocabulary.

6.2 Speech function and lexical density

(6.1)

[Five friends, all university students, three female: <S 01>, <S 04>, <S 05>; two male <S 02>, <S 03>, around the dinner-table.]

<S 01> Well, I've got the other camera so … if Dave … then we can load that and have lots of jolly photographs in the pub.

<S 02> Mm.

<S 03> Mm.

<S 02> Mm.

<S 04> [to <S 02>] It won't rewind.

<S 02> What … the batteries are flat.

<S 04>   ⌞They're not, they're brand new I put them in the other day maybe it's just the way it rewinds.

<S 02> That's the film speed type.

<S 04> I may have over taken one.

<S 02> Well it should have recovered by now.

<S 05> Oh he's licking my feet.

<S 02> What? [laughs] it's only a dog.

<S 05> It's a dog.

<S 01> Woof.

<S 04> Right that should be it, well Amanda.

<S 01> Yeah?

<S 04> Why don't I put your film in here.

<S 01> Okay and I can

<S 04>   ⌞Or put those batteries in the other camera?

<S 01> I can't take it out half way through though and

<S 04>   ⌞Well have you started it? What is it then a thirty-six? … Well why don't I put my batteries in your camera.

<S 01> Yeah … I don't … I mean I don't mind putting my film in there.

<S 04> No well yeah if you want to use the film at some other time.

(5.22)
[<S 02> is making punch for a party. <S 01> is watching him add each ingredient.]

<S 01> [laughs] what you **going to do** with that.
<S 02> Oh it'**ll go** in in a minute I can taste it as I go along and then add the same amounts again.

On the face of it, the pattern of *be going to + will* occurs in examples (5.21) and (5.22). In (5.21), the over-arching situation is 'establishing the correct time', and the predictions about the television provide the 'sequence' (Winter, 1982: 2). But to be more precise, the sequence is also a 'problem-solution' sequence (see Hoey 1983; see section 2.5 for a brief summary of the components of a typical 'problem-solution' pattern), and as such must be distinguished from the preview-detail reports of the newspaper examples (5.16) and (5.17). This may not invalidate the potential for *be going to* and *will* to co-operate at the macro-level; it simply suggests that it would be too simplistic to pair the spoken sequence functionally with our written examples using *be to* and *will*. *Be going to + will* as a framework for problem-solution sequences may well be a common pattern in spoken language, and is intuitively appealing. Hoey (1983: 76–7) has already noted the correlation of *present-perfect + present tense* sequences for the 'response' segments of problem-solution reports (i.e. those which look back at problems now solved); a similar correlation might be posited for *be going to + will* with current problems and their projected solutions, at least in informal spoken mode. However, more contrastive spoken and written data would be needed to validate the claim.

Additionally, *be going to + will* are used in the spoken mode for 'announcements', with *going to* signalling newsworthy items of information. (5.23) and (5.24) below illustrate such contexts:

(5.23)
[<S 01> is a health-service worker informing <S 02> about a new 'patient's handbook' that they are producing.]

<S 01> I'm sort of chairing the working group em [laughs] a document that that it's official name **is going to end up** being something like Patient Handbook [<S 02> yeah] but at the moment it it's lovingly known as the alternative Gideon [<S 02> laughs] you'**ll find** it on the locker next to the bed or something yeah [<S 02> laughs] that, well

that's right yeah I mean that's literally where we want it to be it's **going to be** in every clinic

(5.24)

[Speakers are discussing a currency devaluation.]

<S 01> It's the import bill's **going to rise** usually it'll **double** overnight cos exports'll **be** half the price they are now [<S 02> uh huh] so they'll **have to export** a lot more to get the same amount of money in [<S 02> mhm] so their costs have risen but their revenue's fallen

In the New Year's party example (5.21) above, the speakers co-operatively negotiated the problem of establishing exactly when it would be midnight by discussing current possibilities for action, and this raises the interesting point that grammatical patterns in the spoken mode may be created by more than one participant. Patterns do not only extend across clauses; we should not be surprised to find them across turn-boundaries too. The punch-bowl text (5.22) further underlines the present orientation of *be going to* (<S 01>'s question *What you going to do with that?* could be paraphrased as 'What is your current determination for action?'), in contrast to the point-in-the-future reference of *will*. (5.23) and (5.24) appeared to have a 'headlining' function. (5.21) to (5.24) together would seem to justify claiming a situating potential for *be going to*, even if not in exact parallel to *be to* future. Indeed, Quirk *et al.* (1985: 214) talk of the semantics of *be going to* as indicating 'future fulfilment of the present', thereby suggesting a 'now-relevance', not unlike that posited for present perfect tense.[3] Moreover, they tantalisingly claim that *be going to* tends not to be repeated in a text referring pervasively to the future' (*ibid.*: 218), giving a (concocted?) example of a spoken weather-forecast sequence with initial *be going to* plus sequential *wills*. While this may be so in weather forecasts, repeated *be going to* is by no means impossible, as example (5.23) shows:

(5.25)

[Two young women are getting dressed to go out for an evening on the town.]

<S 01> What are you **going to wear** then.
<S 02> I'm just **going to put** my jeans **on** and a black top I'm **not going to think** about it Sha don't let me think about it I'm **going to be** really boring.

It is possible to interpret (5.25) as a stylistically marked version of what otherwise might be a *be going to* (situation) + *will* (sequence) pattern. This interpretation would rest on the notion of conventionality, rather than determinism, in the kinds of patterns we have been examining. But there is certainly little disagreement among those who have closely scrutinised the *be going to* versus *will* choice that *be going to* projects from a *present* orientation into the future, whilst *will* does not (see especially Lakoff 1970; Aijmer 1984a; Haegeman 1983a: 65; 1983b; 1989; Binnick 1991: 389–90).

5.5 Bringing the arguments together

When we look back over the examples of both written and spoken patterns, a common thread emerges. The situating sentences and utterances, as we have called them, characteristically contain verb-forms whose semantics have something to say about 'now-relevance'. Even *used to*, we have argued, implicitly carries a 'not true *now*' meaning which sets it apart from *would*. This link across the forms enables us to posit a general phenomenon at the discourse level whereby the verb-forms under investigation may be distinguished by their 'situating' versus 'sequencing' potential, and their patterns of co-occurrence may be brought together under these general headings:

Situating	Sequencing
present perfect	past simple
used to	would
used to	past simple (literary examples)
be to	will (written and formal spoken)
be going to	will

The patterns do not have any deterministic length, and may be short, with just one or two sequencing verb phrases, or they may extend over longer stretches of discourse. They are important, though, as illustrations of the potential for describing conversational 'episodes' of talk in the sense of functional units of varying length at levels between the clause/sentence and the whole conversation (Van Dijk 1982; Benwell 1996), some of which may be identifiable by the occurrence of discourse markers, some by intonational criteria. Some of the spoken examples we have looked at also raise interesting questions about the correlation of grammatical choice and adjacency pairs and exchanges.

5.6 Concluding remarks

Winter's work on contextual grammar supports the view that co-occurrence, pattern and sequence of grammatical forms has fundamental significance in the interpretation of consecutive clauses in written texts. What I have tried to do in this chapter is to demonstrate that such sequences occur in spoken data too, and that there is every reason to suppose that similar (even if not always the same) functions are being performed at the macro-level by the particular juxtaposition of tense-aspect choices and the regularity of the ordering of particular elements, but that there may be differences in realisation in the spoken and written. What all the patterns we have noted in this chapter seem to have in common is the creation of a situation anchored to the moment of utterance, followed by details or events which are governed by that situational framework. The situations and their sequence sentences/utterances operate within different temporal frameworks, whether past or future, and represent textual units, both in the written and the spoken mode.

Such contextualised grammatical statements are of great relevance to language teachers for the following reasons:

- They assist in more clearly distinguishing notoriously problematic choices for learners (e.g. *going to* versus *will*).
- They make the study of grammar in texts more truly related to how the grammar builds text itself, rather than just picking out examples of tense/aspect usage in texts for atomistic, local interpretation.
- They can be used to highlight fundamental, generalisable meanings of tenses and aspects in a way that lists or rules, sub-rules (i.e. sub-divisions of rules, as are often found in big grammars) and 'exceptions' often fail to do.
- They correspond to everyday functions that learners are likely to want to realise in their use of the target language, such as narrating, reporting, talking about the future.
- They can assist us in distinguishing what is different between spoken and written grammars, and what features they share. Throughout, I have argued that we cannot simply assume where the differences or

Levinson 1987) and acceptable behaviour in different cultures come to the surface, for example, customs connected with the acceptance or refusal of food, cultural expectations as to whether it will be home-made or shop-bought, etc. Once again, though, it is questionable whether one can effectively 'teach' L2 culture via a presentational methodology, or whether language and cultural awareness activities may be preferable, where the goal is to observe, discuss and come to understand features of interaction rather than to 'learn' or imitate them. Indeed, there are several arguments for advocating such an approach. One is that current models of language and culture have moved away from the notion that culture is simply 'there' in language (the 'colliding cultures' view), and more towards interactional models, where culture is seen as context- and situation-dependent and as something negotiated among interlocutors (Blommaert 1991). The other argument is a pedagogical one: learners probably gain better awareness from exploratory and problem-solving encounters with real data rather than having it interpreted for them and (re-)presented by teachers (see Jackson 1990 for an account of students' own language analyses and a good discussion of this issue).

3.2.2 Interactional features

Under this heading we include those areas of linguistic choice where speakers manage the interaction in less obviously structured ways (in the sense of regular patterned occurrences of restricted choices), in order to proceed effectively towards their goals whilst maintaining relational equilibrium. Amongst many such features, turn-taking, discourse-marking and information-staging are central, and present similar questions as to their 'teachability' as did the more overtly structural features in section 3.2.1.

Turn-taking

Turn-taking, although a universal feature, may cause problems on the cultural plane. Indeed, one might argue that this is one area where English language teaching materials have erred somewhat on the side of seeing the issue as primarily a lexical one. Three problems seem frequently to arise. One is that some cultures seem to tolerate longer silences between turns, for example as is often perceived by other Europeans during conversations in Finnish. Another such example is the rule-conflicts that can cause conversational tensions between 'silence-filling' discourse styles such as that found in American English, and cultures where silence is permissible thinking-time and face-protecting, such as Japanese (Noguchi 1987; Lebra 1987). A second problem is related to acceptable forms of interruption across cultures, for example the preference for direct interruption with markers such as *ma* (*but*) in Italian compared with the indirect use of *well* and/or agreement contrasts in English (Testa 1988). The third problem is that of differing styles of 'back-channel' (the noises and verbalisations made by listeners to show understanding, continued interest, etc.) (Yngve 1970). Spanish speakers often acknowledge incoming talk with what translates to English as a machine-gun-like 'Yes-yes-yes!', and which frequently indicates impatience or irritation with the speaker in British English. There seems again, here, to be a mix of lexical and cultural problems which need addressing in the classroom. And yet turn-taking (and especially interruption) is one area in English language teaching where there is no shortage of lexical advice. Course-books frequently offer conventional phrases for interrupting, such as *Sorry to interrupt* and *Can I just say something?*. Useful though such phrases may be, they are no substitute for close observation of data. When one does this using data from informal conversational settings (and even in some semi-formal contexts) one finds, in the case of English, that an interruption often simply occurs and is then followed or is itself broken off by the interruption marker, as in (3.7) and (3.8):

(3.7)
[<S 02> interrupts a conversation in a corridor between two women.]

<S 01> with Carol and he doesn't even realise
<S 02>   ⌊Helen, **sorry to interrupt**, erm did
     you manage to ring Patrick?
(attested)

(3.8)
[<S 02> interrupts a colleague during a semi-formal discussion.]

<S 01> well it would have to go to a later meeting
<S 02>   ⌊I don't ... for this document,
     sorry to interrupt, but I don't think you can ignore the importance
     of [etc.]
(attested)

(3.4)

<S 05> The nicest pizza I've ever had was in Amsterdam [<S 03> Oh yeah]
    I had a brilliant pizza.
<S 04>   ⌊In Cyprus.

The incoming information has not prompted convergence, but is openly challenged, and it will require work on the part of the speakers to resolve the possible hold-up in the talk. The first part of the adjacency pair predicts the occurrence of a second part, and the second part is seen to fulfil that prediction in some way. In the case of (3.4), we might expect a response showing interest and encouraging <S 05> to go on and describe the wonderful pizza. Instead the unpredicted happens: the information is contradicted. The adjacency pair, in its concern with local decisions by speakers, does overlap with the notion of exchange; the difference is that the exchange is primarily seen as a structural unit building up into higher order units, while adjacency is concerned more with local convergence between participants. Another way of putting it is that discourse analysts working with the exchange are much more interested in the presence of the pattern as a trace in the text for the analyst's purposes, while conversation analysts who work with adjacency are trying to understand local, individual choices from the participants' viewpoint.

There is no evidence to suggest that learners do not orientate themselves to create appropriate adjacency, however imperfectly they may actually realise it, and thus adjacency, as a global notion, is interesting but may not be an essential component of a relevant linguistic model for pedagogy, and probably does not need to be 'taught'. However, once again, a number of adjacency pairs are highly formulaic and can be treated as an aspect of the lexico-grammatical content of the syllabus. One may not need to be taught to 'be adjacent', but one may well benefit from learning a number of ready-made formulae (what Nattinger and DeCarrico 1992 and Lewis 1993: 94 refer to as 'lexical phrases' and 'institutionalised expressions', respectively) which will enable fluent, natural and culturally and pragmatically appropriate adjacency pairs to be realised. Examples that readily spring to mind are reactions of condolence, congratulation-sequences, seasonal greetings, telephone opening conventions, phatic exchanges, etc. In a related way, there is the problem of 'dispreferred' second parts of adjacency pairs (Pomerantz 1984), that is to say responses that do not fit in with expectations, as in the wife's challenge over the pizza in (3.4). For example, how does one disagree with an assertion (see the discussion in section 1.8 on 'disagreeing') or refuse an invitation without causing offence or making the receiver feel threatened? What tends to happen in native-speaker speech is considerable elaboration of the second pair-part (the second part of the adjacency pair) to include reasons for the divergence, and often a preface to the actual 'dispreferred' utterance. These conditions, of course, apply to generally co-operative discourse; people will always exercise their right to be conflictual and rude when they choose to be, or at least fairly direct, as <S 04> feels she can be to her husband in example (3.4). Two further corpus examples illustrate typical co-operative behaviour, the second more direct than the first:

(3.5)
[A young daughter, <S 01>, is being helpful and offering to make everyone toast. Most family members accept two slices. She then addresses her father.]

<S 01> Dad, one piece or two?
<S 02> **One'll do for me**, Jen, if you
<S 01>   ⌊Right, okay.
<S 02> Cos I've gotta go in the bath in a minute, love.

(3.6)
[<S 01> addresses his sister-in-law, <S 02>, and tells her he never realised she made her own Swiss rolls.]

<S 01> And I've never realised that you've made it, I thought this was
    probably, I probably thought it was bought.
<S 02> Oh, you're joking! **It's our speciality of the house!**

The dispreferred utterances are here indicated in bold. Clearly, speakers generally wish to avoid over-blunt refusals, divergences and contradictions, and, once again, considerable lexical effort is expended in elaborating the dispreferred response. In (3.5), there is a risk that the daughter will interpret her father's choice of only one piece of toast as a snub to her efforts to help in the kitchen. We have what looks like an aborted polite conditional and a reason from the father. In (3.6) we have a conventional informal preface of disbelief that softens the confirmation that the first speaker was saying something wildly wrong. Here discourse and culture overlap, and notions of politeness, threats to face (Brown and

<S 02> I'm sure it's got no batteries in, it feels extremely light to me [to
   <S 04>] just put the batteries in that camera.
<S 04> Yes that's what I'm doing.
<S 02> Yeah.[2]

This is a rather typical example of the genre of 'language-in-action' (that
is to say language being used principally in support of actions that are
taking place at that moment, in this case solving a problem with a
camera). As such, the text is lexically quite 'light'. Of its 227 orthographic
words, only 56 (just under 25%) are lexical nouns, verbs, adjectives or
adverbs with content meaning accounting for the topic of solving the
camera problem. If we examine these 56 tokens (individual occurrences
of words), we find there are 40 types (i.e. different vocabulary items); for
instance, *camera* occurs four times, *batteries* four times, *put* six times, and
film four times.

Words which are not fully 'lexical' in the sense of content nouns,
verbs, adjectives and adverbs include:

- 27 items (11.9% of the total words) that refer exophorically to the
  immediate situation, such as '*the other* camera', '*that's the* film speed
  type', 'your film in *here*'.
- 13 discourse markers (Schiffrin, 1987; Fraser, 1990) (accounting for
  5.7% of the total words), small words and phrases that contribute to
  the management and development of the discourse and which perform
  important structural and interactive functions such as marking phases
  in the activity and projecting the assumed state of shared knowledge.
  Examples are: *well, right, I mean*.
- 9 items (3.9% of the total words) that mark modality, expressing
  degrees of certainty about the propositions stated by the content
  words, and expressing the speakers' perceptions of what ought to
  happen or what is a desirable state of affairs. Examples are: *can, may,
  maybe, should, I'm sure*.
- A large remaining number of other function words such as preposi-
  tions, determiners, particles, conjunctions, etc..

Does the fact that there are only 40 different content words (representing 25% of the total orthographic words) mean that the vocabulary
load for a learner wishing to achieve this kind of naturalness in this
kind of situation is likely to be light? Ure's (1971) study suggested that
an average of 40% lexical density could be expected across a wide range

of written and spoken texts, and that a figure less than 30% is lexically light. If vocabulary to be taught/learnt is thought of in the traditional sense of content words, then the answer would be 'yes' to the question of lightness for language-in-action situations such as this one. The 40 types contain many basic-level words (*put, want, day, dog, start*, etc.) and the more topic-specific words are easily arrangeable into interrelated sets (*camera, film, battery*, etc.) which can be taught in a conventional manner. However, there is no doubt that the words referring directly to the immediate situation need to be carefully considered. Notorious problems arise between languages over the usage of items such as demonstratives; deixis with *this* and *that* in English does not always correspond with cognate forms in other languages (e.g. Spanish/German/ Danish; see also section 4.2). Furthermore, if we consider the relational/ interactional dimension, then the discourse markers, the modal items and such features as intensifiers/downgraders (e.g. *just, only*) will also enter into the learning equation. These may require a methodological approach quite distinct from the 'presentation-practice-production' one (the 'three Ps') traditionally used for teaching vocabulary. Without this relational/interactional dimension to vocabulary learning, we run the risk of an over-emphasis on the transactional features of spoken language and of creating a 'reduced' personality for the learner, who may well be able to achieve transactional goals but who may be unable to project his/her personality and create appropriate relationships with interlocutors (for a discussion of the term 'reduced personality', see Harder 1980).

6.3 Repetition, relexicalisation, negotiation of topic

Extract (6.2) raises different issues connected with its vocabulary:

(6.2)
[<S 01> is father in the family. <S 02> is his daughter, <S 03> his wife. They are getting dressed for a family wedding. <S 01> comes in holding the coat of his suit.]

<S 02> That looks very nice put it on and let's have a look at you.
<S 01> I don't like the two buttons I didn't know it had two buttons I
      thought it had three.
<S 03> Well it's the style of the coat Ken.

<S 02> Nick's has only got two buttons.
<S 03>   ⌊It's a low cut.
<S 01>   ⌊All right?
<S 02>   ⌊Very nice.
<S 03>   ⌊It's
beautiful.
<S 02> Lovely lovely.
<S 01> Does it look nice?
<S 02> Yeah it goes very well with those trousers there's a colour in the
jacket that picks up the colour in the trousers.
<S 03> Them others he wears are striped but they clashed, too much
alike
<S 01>   ⌊Two different stripes.
<S 03>   ⌊But
not matching each other if you understand what I mean.
<S 02> Yeah yeah … yeah.
<S 01>   ⌊It's all right then eh?
<S 02> It's very nice Dad it looks very very good.
<S 01> I don't like the I like three buttons you see.
<S 03> Ken it's the style of the coat.

This extract underlines the point made in the prolegomena to our
examination of data: that topics are negotiated in spoken discourse.
While the overall topic of the father's jacket is agreed among the
participants, it is clear that the father himself would like to launch a
discussion of the problematic nature of its having only two buttons (he
opens with the subject and tries to resurrect it again at the end). The
mother and daughter apparently wish to dismiss such talk and are bent
on persuading the father that the jacket looks fine. Where participants
are trying to agree a topic, we often find a significant variation between
exact repetition of vocabulary and what may be called 'relexicalisation',
where content is re-cast in different but near-synonymous words. Firstly,
it is important to note that exact repetition is not always pragmatically
appropriate; the following concocted exchange would be considered by
most people as odd:

(6.3)

<S 01> Hi! Freezing cold today!
<S 02> (with exact same intonation) Hi! Freezing cold today!

<S 02> is much more likely to say something like *Hi! Yes, bitter!* or *Yes, it is freezing!* (see McCarthy 1984 for further discussion). Exact repetition (including syntax, lexis and intonation) often suggests a non-increment to the topical progression of the discourse (increments are things which push the topic forward; a non-increment deliberately stalls it), and can be interpreted as staying with one's present position in the talk, of a refusal to converge or communicatively accommodate (Giles *et al* 1991), with whatever local implicatures that may carry, which can be seen in the wife's repetition of *It's the style of the coat*. This holds up the discourse from reaching its goals, in this case, those of the genre of 'checking/ approving appearances', and places a strain on the relationships of the participants. The socially co-operative norm in non-ritual, non-copying adjacency pairs is typified by (6.4) below, where repetition is accompanied by relexicalisation (as indicated by the items in bold face), and convergence is achieved:

(6.4)
[Two middle-aged male teachers are gossiping about a female ex-colleague.]

<S 01> There was this guy that she was really **madly in love with** that went on and ended up working on an oil rig somewhere.
<S 02> Really.
<S 01> Oh yes she really was really loyal, **very struck on** him.
<S 02> **Smitten.**
<S 01> **Smitten with** him, had he, had he asked her at that particular time er I think she would have probably married him.
[later in the same conversation]
<S 01> And this is going back to the time when she was living in oh
<S 02> **Southampton.**
<S 01> **Southampton** yeah.
<S 02> In that **big house**.
<S 01> In that **huge house**, I mean she's got an **awful lot** to offer, **tremendous amount**, I mean what a personality.

In (6.2), it is precisely the cases of exact lexical repetition which focus most sharply the stubborn stance of the conflicting parties and the frustration of the goals of the episode. This may be contrasted with the more solidary, supportive and convergent exchanges, where repetition gives way to relexicalisation:

<S 01> All right?
<S 02> Very **nice**.
<S 03> It's **beautiful**.
<S 02> **Lovely lovely**.
<S 01> Does it look **nice**?

Here the speakers vary one another's lexis and also pick up one another's words (note how <S 01> takes up *nice*: repeating across three speaker-turns). Notable too is the occurrence of paraphrase (which is, by definition, a type of relexicalisation, but which affects longer stretches of language than single words or phrases) within speaker-turns, rather than exact repetition. This can be seen as a co-operative gesture by the speakers, 'explaining themselves' for their listeners:

<S 02> Yeah it **goes very well with those trousers there's a colour in the jacket that picks up the colour in the trousers**.
<S 03> but **they clashed too much alike** … but **not matching each other** …
<S 02> **It's very nice** Dad **it looks very very good**.

What we may observe in (6.2) and (6.4) is the importance of the interweaving of lexical repetition and relexicalisation. The ability to vary one's lexis while still saying more or less the same thing pushes the discourse forward and gives out important interactional signals. It is a fundamental feature of lexical competence and is one of the basic characteristics of vocabulary patterning in everyday talk. Learners often need practice in variation, but they cannot be expected to vary their choice of word if their word-stock is impoverished. Here lies the opportunity for motivated vocabulary building, bringing abstract notions such as synonymy, antonymy and hyponymy to life. If we can see how these lexical relations are exploited interactively in real contexts, then there is a good reason for learning synonyms and other sense groupings; if we do not have them available as speakers for just the kinds of everyday functions highlighted here, we may end up sounding very unnatural indeed and may become victims of socio-pragmatic breakdowns in communication, even though, on the purely transactional level, we may survive.

The ability to vary one's lexis applies not only across speakers, it will be noted. When speakers are unsure of the best wording or are offering particular meanings for words in context, they will often explore various lexical possibilities, including negated opposites, in an attempt to put across what they want to say:

(6.5)
[<S 01> is describing the landscape of his part of England to a Welsh person who has never been there.]

<S 01> It's **flat** you know it's **not** er **hilly** like Wales but [<S 02> mm] you get used to that strangely enough after a while, I mean it's **not as flat as a pancake** it's kind of **undulating** and lots of little villages

Exploiting lexical alternatives in this way is only possible if one has an adequate vocabulary of synonyms and antonyms, and the ability to retrieve them in real time. If possible, the vocabulary class, especially at the advanced level where many words are known but often in an atomised way, should offer activities where learners have the opportunity to string alternatives together to produce meanings. So often, the opposite is the case, with learners being unable or unwilling to utter words unless they feel they are the 'right' ones, and with so many exercises demanding just one, right word as the answer. Dialogue games where repetition is 'forbidden' can force learners to look for alternatives, as can games where contradiction or agreement (without repetition) is required.

6.4 More than one speaker: the listener's contribution to lexical patterning

In this section, we shall consider an area often underplayed in discussions of spoken language: how listeners behave. We shall use a typical situation where the contribution of listeners comes most to the fore – everyday storytelling. (6.6) is a typical professional anecdote of the kind exchanged among friends and colleagues:

(6.6)
[A woman is telling a funny story about a conference she attended.]

<S 01> Well, the conference theme was the 1990s and they did this talk and there was this amphitheatre that seats 2,000 they started off this sort of slide and sound sequence
<S 02> Ah Son et Lumiere.
<S 01> Son et Lumiere.

\<S 02\> I see and they zapped it to you.

\<S 01\> It starts off with this tiny black, we're all in the dark you see and tiny little ... and we hear this click-click and you see this little coloured pattern and this coloured pattern gets bigger and bigger.

\<S 02\> What was this projected by, a movie projector or video or what?

\<S 01\> No it was ... erm ... a slide sequence but it was one after another ... anyway the very funny bit was that the sound went.

\<S 02\> [laughs] That's the trouble when you rely on technology.

\<S 01\> Yeah and that was very very funny and we're all sitting there in the dark and this picture thing going on you see, obviously going ahead of the sound and him saying 'Why can't we hear any sound? Why is there no sound, technician?' you know, chaos and a great big smile on everybody's face.

\<S 02\> Especially the other companies.

\<S 01\> And anyway they got it going again and you heard this 'click-click' again and this coloured thing suddenly reveals itself to be the Berlin Wall with people on the top of it.

\<S 02\> That's a novel idea. Was Pavarotti singing as well?

\<S 01\> Oh yeah yeah.

Much of the literature on spoken language focuses somewhat unduly on what *speakers* do, and those whose main role in the discourse is to listen to and support current speakers are often neglected (see, however, Bublitz 1988; McGregor and White 1990; Duranti 1991). One good context in which to examine the role of listeners is oral narrative, since the speaker who takes the role of storyteller has the main speaking role. Those on the receiving end of the story have reduced turn-taking rights and may only interrupt at specified places (Houtkoop and Mazeland 1985). Nonetheless, listeners are by no means expected to remain passive and silent throughout.

It may be helpful first to view the anecdote in (6.6) in terms of Labov's (1972) generic model of narrative, one of the most important components of which is *evaluation* (see section 3.2.3). The story must be made interesting, funny, shocking, appalling, or whatever, in order constantly to keep at bay the possible objection 'well, so what?' on the part of the listener(s). The teller therefore must work hard to evaluate the story. At the lexical level, this may include choices of expressive vocabulary, intensification, hyperbole, onomatopoeia, all of which may stretch the teller's lexical talents.[3] Note some examples of these phenomena in (6.6):

> *tiny little*
> *click-click*
> *great big smile*
> *very very funny*

as well as the explicit marking of the high point of the story by the teller: *the very funny bit was*. But the listener is not passive in evaluating the story either. He comments on the story as it progresses:

> *and they* **zapped it to you**
> **that's the trouble** *when you* ...
> **that's a novel idea**

Another characteristic that may be observed in (6.6) is the use of several items by the teller which seem to be deliberately vague and to make her account less precise:

> *this* **sort of** *slide and sound sequence*
> *this picture* **thing**
> *this coloured* **thing**

Vague and rather general words like those highlighted are frequent in everyday talk. Channell (1994) has made a thorough study of some aspects of vague language, confirming its widespread occurrence (see also Aijmer 1984b and many annotated examples in the conversational extracts in Carter and McCarthy 1997). *Thing* is certainly a frequent and very useful word in spoken language; it can substitute for a wide range of names of objects, processes, entities and even persons in discourse (see Fronek 1982). Despite their vagueness of denotation, such words rarely cause problems for listeners and pass unnoticed, but they do seem to make an important contribution to naturalness and the informal, convergent tenor of everyday talk. Indeed, the listener would be considered irritating and unco-operative if he/she constantly demanded clarification and specification of vague language items.

   Listeners can also show convergence with speakers by predicting what the speaker is about to say:

(6.7)
[Two men are discussing domestic pets.]

<S 01> Well of course people who go to the vet's are [<S 02> mm]
   interested in the cats and dogs ain't they?

<S 02> Yeah but the people that first have pets, kit-, pets er don't realise
what's involved do they?

<S 01>   ⌞Care,

well it sorts them out you know those that don't care that's
it so [<S 02> mm] but [<S 02> mm] if you wanna you know,
somebody that's keen on having [<S 02> mm] a pet [<S 02> mm]
and want it in good order.

<S 02>   ⌞Done … done properly that's right yeah.[4]

Here we see that it is not only in 'monologic' modes such as storytelling
that listeners have a role in creating the lexical patterns of a text. The
effective listener is constantly predicting the upcoming discourse, and
quite often these predictions are verbalised, as if to say: 'I know what you
are going to say and I think this is what you will say'. Each of the speakers
does this in this extract:

<S 02> … pets er don't realise
<S 01>   ⌞Care
<S 01> … and want it in good order.
<S 02>   ⌞done … done properly that's right yeah.

Usually the predicted words are near enough to the speaker's intended
ones not to impair communication. The phenomenon of prediction is
very common; we may note here that each speaker does it to the other.
Once again, this is evidence that listeners are not passive in constructing
the lexical fabric of a conversation; conversational convergence (in terms
of both goals and relationships) is necessarily a joint responsibility, and
the lexical choices are significant signals of attempts to converge.

6.5 Fixed expressions

In (6.8), we may observe another dimension of vocabulary choice in
conversational language, namely the number of fixed (including idiomatic), ready-made expressions the speakers use (idioms are investigated
in greater depth in Chapter 7):

(6.8)

[<S 01> has just come back from a holiday where he had trouble with his
luggage going astray. He is about to go off on another trip. <S 02> is his
neighbour.]

<S 02> When are you heading off again Bob?

<S 01> A week today ... I shall be off to Munich this time ... so I'm just wondering where the luggage is going to go and looking at my case now, I find that it's burst open and whether it's fair wear and tear I don't know, because last time I saw it it was in perfect nick.

<S 02> You reckon it might have suffered from its journey.

<S 01> Oh they get slung about you know, I never used to get a decent case I buy a cheap one.

<S 02> Mm.

<S 01> Because they just get scratched.

<S 02> Mm.

Informal conversation is marked by a high occurrence of fixed expressions and idioms of various kinds, some more transparent than others, though still quite fixed in their syntax and lexical form. We may note some examples here:

when are you **heading off**	(phrasal verb)
a week **today**	(fixed adverbial frame)
I shall **be off** *to Munich*	(phrasal verb)
it's **burst open**	(phrasal verb)
this is **fair wear and tear**	(irreversible binomial)
it was **in perfect nick**	(restricted collocation)
they get **slung about**	(phrasal verb)

Idiomatic fixed expressions are by no means equally distributed in discourse (see Chapter 7; also McCarthy and Carter, 1994: ch.3) and an over-concentration on written text in language learning may well present an unbalanced view of their significance in communication. They are always evaluative in the sense that they are not neutral alternatives to their literal counterparts but include some attitude or comment on the entities and phenomena they describe and project an informal relationship between conversational participants. Observing how, when and where such expressions occur is a major challenge to research in the spoken language (see Nyyssönen 1992), and available evidence so far is scarce (exceptionally, see Strässler, 1982; Powell 1992). Chapter 7 will attempt to remedy that situation by looking at idioms in spoken data. But apart from opaque idioms, a good deal of semantically transparent vocabulary is also fossilised into fixed, multi-word expressions and restricted collocations (see Aisenstadt 1981) and compounds. Some of these are highlighted in (6.9):

(6.9)
[<S 01> has been telling a story about a road accident involving her car and a tramp.]

<S 01> And **of course** the **police officer** came and I was **a bit** shocked and he said **get in the passenger seat** and he drove me to the **police station you see**, somebody **sent for an ambulance** and there was all **activity going on** this man was **propped up at the side of** the wall he looked pretty **you know** he wasn't bleeding **or anything**

<S 02> Wasn't he?

<S 01> No no

<S 02> How fast were you going then?

<S 01> I wasn't going very fast **you see you know** it was I'd **only just turned the corner more or less** here, and there was **a bit of a line of traffic** and then

<S 02> So **it was a bit of a miracle** he wasn't hurt wasn't it

<S 01> Apparently it was his party no it was his **party-piece** because the police told me that he'd done it very often this 'cos it **got him a bed for the night, you know** it got him **in hospital** [<S 03> [laughs]] and when he were **getting a bit fed up**, he'd already **had them there** that morning apparently saying the IRA had put a bomb under his bed but then he **picked on** me and er **it got him a bed for the night in hospital** and that was his he did it regular

<S 03> **Good grief**

<S 01> **You know** but the thing to laugh

<S 02>   ⌊**It's a wonder he didn't break every bone in his body** isn't it

<S 01> It was just, well the **police woman rang up** I was there because I were very **upset at the thought** I'd hurt him **you know** and she said oh he's only **cuts and bruises** they're used to him and **you mustn't bother about this sort of thing** but I was **pretty upset at the time**

<S 02> Yeah yeah.

This kind of 'off-the-peg' vocabulary assists fluent production in real time, and seems to be just as significant as the single-word elements that go to make up the text. Indeed, it is hard to envision the notion of fluency having any real validity if language could not be (at least in part) produced ready-assembled in this way (see Bolinger 1976). Thus spoken language pedagogy cannot afford to neglect the multi-word items that are found in data. Only close observation of real data can raise awareness of the centrality of such phenomena, and confronting data may be a necessary preamble to the more conventional teaching and learning strategies that are found in typical vocabulary lessons.

6.6 The spoken vocabulary syllabus

The question often arises as to how teachers with little or no access to large amounts of real data can get access to relevant lexical facts about the spoken language. One solution (though limited in what it can tell us, as much of the necessary qualitative interpretation in this chapter underlines) is the use of ever-increasingly available computer-generated word lists. Computational analysis enables the creation of automated word lists which can be used alongside the manually-compiled word lists that often appear in syllabuses as a checking mechanism, or to compare with computer-generated word lists for written language. Frequency lists for spoken language do differ considerably from those dependent on written databases, especially journalistic ones (such as Zettersten 1978). The following lists are each based on approximately 100,000 words of data, and reveal interesting differences (for a fuller discussion, see McCarthy and Carter 1997a):

	Written	Spoken
1	the	I
2	to	the
3	of	and
4	a	you
5	and	it
6	in	to
7	is	that
8	for	is
9	it	a
10	that	yes
11	was	of
12	on	in
13	he	was
14	with	know
15	as	have
16	his	they
17	be	no
18	but	but

19	at	like
20	by	she
21	have	so
22	has	do
23	from	well
24	are	on
25	I	oh
26	this	there
27	they	what
28	not	he
29	an	for
30	will	got
31	who	this
32	been	all
33	their	be
34	had	don't
35	one	not
36	which	just
37	you	go
38	all	at
39	last	with
40	her	think
41	said	about
42	were	one
43	we	really
44	when	then
45	more	said
46	there	get
47	would	or
48	she	if
49	or	right
50	up	up

Figure 1: The 50 most frequent words from 100,000 words of written data (newspapers and magazines)[5] and 100,000 words of spoken data (CANCODE). The shaded cells in the spoken column indicate forms which occur significantly more frequently in the spoken than in the written

Notable in these lists are both the similarity of rankings of basic words and some differences which give the two modes of language their characteristic qualities. The written list consists of mostly function words, but the spoken list seems, on the face of it, to include a number of lexical words such as *know, well, get/got, go, think, right*. However, most of nese prove to be elements of discourse markers (e.g. *you+know, I+think*) or single-word markers (*well, right*) (see Stenström 1990 for a discussion and further examples). This suggests that any teacher wishing to incorporate insights from vocabulary analysis of the spoken language has to decide the status in the syllabus of discourse markers. As well as these lexical words, a number of items which are often classified as conjunctions in sentence-grammar may have to be re-assessed owing to their extremely high frequency of occurrence as markers in the spoken language (e.g. *so;* see also the discussion of subordination and words such as *because*, in section 4.5). Other items will need re-examination too. What are the commonest functions of the frequent spoken uses of *get*? Is *get/got* used differently in spoken language as compared to written? To answer this last question, let us consider some statistics for the form *got. Got* occurs approximately 14 times more frequently in our spoken sample than in the written. By far the most frequent use of *got* in spoken is in the construction *have got* as the basic verb of possession or personal association with something. Some examples follow, concordanced for the subject pronoun *I* plus *'ve*:

4684 03	en or something Yes cos	I've got	the cross-London transfer anyway A
2028 01	ipe it Erm not yet cos	I've got	to make the bread when I've finish
7782 01	is born in July, 'cos	I've got	so many birthdays in July. All
551 03	know. I've got it down	I've got	it somewhere that outside the er c
481 02	um I tell you what else	I've got	Chris do you know we made an album
8552 02	West. Yes so am I. Er	I've got	an agreed overdraft limit of five
102 01	aying about the fellah	I've got	you She would marry him if he wor
1986 01	you know a sore finger	I've got	a great big bloody hole It's not
4544 02	called Hearts of Fire	I've got	that on video But they took off a
4047 01	ome of the upper fours	I've got	erm a magazine and it had like sui
8899 02	l got them. Yes I have	I've got	them they must be around out here.
3627 02	hat's why it's so heavy	I've got	like That's why cos cos you got,
950 01	ildren I don't know how	I've got	it unless you don't go to the danc
6644 01	ewed. . I'll tell you I	I've got	a choice between three months in t
482 02	Switzerland you did it	I've got	that upstairs. That was dreadful
990 04	eah it does doesn't it	I've got	two now yes it does always disappe
6604 01	ve got jobs. Go for it.	I've got	a job. Not yet. Do you want one? M
2579 04	rop Sorry Warwick No	I've got	some thanks Cheers Nice Mm Ver
6686 01	you got? Sweden's not.	I've got	eleven. Norway. Norway isn't eithe
1768 02	ah That's the only one	I've got	Yeah that's fine Yeah d'you mind
6794 01	t . That's the only one	I've got	I haven't got any of the small one
478 02	some I'll get some out	I've got	some up in the cupboard haven't I

Figure 2: Sample concordance lines for *I've got* (spoken)

Not only *got* displays differences in distribution between written and spoken; we can expect many other words to display significant differences too, especially apparently synonymous words such as *start* and *begin* (Rundell 1995) and *too* and *also*. Other individual words too will occur differently. For example, in our samples, the modal adverb *probably* occurs six times more frequently in the spoken data than in the written, and is thus one of those words that may have far greater importance in the spoken vocabulary syllabus than it might have attracted in a syllabus based only on written data. Meaning and use as well as frequency may be different between written and spoken data. In the concordance for *I've got*, above, the line '*cos I've got so many birthdays in July* is typical of the rather vague types of meaning that can be expected to be more frequent in informal spoken language. Another example of contrast between spoken and written is the verb *tend*, which occurs nine times more frequently in our spoken sample than in our written one, and there is evidence to suggest that (especially among younger speakers when the speaker designations are traced back to the archived information on speaker age/gender, etc. in the CANCODE corpus) it is becoming grammaticised, and being used to express habitualness or regular occurrence rather than proclivity or bias towards an action. Again, the spoken concordance reveals this pattern:

4783 02	chool Erm yeah but we don't	tend to go very often because it I mea
4789 02	quite far away Mm but I	tend to like to save my money and spen
5768 37	up the drift The thing is I	tend to borrow things off Tim and he t
3073 04	on I tend not to use names I	tend to use direct names very little b
297 01	that? Rock seaside rock. I	tend to buy it and then wait a year so
7842 01	straight to bed Yeah What I	tend to do is read or watch television
7281 01	to look too Do you like it,	tend to like it slightly sort of forwa
7026 01	ke that with parties, people	tend to not turn up Mm until after
4676 01	That's right Yeah the shops	tend to open about eleven o'clock
2050 02	ionally if I do buy bacon we	tend to have it for a lunch you know w
5761 37	got six good glasses but we	tend not to use them She was saying s
2151 02	ty seven Well that's how we	tend to go every fortnight and we spen
4771 02	re a couple of times and you	tend to find that a lot of the London
7276 01	se, yeah Yep, How do you	tend to like to dry it, do you like it
5763 37	e about half past six and he	tends to clean the windscreen then Su
3002 03	in Cardiff it tends to be it	tends to be quite wet it wasn't too ba
7848 02	off straight back because it	tends to flop, urm certainly tightene
6884 02	I think when it's shorter it	tends to, you notice it growing more a
7283 02	ith that a bit down, or that	tends to go back I don't quite know wh

Figure 3: Sample corcondance lines for *tend* (spoken)

Many of these concordance lines suggest a focus on regularity or habitualness rather than on the meaning of bias towards an activity, or 'hedging' of a proposition (as Low 1995 interprets his questionnaire respondents' use of *tend*). One might especially note *we don't tend to go very often, what I tend to do is read or watch television, we tend to go every fortnight* and *he tends to clean the windscreen*. It is not that grammars or dictionaries necessarily fail to pick up these distinctions of sense (e.g. see the excellent sense distinctions for *tend* in the COBUILD 1995 dictionary, where corpus evidence informs the dictionary, and where the 'habitual' sense is foregrounded). The importance for the present discussion is rather the prominence of *tend* with this sense in the spoken corpus, and, above all the much higher frequency of *tend* in the spoken, which suggests that its marginalisation in most grammars may give less than a true picture of its use in everyday language. For example, Quirk *et al* (1985: 236) relegate *tend* to a mere mention in a category labelled 'other' among the marginal auxiliaries, and yet *tend* is three times more frequent in the spoken sample of 100,000 words than *ought*, which gets much more attention in large grammars and in English language coursebooks.

Computational analysis of language corpora can point up some interesting and pedagogically useful differences between spoken and written vocabulary use, and even relatively small samples (by today's standards) can yield original insights or can raise awareness for future observation and verification in the field.[6] But computers are not very good at picking up the interactive features of lexical choice and are no substitute for keen observation and qualitative interpretation. Having said that, the combination of good quality observation and sophisticated computing power, along with carefully targeted corpora, can be an extremely effective tool in assisting progress towards our goal of discourse-oriented language descriptions for pedagogical purposes. And yet the corpus should not exercise a tyrannical hold on the syllabus. For example, it is unlikely that the names of all seven days of the week will occur with exactly equal frequency in any corpus (see Martin 1988), yet no-one in their right mind would seriously doubt their equal status (from a psycholinguistic point of view) as target items in the lexical syllabus. Many other intuitively related word-sets may have to be considered in this way too, and the syllabus should be corpus-informed rather than corpus-driven (for discussion of this distinction, see section 1.9). It is also worthy of note that, although we have concentrated on high-frequency spoken items, there is still a huge lexical load of infrequently occurring words in everyday conversation: the Davis-Howes word-count of spoken English (Howes 1966) (see section 1.3) has already shown that getting on for half of all the words listed in its 250,000-word corpus occur only once. What is important in the case of automated analysis of spoken language is to achieve a degree of objectivity of observation that real-time participation in conversation denies us most of the time to a far greater extent than reading written text does, and it is here that a corpus of spoken language comes into its own.

6.7 Conclusion

Our conversational extracts have illustrated different aspects of the lexical characteristics of everyday spoken language, and one does not need much data to see the same features constantly recurring. A view of language which starts from the premise that language forms in contexts create the discourse process, helps us to locate and explain those features in terms of the kinds of constraints which differentiate conversational language from the composed, single-authored written text mentioned at the beginning of this chapter. The differences are many, and here we have only considered the implications for lexical patterning and, in turn, what broad implications for vocabulary teaching and learning such a view of lexical patterning holds. We have also seen in Chapters 4 and 5 that the same applies to grammar. The grammar of spontaneous spoken language is different in crucial aspects from that of carefully composed written text, and operates under the same constraints related to participants, goals and settings as lexical selection. A discourse-based view of language forces us to change our understanding of formal patterns but also raises important questions about how one communicates such knowledge to learners and, above all, equips them with the appropriate resources to enable them to converse naturally in conversation in the target language. I have suggested that the kinds of features highlighted here may provoke a reconsideration of methodological assumptions in vocabulary teaching. It may not be enough to present, practise and produce words (or even words in sentences) when we are dealing with the kinds of lexical features we have argued to be central to conversational language. A language-awareness approach may be more effective and appropriate at the outset, and encouraging the 'learner-as-researcher' may be the best long-term strategy for empowerıg the learner to become a natural user of the target spoken vocabulary. The lexical load may not necessarily be greater in spoken language programmes, but it will certainly have different priorities and emphases, and will be based on what real data can tell us, rather than intuitively constructed word lists and sentences. Above all, the syllabus will recognise that the vocabulary of a language is an integrated resource (as we have argued for features such as synonymy and antonymy) which serves the progression and development of topics and participant goals, and just as importantly, the construction and maintenance of social relations.

Notes

1 This chapter is a much revised version, with new data and expanded references, of a paper published in Longa, H. P. (ed) (1994) *Atti del Seminario Internazionale di Studi sul Lessico*, Forli – San Marino, 1992. Bologna: CLUEB, 119–30.

2 I am grateful to Faye Wadsworth, formerly of the Department of English Studies, University of Nottingham, for permission to use this piece of data, recorded in 1990.

3 Lexical creativity in oral narrative and other genres is further discussed, with corpus examples of morphological creativeness, in Carter and McCarthy (1995a).

4 Data kindly supplied by Jim Lawley, formerly of the Department of English Studies, University of Birmingham, 1987.

5 Sampled from the 100-million-word Cambridge International Corpus; © Cambridge University Press.

6 The question of optimum corpus size is largely irresolvable, and seems to be dependent on the current size of major competing corpus projects (see the discussion in Chapter 1). We may confidently predict that the present-day rush for corpora of tens and even hundreds of millions of words will be ridiculed within a decade by those who will argue that anything less than a billion words is inadequate. Carter and McCarthy (1995b) demonstrate that even relatively small samples of 20–30,000 words of spoken language, if carefully targeted to particular goal- and relation-types, can yield grammatical insights overlooked by analysts of corpora many times that size, and can be pedagogically useful and relevant.

7

Idioms in use: a discourse-based re-examination of a traditional area of language teaching

7.1 Introduction

In an earlier paper on this subject,[1] and in McCarthy and Carter (1994: 109), we noted that idiomatic expressions of various kinds have long preoccupied language teachers and learners, and that publishers regularly devote special supplementary teaching materials to idioms and put out dictionaries of idioms aimed at language learners (e.g. Cowie and Mackin 1975; Longman 1979; Cambridge University Press 1998). We also noted that, compared with the amount of research into features of spoken language in general, including such areas as turn-taking (Sacks *et al.* 1974), topic-management (Gardner 1987), and lexical patterning in general (small though work in this last area has been, as was examined in Chapter 6), we still seem to know very little about how idioms are actually used in everyday talk. Instead, we tend to continue to teach them as curiously disembodied items, detached from any contexts other than imagined and contrived ones which may or may not bear any resemblance to their real use. Learners tend to treat them as an oddity, a whimsical feature of the target language, something to collect and hoard, list-wise, in the vocabulary notebook. In this book, I have consistently argued that language teaching and applied linguistics in general can benefit from a spoken discourse-based orientation towards language description, and that language teachers should concern themselves critically with the descriptive approaches that generate raw material for teaching. But the temptation is often to attempt to incorporate the more exciting insights of discourse analysis, such as models of turn-taking and the like (see section 3.2.2), and to leave traditional areas of interest, such as pronunciation teaching and vocabulary teaching to the traditionalists. However important and fruitful that line may be, an even greater challenge exists in the re-modelling of traditional areas of teaching, especially those embedded in largely unquestioned assumptions. This chapter, therefore, attempts to look at some natural spoken contexts of use for idioms, and to examine what sorts of discoursal functions idioms perform. It extends the work reported in McCarthy (1992b) and McCarthy and Carter (1994), and tries to draw the threads together into a coherent theory of idiom use.

In the earlier work referred to, we used the word 'idiom' to mean strings of more than one word whose syntactic, lexical and phonological form is to a greater or lesser degree fixed and whose semantics and pragmatic functions are opaque and specialised, also to a greater or lesser degree. An example of a string where all elements are fixed is the expression *rough and ready*. The expression must be uttered with that particular word-order, those particular words and with one single tone-unit (/^{2}ROUGH and ^{1}REAdy/ [^{1} = primary stress; ^{2} = secondary stress; / / = tone-unit boundary]); its meaning is fixed and largely non-negotiable (see Cowie 1988 for an extended discussion of this feature of fixedness). Other expressions may be more flexible in one or more respects along the possible continua of lexico-grammatical, phonological and semantic/pragmatic fixedness. The expression *to turn a blind eye (to something)* was recently nominalised and pluralised by an interviewee on a BBC radio programme, when he replied that '*Blind eyes have been turned* all the way along to breaches of safety regulations ...', revealing a degree of acceptable syntactic flexibility. The cut-off point where fixed expressions become open, freshly synthesised lexico-grammatical configurations (created anew each time, as it were), and where opaque idiomatic meaning becomes transparent and more and more literal is problematic and ultimately impossible to pinpoint. But a definition of idioms that has blurred boundaries has advantages as well as disadvantages: it usefully enables us to incorporate within the term a wide range of fixed expressions over and above the clause-idioms (of the type *verb + complement*, e.g. *hit the sack* in English, meaning 'to go to bed') and idiomatic phrasal verbs (e.g. *take (sb) off*, meaning 'to mimic'), which are traditionally most often focused upon in language teaching materials. These extra categories of idioms include:[2]

1 Prepositional expressions: *in two shake's of a lamb's tail* (meaning (to do something) very quickly).
2 Binomials and trinomials: usually irreversible combinations with *and* or other conjunctions whose order may vary from language to language: *black and white* film (cf. Spanish *blanco y negro*, 'white-and-black'), *ready, willing and able, give or take, safe and sound* (see Malkiel

1959; Gustafsson 1975; Norrick 1988; Fenk-Oczlon 1989 for further examples and discussions).[3]

3 Frozen similes; usually formally identified by the removability of the first as: *(as) keen as mustard, (as) cold as charity* (see Tamony 1982; Norrick 1986).

4 Possessive 's phrases: *a king's ransom, the cat's whiskers*.

5 Opaque nominal compounds: *blackmail, a mish-mash, the back of beyond*.[4]

6 Idiomatic speech routines, gambits and discourse markers, which are very frequent in conversational data: *by the way, how's it going?, that's that, mind you*.

7 Cultural allusions; these include a wide range of quotations, slogans, catch phrases, proverbs, all instantly identifiable to those who share the cultural context: *to be or not to be ..., sock it to me, every cloud has a silver lining*.

What is important to note from this list is that idioms cannot always be uniquely identified by their formal properties, especially the phenomena listed in 7, where a wide variety of formal types are found (phrases, clauses, sentences, whole texts) and which are held in common by the members of speech communities as references to their shared culture. Ultimately, intuition also has to play a role, especially in borderline cases, in the identification of idiomatic strings of words (see Rressan 1979 for an extended discussion of the problems).

7.2 Idioms in use: evaluative force

All of the types of idiomatic expression listed above may be found in greater or lesser number in real spoken and written language. In the literature, discussion usually centres upon the semantics, the syntax, the cross-linguistic differences and the universality of such expressions (e.g. see Makkai 1978; Fernando and Flavell 1981; Reagan 1987), and I shall not gainsay the pedagogical use to which such insights may be put. What is almost always lacking, though, is an attempt to examine function and distribution in real contexts of use. Conversational routines, gambits and discourse markers are an exception (see Coulmas, 1979, 1981a; Schiffrin 1987) and need little further comment here. There is often an underlying assumption that idiomatic expressions are merely rather informal or colloquial alternatives to their semantically equivalent literal free-forms. This may well be true insomuch as the kinds of data where idioms occur often reflect a high degree of informality at the interpersonal level between speaker and listener, but this does not go anywhere near far enough to tell us why speakers choose idioms instead of literal, transparent counterparts at particular points in a discourse. The question to answer is: why should languages 'duplicate' ways of saying things, offering the literal and idiomatic options that seem to operate (theoretically at least) in free variation at many places in discourse? Certainly, real data seem to indicate, as I shall attempt to demonstrate below, that idiom selection is not random and unmotivated, and can be linked to features of language choice at the discourse level. Considerable support for this claim is already available from computational analysis of written texts of a wide variety of types, where the function of idioms as evaluative devices, correlating with authorial comment segments in texts, seems to be a regular pattern (see Moon, 1992). In spoken data, the distribution and functioning of idioms is even more fascinating and less well-researched. A spoken corpus enables us to observe idiom use in everyday talk at close quarters across a wide range of speakers of diverse ages and social classes, in different situational contexts.

One of the very few analysts to attempt to describe idiom use in naturally-occurring spoken English is Strässler (1982) (and more recently, see Powell 1992).[5] Strässler does what the present chapter advocates and departs from the traditional way of analysing idioms as a semantic problem and looks at the pragmatics of idiom use. Strässler found that idioms were, relatively speaking, infrequent (they occur on average once per 1,150 words in his data). This might immediately suggest, for the learner needing to concentrate on spoken skills, that they are less of an obstacle to native-like fluency than they are often believed to be. But where idioms did occur in Strässler's data, they did so with a degree of predictability, not randomly. Idioms, Strässler maintains, are much more likely to occur when a speaker is saying something about a third person or about an object or other non-human entity, rather than about the speaker him/herself or about the listener(s) (1982: 103). This he attributes to the evaluative function of idioms and the risks to 'face' and interpersonal relations which can stem from the self- or other-abasement which idioms often entail (Strassler 1982: 103, 109) ('face' here is understood in the sense propounded by Brown and Levinson 1987). To say to someone *I'm sorry to leave you twiddling your thumbs* (instead of *I'm sorry to keep you waiting*) expresses a certain dominance and confidence (and flippancy?) on the part of the speaker and a potential offence and loss of face to the listener, which alternative, more transparent, 'literal' renditions seem to guard against. Indeed, when speakers do use idioms directly about their interlocutors, they may explicitly gloss their usage to guard against threats to face, as in (7.1):

(7.1)
[Speaker <S 01> is telling his listener how he envied him and another colleague their ability in their job.]

<S 01> Well you and Aubrey used to **make me sick** actually, **in the nicest possible way.**

Strässler's study and example (7.1) indicate the direction of the present chapter: the potential for the integration of levels between lexical form and communicative function (to include interpersonal elements such as politeness and face). We shall also be interested to see whether genre has any implications for the use of idioms.

(7.2) illustrates the evaluative function in action, with the use of an idiom (in this case a frozen simile) to a third-person, non-participant entity:

(7.2)
[The speakers are exchanging views about political dominance by the Conservative Party in Devon, in the south-west of Britain.]

<S 01> But living down here in Devon there's no way
<S 02> We're disenfranchised completely.
<S 01> You know there's such an enormous Conservative majority I mean today I had to ring up one of the local councillors he's **as thick as two short planks.**[6]

Here we have a factual observation, followed by an evaluative comment. This pattern, as we shall see later, is a recurring feature of idiom use. This general 'observation plus comment' function, as I shall refer to it, has a specific type of manifestation in oral narratives, to which we shall now turn.

7.3 Idioms in everyday stories and anecdotes

In this section, we consider oral narrative as a clearly defined generic activity with an identifiable discourse structure (see Labov 1972, and the brief summary of Labov's model in section 3.2.3). Idioms do seem to occur at important junctures in everyday stories, not just randomly. They often occur in segments where the teller and listeners step back and 'evaluate' the events of the narrative, rather than in the reports of the events themselves. Evaluation in Labov's model refers to the function whereby storytellers make the events they are telling worth listening to. Evaluative clauses in narratives forestall the embarrassing question *So what?* (*Why should I want to listen to this story? What's exciting/special/funny about it?*). Equally, listeners add their evaluation of events, commenting on the story's general worth, its effects on them, and so on. Evaluation is not an optional extra in storytelling; without it there is no story, only a bland report. In the following examples, the contrast between 'events' and the evaluation of them is underlined by the shift from neutral expressions to idioms:

(7.3)
[The teller, <S 01> introduces a new character into his story.]

<S 01> And Guss Hughes came along one day and we were always **taking the Mickey out of** him he was you know he was one of these the lads that always **got taken** so we all knelt down

(7.4)
[<S 01> (Mary) is recounting a story that happened when she was on holiday with her friend, Dulcie.]

<S 01> I said what would you like to do this afternoon Dulcie she said oh Mary let's go to bingo now bingo is **never** ever **my cup of tea** [<S 02> no] but seeing that I was supposed to be with her
<S 02>   ⌊Supporting her yeah
<S 01> I'd to **fall in with** her [<S 02> [laughs]] all right then Dulcie where do we go now to bingo.

In (7.4) the transition from event segment to evaluative segment is further reinforced by the discourse marker *now*. We may conveniently represent the event line and evaluation line (which simply represent a more specialised version of the 'observation plus comment' function) diagrammatically:

Event line	Evaluation line
(7.3) and Guss Hughes came along one day	
	and we were always **taking the Mickey out of** him he was you know he was one of these the lads that always **got taken**
so we all knelt down	
(7.4) I said what would you like to do this afternoon Dulcie she said oh Mary let's go to bingo	
	now bingo is **never** ever **my cup of tea** but seeing that I was supposed to be with her I'd to **fall in with** her
all right then Dulcie where do we go now to bingo	

In everyday stories, idioms often occur in codas (again in Labov's sense; the 'coda', at the end of a story, provides a bridge between the story world and the real world of the teller and listeners; see also Chapter 3). Here are some examples from corpus data, with relevant idioms highlighted:

(7.5)

[End of a story by speaker <S 02> of how a job opportunity she took represented a big step in her career.]

<S 01> Still that's the way it all started for you.
<S 02> That's right
<S 03> **The big break** wasn't it.

(7.6)

[End of a story by speaker <S 01> in which she and a friend benefitted from half-price food during a 'happy-hour' at a restaurant.]

<S 01> And that was drinks [<S 02> yeah] but that was half price it would have been sixteen pounds each [<S 02> yeah] had it been later.
<S 03> Well that's **fair enough** isn't it.
<S 02> **You can't go wrong with that** can you.

(7.7)

[End of a story where speaker <S 01> has recounted a coincidence of seeing once again a stranger she had felt attracted to but whom she thought she would never see again.]

<S 01> I thought oh am I never gonna see you again and on the
      Wednesday I was just walking past the bank and I saw him [laughs]
      so he must have lived in Carmarthen.
<S 02> [laughs] that's a bit odd
<S 03>   ⌐**Small world.**
<S 02>   ⌐when things like that happen
      isn't it.
<S 01> I just sort of go I know him from somewhere and **it clicked**.

(For further examples see McCarthy and Carter 1994: 111.) In (7.5), the idiom evaluates the whole narrative, summarising the main events and relating them to the teller's current career position. Idioms in (7.6) and (7.7) similarly perform a summarising function. As I have argued elsewhere (McCarthy 1991: 139–40), storytelling is normally a collaborative enterprise, and listeners have the right (one might say responsibility) to evaluate the events, and to ensure a smooth passage for all participants from story world back to conversation world when the story has ended. (7.5), (7.6) and (7.7) all have listeners using idioms to contribute to the coda. But where listeners do use idioms for this purpose, they will have to be ones that are careful not to abase the teller, unless the relationship between teller and listener(s) is very relaxed and on equal and/or intimate terms. The kinds of idioms we see in codas (often clichés, proverbs, sayings of various kinds) partake of the 'sheltering behind shared values' that Moon (1992) observed in idiom usage in her written data (see also Loveday 1982: 83), and reinforces the importance of observing the cultural contexts of idioms, in the broadest sense of the word 'culture' (see McCarthy and Carter 1994: 114–17). Narrative codas are essentially no more than a specialised example of a more general class of points in discourses where gist is summarised, providing the opportunity for participants to agree on what they have achieved so far, and to move on to new topics (see the discussion on 'formulations' in section 2.3). It is no surprise, therefore, that sociolinguists and conversation analysts, coming at talk from an angle of trying to understand the social significance of the precise moment of placement of particular items, should find that idiomatic expressions occur regularly at topic-transitions (Drew and Holt 1995) and as summaries of gist in sequences such as the formulation of complaints (Drew and Holt 1988). The motive of these researchers is sociological; however, language teachers can learn a great deal from such analyses. Drew and Holt's work underlines the non-random occurrence of idioms and strengthens the argument which is at the heart of the present chapter: that we have much to gain by closely observing how and when idioms are used, not just their formal characteristics.

Another noteworthy feature of idioms in everyday talk is the way speakers use them creatively, by a process of 'unpacking' them into their literal elements and exploiting these. McGlone, Glucksberg and Cacciari (1994) argue that speakers cannot ignore the non-idiomatic meanings of individual words in idiomatic expressions, and that even in opaque idioms, literal meanings of component words are in some sense activated, or at least are potentially available. In (7.8) two middle-aged school-teachers are reminiscing about the early years of their careers; one of them comments on a class he had:

(7.8)

<S 01> The second year I had, I started off with 37 in the class I know that, of what you call **dead wood the real dregs** had been taken off the bottom and **the cream the sour cream in our case up there had been creamed off the top** and I just had this **dead wood**, I mean it really was and he was so impressed with the job that I did with them and the way that I **got on with** them and he immediately said right how do you feel about taking a special class next year and I took one from then on.

<S 02> **Rather you than me.**

The shift from the event line to the evaluation line is quite clear here again, with idioms occurring in the evaluative segments. The idiom *to cream off* and the idiomatic noun phrase *the cream*, are exploited by re-literalising the notion of cream and adding *sour* as an ironic evaluation[7]. The listener then characteristically adds his evaluation/coda with the expression *rather you than me*. Items such as *the cream* and *cream off* in (7.8) do admittedly raise problems concerning the borderline between fully institutionalised, 'fossilised', opaque idioms and extended metaphors which are perhaps not yet fully fossilised and retain some transparency of meaning (on this fuzzy borderline see Choul 1982; Fernando and

Flavell, 1981: 44–7). But this is not the issue of our present discussion, and recent work on metaphor stresses the interpersonal and evaluative functions of metaphors, so underlining their common ground with more opaque idioms (see especially Low, 1988). Not least, the study of metaphor must also confront the apparent duplication of meaning in the vocabularies of languages and attempt to understand its functioning in exactly the same way as the study of idioms should do.

(7.9) is an example of the exploitation of semantic connections between two idioms to elaborate the coda:

(7.9)
[End of a story by a couple, speakers <S 02> and <S 03>, of how they were involved in a consumer survey.]

<S 01> So you were Mr you were that **Mr and Mrs Average** they're always
     talking about then.
<S 02> Yeah.
<S 03> Yeah.
<S 01> **The man and woman in the street.**
<S 03> Yeah.

In (7.10), the teller and listeners create a series of puns to act as coda to a spooky story about a ship being sunk in battle. The end of the event line (the 'resolution' of the narrative in Labov's terminology) is that all on board the ship were killed, except the teller's father, who had had a premonition and refused to sail on the ill-fated voyage:

(7.10)

<S 01> Everyone, everyone died
<S 02> Anyway **all hands lost** but legs saved.
[laughter]
<S 03> Well sailors were always **getting legless** weren't they anyway.
[laughter]
<S 01> **Finding their sea legs.**
<S 03> Yeah

The euphemistic *all **hands** lost* (= all crew dead) gives rise to association with *legs*, in turn connecting with *get **legless*** (= get drunk) and with *finding their sea **legs*** (= becoming accustomed to being on board ship). Such punning and word-play memberships participants as 'belonging' culturally, and may make 'non-membershipped' participants (e.g. non-native speakers/speakers of other varieties with different idiom sets) feel quite excluded. Indeed, idioms are often created among small groups or those with shared interests (for example see Gibbon 1981), right down to partnered couples, where intimacy is reinforced by 'private' sets of euphemistic and humorous expressions (see the data in Hopper, Knapp and Scott 1981).[8] Humorous unpacking and semi- literalising of idioms is by no means rare in the CANCODE corpus. Another example involves a cultural allusion to the (at the time) popular media icons, the Teenage Mutant Ninja Turtles:

(7.11)
[Two young women discussing having children. A *ginger nut* is a kind of biscuit with a ginger flavour, and a nickname for people with ginger hair.]

<S 01> There's twins in our family.
<S 02> Is there.
<S 01> Yeah.
<S 02> Oh right so you might have a twin.
<S 01> And there's **ginger nuts**.
<S 02> Nothing wrong with that.
<S 01> My mum reckons I'm gonna have ginger twins.
<S 02> Mind you one of my best friends at home **Ninj** we call him
    because he's ginger you see, **Ninja**. [pron: /ˈnɪndʒə/]

Other cultural allusions assume shared knowledge of whole expressions by only saying part of them; this is a particularly exclusive form of membershipping:

(7.12)
[The same two teachers as in (7.8), reminiscing about a room at their old school, which <S 01> thinks now looks somewhat shabby.]

<S 01> I said I remember this when it was a woodwork room, her room
    and I said cor crikey it looks as though **it could do with one or two**
    yes she said they **rearrange the deckchairs** round the edges every so
    often but that's as far as it goes.

It could do with one or two is understood as continuing ... *coats of paint* (i.e. it needs redecorating), while *rearrange the deckchairs* is a partial rendition of *to rearrange the deckchairs on the Titanic* (meaning to make temporary solutions that do not solve the major problems that lie ahead: the ship *Titanic* sank, even though it was thought to be unsinkable).

7.4 Idioms in *collaborative ideas* discourses

One of the most frequent conversational activities is what we referred to in section 1.3 as *collaborative* ideas, where participants share views of the world, discuss matters of interest, etc. Often, conversations just grow out of observations about the world and evaluations of those observations, one observation following another. This type of conversational activity differs from narrative in that there is not necessarily any kind of chronological report. Speakers simply make statements of fact or of perception about the world and accompany it with a comment indicating their stance towards those observations. This often happens in talk marked by topic drift, where participants may be 'fishing' for topics and simply casting their minds around, making general and local observations. Not surprisingly, the place of idioms is firmly in the 'comment' segments in such discourses. Some examples are given in diagram form to underline the functional shifts:

Observation	Comment
(7.13) <S 01> I wouldn't come back and live in a big town not at all they're dirty they're noisy	
	<S 02> **All this hustle and bustle**
(7.14) <S 01> and so I go into his bed and he comes back in	
	so to my bed and his bed and **chopping and changing**
(7.15) <S 01> See, the folly of leaving the company, you know,	
	you would have been **jetting off** <S 02> Yeah **left right and centre** [<S 01> yeah] Andorra one day Hong Kong the next

(7.16)
<S 01> Left here at four,
[<S 02> oh yes yeah] ... three, three
and a half hours

> He must have **driven like the clappers**

(7.17)
<S 01> I don't know, I feel a bit
nervous now [laughs]

> <S 02> Do you, **stage fright** is it

<S 01> I think so yes

(7.18)
<S 01> Mm what about something
like erm ... forensic linguistics
<S 02> Mm I mean, I think the thing is

> <S 03> Kind of thing like **who dunnit**
> on the trial [*a who dunnit* is an
> idiomatic compound noun meaning a
> mystery murder novel or film: i.e. 'Who
> has done this murder?']

<S 01> That's right

(7.19)
<S 01> I don't usually have chips
I usually have jacket potatoes

> <S 02> **Like mother like daughter**

While the comment usually follows the observation, it may also precede
it, as in these examples:

Comment	Observation
(7.20) <S 01> Julie's got a very **cushy number**	
	she's off to Mauritius
(7.21) <S 01> Thomas **is a bit of a pain**	
	all sorts of things frighten him you know, <S 02> Yeah] wakes up with nightmares and that

(cont.)

(cont.)

Comment	Observation
(7.22) <S 01> I think she ought to be **told the time of day**	
	when I was 21 I didn't have a car
(7.23) <S 01> I think **there isn't a magic formula**	
	it's something that just happens
(7.24) <S 01> **you're left to your own devices** that's it	
	you get no, no further training nothing

Once again, it is to be noted that the 'observation-comment' function may be split between participants in the conversation, creating cultural solidarity between speakers and their listeners (on the supportive roles of participants, see Bublitz, 1988).

In addition to the 'observation-comment' function in the more temporally displaced kinds of exchange of facts and perceptions illustrated in the table, the 'comment' may be immediately referential, referring to the here-and-now situation of the participants:

(7.25)

[<S 01> and <S 02> are house guests and are waiting to be called to table for dinner]

<S 01> We're the privileged guests you know you and we're
<S 02>   ⌊How nice
<S 01>   ⌊We're
    allowed to just sit here and **swan it**

(7.26)

[<S 01> is relaxing just before a family party, after working hard to prepare it.]

<S 01> [yawns] well this is **the calm before the storm** isn't it what time is
    it

(7.27)

[<S 01> and <S 02> are looking at an old photograph of themselves from 1967.]

<S 01> It **says it all** doesn't it.
<S 02> Absolutely 1967.

7.5 Idioms, negotiation of meaning and convergence

Another feature of idiom use that emerges from close examination of conversational data is the role idioms play in segments where lexical meaning is being negotiated among participants. In a way, this is also true of the more specialised uses of idioms we have been concentrating on up to now. Oral narrative functions such as evaluations and codas are negotiated among participants, and attitude and stance do not simply exist in discourse, but are usually negotiated and worked at, owing to the potential threats to face, the interpersonal exigencies of real-time, face-to-face interaction, and the normal desire for conversational convergence (see glossary p. 177). Throughout our data we can observe idioms being put to service to support the negotiation of lexical meaning. I have discussed elsewhere (McCarthy 1988; see also section 6.3) how lexical reiteration performs important negotiating functions. Idioms, with their often rather vague and general meanings, can stand in for more precise values in discourse where speakers work towards convergence and mutual understandings. Some examples follow. (7.28) gives to the idiomatic compound *knick-knacks* an instantial 'equivalence' to the candles bought by <S 02>. (7.29) uses the idiomatic simile *as flat as a pancake* in a relation of 'opposition' to the precise topographical description, and (7.30) uses the binomial idiom *life and death* in opposition to the speaker's preferred term. These latter are characteristic uses of antonymous expressions in the negotiation of lexical meaning (for further examples see McCarthy 1988):

(7.28)

[Speakers are discussing <S 02>'s day's shopping.]

<S 01> Sounds like it cos you bought your little **knick-knacks** there today
    didn't you.
<S 02> The candles.
<S 01> Yes yes.

.29)

[Speakers are discussing the Eastern part of England.]

<S 01> It's flat you know it's not er hilly like Wales but [<S 02> mm] you get used to that strangely enough after a while, I mean it's not **as flat as a pancake** it's kind of undulating.

(7.30)

[Speakers are discussing the decisions speech-therapists have to make in their work.]

<S 01> That's what Ana-Maria says, she's sort of making not quite **life and death** decisions but real life enhancing decisions among you know dozens of priorities.
<S 02> Yeah.

Knick-knacks in (7.28) is typical of many idiomatic expressions which enable speakers to avoid precise reference. In (7.31), a hostess at the dinner-table wants her guests to take vegetables and condiments and to start eating. Too precise a reference to these items may have sounded rather commanding; the idiom she chooses is sufficiently oblique to avoid any threat to her guests' face:

(7.31)

<S 01> Look get started you know putting all the **bits and pieces** on.

The same binomial idiom occurs in (7.32), where the speaker is re-counting how he got lavish presents at a job-leaving party, while another colleague also leaving got nothing. *Bits and pieces* defocuses from the precise meaning and tones down the possibly boastful (and thus face-threatening to the teller) interpretation of the event:

(7.32)

<S 01> As I say I collected all these **bits and pieces** all these goodies and everything and she got virtually nothing.

7.6 Drawing the threads together: the overall functioning of idioms in discourse

Although the division of this chapter so far may suggest rather discrete functions for idioms, there is clearly an overlap between the notion of narrative evaluation and the evaluations found in non-narrative observation-comment discourses. In section 7.5 I have also suggested that the negotiation of lexical meaning has preoccupations in common with other uses of idioms (e.g. the need to protect face, participant orientation, etc.). We have now reached a point where more over-arching conclusions can be drawn, as a framework for pedagogy. What seem to emerge most usefully from our data are the following insights:

- Idioms are never just neutral alternatives to literal, transparent semantically equivalent expressions.
- Idioms always *comment* on the world in some way, rather than simply *describe* it. They are evaluative and frequently involve potential threats to face.[9]
- Speakers are aware of the face-threatening potential of idioms and are careful to use idioms generally only for third-person reference, or to mitigate threats to face in first- and second-person reference.
- Idioms are communal tokens that enable speakers to express cultural and social solidarity; this is particularly so of those that are direct cultural allusions such as proverbs, quotations, etc.
- Idioms may be relatively infrequent in occurrence, but it is possible to predict where they are likely to occur (e.g. in particular genres and at particular places).
- Idioms occur in a wide variety of forms, not just the *verb + complement* type. In our data samples we have seen idiomatic nominal compounds, frozen similes, binomials, phrasal verbs, and clausal idioms.

Another point that could be made, but which has been beyond the scope of the present, necessarily limited discussion is that idioms are sociolinguistically marked: the overwhelming majority of idioms in the CANCODE corpus are spoken by speakers over 25 years old. This may make their teaching as *productive* vocabulary for younger age-groups inappropriate.

The six main points above, and others raised along the way, have implications for pedagogy. Firstly, it would be unwise to ignore idioms just because they are not terribly frequent, for where they do occur seems to be in very ordinary, everyday contexts such as storytelling, and at crucial junctures such as evaluations and codas, and other transition points. What is more, in these and other contexts where they occur, we have been able to observe how the workload of idiom selection is shared among participants: in oral narrative, for example, it is certainly not just tellers who use them, but listeners too. This suggests that idioms are highly interactive items, and are therefore best looked at in context and, if possible in interactions of the kinds I have exemplified. The importance of looking at idioms in context actually has benefits for the recognition of recurrent formal features too, as Coulmas (1981b) has argued. In English, for instance, certain verbs such as *take* and *get* seem to be 'idiom-prone', and regularly combine with many other words to form expressions with specialised pragmatic functions which can only be fully appreciated in context. Elsewhere Coulmas (1981a: 5) asserts that all fixed expressions are better explained in terms of their use rather than their semantics. More directly referring to pedagogy, Lattey (1986) advocates contextual organisation of idioms on the basis of recurring pragmatic functions related to the interaction of speaker and listener, speaker and the outside world, positive evaluations and negative evaluations of people and phenomena, etc. Similarly, McCarthy and O'Dell (1994) try to put into practice both a formal and functional categorisation of idioms in the organisation of self-study units on idioms for upper-intermediate learners of English. Our categories there include 'Idioms connected with praise and criticism', 'Idioms for describing people', 'Idioms connected with problematic situations'. In short, it is a matter of seeing idioms as a communicative resource, rather than as a mere formal quirk of the language (for further discussion, see Fernando 1996: ch. 6).

However, language teachers often quite justifiably ask the question: how do I do *controlled* practice of items which are highly interactive? One of the problems associated with any discourse-oriented approach to language teaching is the implication that everything must be practised in real interactive contexts or at the very least in well-designed simulations. Teachers at the chalk-face know that such free production can usually only work after an intensive period of controlled practice of some sort. It is simply unrealistic (and likely to produce disastrous results) merely to say 'get into groups and use idioms with one another in this activity'. But the answer to the plea is a complex one. Firstly, discourse-oriented pedagogical approaches tend to demand something more than just a 'presentational' phase as the lead-in to practice. Because discourse-based methods often go strongly against learner expectations, awareness-raising may have to be the first step. In this case the awareness-raising is concerned with why idioms are there, and how speakers use them, before the 'vocabulary-learning' task is undertaken. This may involve examining data extracts just as we have done in this chapter, focusing on function rather than just meaning, observing the tendency towards third-person reference, how face is protected, etc. A controlled practice phase could then utilise just the sort of segmentation I have used in the tables that illustrate the division between, say, event line and evaluation line in stories, or 'observation' and 'comment' in collaborative ideas discourses. Gap-filling and multiple-choice activities using idioms (provided as vocabulary input in the normal ways) in such tables is then clearly controlled and related to function, avoiding the scatter-gun effect of simply substituting idioms randomly throughout texts and avoiding decontextualised focusing just on semantic meaning. Narrative contexts can be re-created by providing summaries of stories and giving alternative listener evaluations or codas, for example:

> A friend tells you a story about how she discovered that a colleague she has worked with for ten years went to the same school as her thirty years ago, even though they had never realised this before. What could you say at the end of her story? Which of these idioms would be suitable and why?
> a 'Oh well, that's life'
> b 'It's a small world, isn't it'
> c 'I bet you were on cloud nine when you heard'
> d 'You live and learn, don't you'
> e 'Well, would you believe it!'

During the more controlled phases of practice, it may be beneficial to encourage learners to connect idioms with their own personal experiences, as Bergstrom (1979) advocates, since we have seen how often they occur in personal narratives. While it may never be possible to re-create in the classroom the precise natural conditions under which idioms occur, even the most traditional kinds of exercises and activities can benefit enormously from an awareness of how idioms are used in real discourse. Shying away from that fundamental question will get us nowhere in the quest for more engaging and authentic contexts in which to teach an area of vocabulary that seems naturally to interest learners, but which for too long has suffered from being considered a mere problem of semantic and syntactic perversity. Chapters 6 and 7 together, I hope, reinforce my argument that vocabulary choice is not something that should be neglected as beyond the purview of discourse analysts. Without it, there would be no discourse to analyse.

In Chapter 8 we turn again to grammatical issues, addressing an area regularly included in pedagogical grammars and language coursebooks in English language teaching: reported speech. There we shall see once again that observation of spoken data, both quantitative and qualitative, paints a somewhat different picture from the descriptions of reported speech that have come to us via the study of written texts or from concocted sentences.

Notes

1 This chapter grew out of an earlier paper (McCarthy 1992). The present version is fundamentally revised and concentrates on spoken data only.

2 Though it is worth noting that not all would agree with the inclusion of nominal compounds and phrasal verbs in the category of idioms. Gottlieb (1992), for example, would exclude them, for practical lexicographic reasons.

3 I am aware of the debate on iconicity in the word-order of binomials, a recent, useful contribution to which is Birdsong (1995). There do sometimes seem to be some iconic principles at work, such that the first element is often speaker-centred (e.g. *here* and there, *now* and then, *back* and forth), or moving from unmarked to marked term in antonymous pairs (e.g. *high* and low, *good* and bad), or displaying phonological 'strength' in the second element (e.g. wine and *dine*, huff and *puff*). However, it is a matter of debate whether such principles can usefully be incorporated into teaching, or whether binomials, because of their idiomaticity, are best taught and learnt as unanalysable wholes, just like monomorphemic words.

4 Here I have focused only on semantically opaque compounds. It has been argued, however, that all compounds are idiomatic in the sense that they have developed some sort of semantic or pragmatic specialisation in the process of institutionalisation as compounds (see Kooij 1968).

5 Additionally, Norrick's (1988) study of binomials uses real conversational data. On the written side, Moon (1992) and Vorlat (1985) also examine real data.

6 I am grateful to Beth Sims, former student at the Department of English Studies, University of Nottingham, for permission to consult and use her data, from which this example is taken, as part of the CANCODE project.

7 See Ernst (1980) on the use of 'extra' adjectives in idioms.

8 In the study of written text, the clever, often humorous use of idioms 'hidden' in advertising, titles and headlines is well documented (see Moeran 1984; Diaz 1986; McCarthy and Carter 1994: 114–15).

9 Černák (1994) suggests that the subjective, evaluative and emotional aspects of idioms are unparalleled elsewhere in the language.

8

'So Mary was saying': speech reporting in everyday conversation

8.1 Introduction

In a small village in County Tipperary, Ireland, there dwelt a local character whose nickname was 'So-Mary-was-saying', since this was his stock response when greeted with any piece of news or village gossip; he had always heard it already, from Mary, the hub of all information in the small, tight-knit community.[1] News, gossip, stories, indeed the whole fabric of everyday conversation depends heavily on quoting or referring to the words of others, and it is hard to imagine a day of our lives when we do not at some point support our discourse with direct or indirect reference to someone else's words. It is equally hard to imagine, therefore, any second language pedagogy claiming real adequacy that did not take the matter of speech reporting very seriously and did not give it a place in the syllabus. As I have argued throughout this book, central to any investigation of language with a claim to pedagogical usefulness is the close observation of how the most common, banal, everyday functions of linguistic communication, such as speech reporting, are actually carried out. Equally important is the willingness to approach real data with an open mind, unencumbered by preconceptions arising from sentence-based analysis or the evidence solely of written texts.

Hardly any stretch of casual conversational data is without reports of prior speech, and it is hard to conceive of achieving any intermediate level of competence in a foreign language without needing to know how the speakers of that language make speech reports. Thus language coursebooks can be relied upon to contain lessons on speech reporting and to offer opportunities to practise reports. Yet there is evidence to suggest that many books give an impoverished and inadequate coverage of what really happens in everyday data, probably because of the continuing influence, whether overtly acknowledged or not, of sentence-based grammatical models, of an over-reliance on written data, and because of a lack of observation of everyday language. This chapter, like the other chapters, will base its evidence on the first one million words of the CANCODE spoken corpus. That is not to say that such observations as are made below cannot be arrived at by careful listening to native-speaker talk; as we have discussed before, computers simply make it easier to look at a lot of data in one go, but one usually needs to have some idea of what sort of thing one is looking for in order to use the power of the computer most efficiently. The particular strength of computerised corpora is that they offer the researcher the potential to check whether something observed in everyday language is a one-off occurrence or a feature that is widespread across a broad sample of speakers. This book does not take the line that experienced language teachers are stupid and need to have their eyes opened by the findings of academics investigating huge corpora vastly beyond the means of practising teachers to emulate.

The CANCODE corpus confirms the common-sense intuition that speech reporting is exceedingly common in everyday language. It also demonstrates that the ways in which speakers effect reports are many and varied. These overlap to a considerable extent with those which fiction writers recreate in their stories (see Page 1973 for a seminal discussion) and which journalists use to report the words of politicians and other newsworthy figures (e.g. Zelizer 1989; Waugh 1995; Thompson 1996). But spoken data also exhibit choices which are rarely, if ever, found in written-text reports. What is most striking is that everyday conversational resources for reporting are much richer than is suggested by sentence-based accounts of the structure of direct and indirect speech.

In this chapter I shall take the terminology proposed by Genette (1988) as articulating a convenient framework for the differentiation of basic types of speech reports, viz:

Type	Characteristics
Direct:	Reconstructions of quoted speaker's words, usually form-focused,[2] syntactically independent from the reporting clause, e.g.: *I said 'What would you like to do this afternoon, Dulcie?'* The punctuation here is for the sake of illustration; the original CANCODE corpus transcripts are not punctuated in this way, and, in a spoken corpus, many types of audible and contextual cues have to be taken into account in attributing the function of direct speech report to any given string of words. For the purposes of the present chapter, the original tapes were consulted to confirm the attribution of speech-reporting.

Type	Characteristics
Indirect:	Reconstructions syntactically dependent on the reporting clause, frequently accompanied by changes in tense, deixis, pronouns (see Banfield 1982: 25); heavily context-dependent for interpretation, e.g.: Cos *a friend of mine, he asked me if he could stay there* and I said 'Yes' It is impossible to know whether the original words were 'Can/could I stay here/there?', but it is usually unnecessary for successful communication for the original words to be reproduced.
Narratised:	Reports of an act of speaking, without speaker's words being quoted, summarising the event, e.g.: Oh my doctor came and *she rang up and complained at the way that I'd been treated* Baynham (1991), who uses a similar tri-partite division of speech-report types, refers to this third type as 'the lexicalisation strategy'.

Lucy (1993: 18–19) makes the further distinction that direct speech reports are made within the framework of the 'reproduced speech event', while indirect reports operate within 'the perspective of the reporting speech situation' and are relevant to 'the concerns of the current event'.

8.2 Speech and writing

Let us begin with two rather extreme examples of data containing speech reports. Extract (8.1) is from the classic novel *Ivanhoe*, by Sir Walter Scott; (8.2) is from an anecdote in the CANCODE corpus. *Ivanhoe* is an extreme choice, but around the world, many learners of foreign languages get much of their main exposure to speech reporting from classic literature, as I myself did in Spanish and French as a student. What is more, although modern novelists writing in English often experiment with alternative ways of depicting speech, the rather stilted (to our ears) manner in which it is done in *Ivanhoe* is still alive and well in many examples of popular fiction published in magazines:

(8.1)

> Rebecca again looked forth, and almost immediately exclaimed,
> 'Holy prophets of the law! Front-de-Boeuf and the Black Knight
> fight hand to hand on the breach, amid the roar of their followers,
> who watch the progress of the strife – Heaven strike with the

cause of the oppressed and of the captive!' She then uttered a loud shriek, and exclaimed, 'He is down! He is down!'

'Who is down?' cried Ivanhoe; 'for our dear Lady's sake, tell me, which has fallen?'

'The Black Knight,' answered Rebecca, faintly then instantly again shouted with joyful eagerness – 'But no – but no! – he is on foot again, and fights as if there were twenty men's strength in his single arm – His sword is broken – he snatches an axe from a yeoman – he presses Front-de-Boeuf with blow on blow – The giant stoops and totters like an oak under the steel of the woodman – he falls – he falls!'

'Front-de-Boeuf!' exclaimed Ivanhoe.

'Front-de-Boeuf,' answered the Jewess; his men rush to the rescue, headed by the haughty Templar – their united force compels the champion to pause – They drag Front-de-Boeuf within the walls.'

'The assailants have won the barriers, have they not?' said Ivanhoe.

'They have! – they have! – and they press the besieged hard upon the outer wall; some plant ladders, some swarm like bees, and endeavour to ascend upon the shoulders of each other – down go stones, beams and trunks of trees upon their heads, and as fast as they can bear the wounded to the rear, fresh men supply their places in the assault.'

'Who yield? – who push their way?' said Ivanhoe.

'The ladders are thrown down,' replied Rebecca, shuddering; 'the soldiers lie grovelling under them like crushed reptiles – The besieged have the better.'

(8.2)

[The speaker is recounting how, while on holiday with a friend, they accidentally ended up as extras in a film, instead of playing bingo, which they thought they were queuing up for.]

<S 01> So we'd been wandering round in the morning doing the usual thing came back and had lunch and she, I said what would you like to do this afternoon Dulcie she said oh Mary let's go to bingo, now bingo is never ever my cup of tea [<S 02> no] but seeing that I was supposed to be, with her

<S 02>　　　　　└Supporting her yeah.

<S 01> I'd to fall in with her [<S 02> [laughs]] all right then Dulcie where do we go now to bingo, I don't know she said but we'll find out so we walked along and we saw this hall and she said I think that's it so I saw a lot of people and I said I don't know Dulcie, doesn't look like a bingo hall so she said well go in the queue she said and find out what's happening so I go in this queue and I'm waiting so I saw them taking names and writing things down so I had this feeling I was in the wrong place [<S 02> [laughs]] so I thought to myself oh I'm going from here but as I was stood at the table this person said er now then you're next so I said excuse me is this the bingo hall and he said no my dear oh so I said oh I'm sorry and I started to walk away but he said hang on a minute he said erm how would you like to be an extra I said an extra for what [<S 02> [laughs]] he said for a film he said [<S 02> no] we're doing a film [<S 02> get away] so I said me he said yes he said [<S 02> yeah] want lots of people [<S 02> yeah] so I said oh I can't really I'm sorry because I've got my friend with me [<S 02> yeah] that's all right he said ask your friend to come up so I said well before you take any more details I'll ask her to come up with me now, so I go back to Dulcie and she says all right Mary is, will the bingo be starting soon I can't see any chairs and tables no I said we're in the wrong place Dulcie [<S 02> [laughs]] and I said they've asked us if you'd like to, like us to be in a film what d'you mean she said well I said don't know the story as yet [<S 02> mm] I said but erm but I said I think it'll be a laugh oh she said I'd love it.

Both extracts are rich in speech reports. Both in different ways stage the speech reported as if it were happening before the reader's/listener's eyes. Both are a conventional fiction in the sense that neither is likely to be a true and accurate account of someone's words.[3] The written text is fictional because the characters are fictional anyway; the spoken text (although told as a true story) is also a fiction, because we know the speaker can do no more than attempt a reconstruction of what (s)he considers the characters' important original words to have been, even if direct speech reports may be argued to be as less of a distortion of the original words than the necessary paraphrasing of indirect speech (see Coulmas 1985a). Indeed, it hardly matters whether the words are a true re-statement; spoken storytellers' reports are open to challenge, but are usually only challenged if they stretch credibility or if another witness to the original event(s) chooses to question their accuracy.[4] The *Ivanhoe* text represents a particularly traditional and stylised type of speech reporting, and I would reiterate that I certainly do not suggest that it is typical of modern fictional literature. Most readers will be familiar with writers who report speech by a mixture of direct speech and indirect speech, and either by using the kinds of speech reporting verbs seen in both extracts above or by simply indicating characters' speech by using quotation marks or paragraph indentations, without any reporting verbs. The two extracts are chosen purely for illustration of how wide the gap *can* be between written and spoken speech reporting. Let us consider what features make them so different. The following lists show the use of reporting verbs and any accompanying modification in each extract:

Ivanhoe *text*

> *exclaimed* (3 times)
> *uttered a loud shriek*
> *cried*
> *answered faintly*
> *shouted with joyful eagerness*
> *answered*
> *said* (twice)
> *replied shuddering*

Spoken story

> *said* (29 times)
> *says*
> *asked*

The two extracts are not the same length (being approximately 300 and just over 400 words respectively), but it is clear that the written text avails itself of a range of reporting verbs and of adverbial modifiers which add specific characteristics to the reported words (e.g. acoustic parameters: *loud, faintly*). The spoken text seems to rely almost entirely on the verb *say*, though it does vary its tense, using present simple on one occasion, and an indirect report with *ask* embedded in a direct report.[5] If we take the reporting verbs used in the *Ivanhoe* passage, we find that their occurrence in the conversational corpus is quite different. In just over one million words of CANCODE data, the verb *exclaim* does not occur at all, and *utter* only occurs once in a quasi-speech reporting function, when a speaker is attributing authorship to a pun that crops up in a casual conversation.[6] *Cry* never occurs as a speech reporting verb, and *answer* never occurs reporting direct speech. There are 250 examples of *reply/replying/replies/replied* in the corpus, but all but two refer to *written* replies to letters. The verb *shout* occurs 53 times in the corpus, reporting speech both directly and indirectly. Five illustrative examples occur in one conversation where a woman is recounting her experience giving birth, surrounded by people urging her on:

(8.3)

<S 01> I can remember them all **shouting** at me to push and I was
     getting so fed up with them all like, that girl, that, I mean she didn't
     even know me and she was telling me to push and I was thinking
     what's it got to do with you you know and Doctor Hill's **shouting** in
     the other ear and they were just, meant [<S 02> mm] nothing to me
     ... but like Nancy Carr was really, she was being horrible really cos
     she had to to make me do it and afterwards she said like you done
     really well and she said [<S 02> mm] sorry if I **shouted** at you ... but
<S 02>   ⌊Who who was
     being horrible to you, Nancy Carr?
<S 01> Nancy Carr like **shouting** at me to push and that
<S 02> Mhm.
<S 01> And she said afterwards em sorry if I kept **shouting** at you but if
     she just said push like that you wouldn't bother would you you
     wouldn't try.

It will be noted that *shout*, as well as reporting indirect speech with the original words reconstructed (e.g. *shouting at me to push and that*), also occurs in narratised reports (*and M's shouting in the other ear; sorry if I shouted at you*). When used for direct speech reports (in seven cases), *shout* is used in the continuous (*-ing*) aspect, which may be a reflection of the greater vividness generally found in conversational speech reports (Tannen 1986), for example:

(8.4)

[<S 01> and <S 02> are describing how one of their children fell off a wall and was injured by a loose brick.]

<S 01> The doorway opened and we heard somebody **shouting** help me
and then we seen him like crawling in but he had er pla, er a plaster
thing on his arm didn't he.
<S 02> Yeah for about a week.
<S 03> Yeah.
<S 02> To make sure there was nothing broken.

(8.4)
[<S 01> is describing a female neighbour who has learning difficulties.]

<S 01> She had somebody knocking at her windows **shouting** fire fire
and it was just a ruse to get her out the house you see.
<S 02> Mm.
<S 01> And er she was very sensible the old lady was she phoned.
<S 02> Good.
<S 01> And how we heard about this it was the following morning the
window cleaner came I told him about it he couldn't clean the
windows detectives were there detectives come to that's how we
heard about er that.

Thus we see that a spoken conversational corpus may well produce a
different set of usages compared with the kinds of speech reports found
in classic or popular fictional literature, with the *Ivanhoe* text displaying
well-documented literary devices (see Tannen 1988 for further examples
and a discussion). As noted above, although writing styles have changed
since the time of Sir Walter Scott, the kinds of graphic speech reporting
verbs and adverbial modifiers illustrated in the *Ivanhoe* extract are still
in common use, though perhaps more so in popular fiction (e.g.
magazine romances; see Nash 1990: 29–34 for examples; see also
Oostdijk 1990 for a general discussion on natural speech features versus
fictional speech) than in canonical literary works. As Hughes (1996: 49)
points out, literary conversations 'are constructed by writers for
readers, rather than by interlocutors for one another', and so we can
expect the literary author, with all the compositional time and reflection available, to exploit the full potential of reporting verbs and
adverbials to constrain the reader's interpretation of characters' spoken
words.

But does (8.2) above suggest that speech reporting in everyday conversation may be expected to be an anodyne affair, endlessly repeating an
impoverished range of options? If so, then the teaching of speech

reporting in spoken contexts would seem a simple task, perhaps concentrating on a limited repertoire of declarative reports involving the verb *say*, with further explorations into verbs such as *tell*, *ask* and *shout* at a later stage. To answer the question, we need to look at more data, and to take another, closer look at the strategies used by the speaker in extract (8.2). We may list the following features of the speech reports in (8.2) as potentially relevant:

1 The teller uses *say* not only to report statements, but questions too, e.g.: *I said what would you like to do this afternoon Dulcie* (reported question)
she said oh Mary let's go to bingo (reported statement/response)

2 The teller uses the zero-quotative option (i.e. simply reporting speech without any reporting verb or explicitly naming the speaker), e.g.:
all right then Dulcie where do we go now to bingo
We may note that this also occurs in the *Ivanhoe* passage, in the paragraph beginning 'They have! – they have!'. Zero quotatives are usually not problematic: the simple rules of two-party turn-taking which indicate 'next speaker' usually allow the receiver to interpret who is being quoted (see Mathis and Yule 1994), along with general semantic/pragmatic assumptions made by the listener that attribute the speaker's reports to sources already indicated, unless told otherwise (see Palacas 1993 on 'attribution' semantics). In the written text, Ivanhoe is attributed as speaker before and after the zero-quotative turn, thus we assume it is Rebecca speaking, and in the spoken text, the teller names the addressee (her friend, Dulcie), thus we assume it is the teller quoting her own words.

3 The reporting verb may be placed initially, medially or finally, or in more than one place in quoting any particular turn-at-talk:
she said I think that's it (reporting verb initial)
I don't know she said but we'll find out (reporting verb medial)[7]
what d'you mean she said (reporting verb final)
so she said well go in the queue she said and find out what's happening (reporting verbs initial and medial). Initial, medial and final placement, though not combined, also occur in the *Ivanhoe* passage.

4 The reporting verb may be in historical present tense (i.e. a present-tense form reporting a past event), just as other verbs in the narrative may switch to historical present, e.g. *so I go back to Dulcie and she **says** all right Mary is, will the bingo be starting soon.*

5 The reported words attempt to resemble natural conversation as closely as possible, for example, discourse markers are often included in the report in the way they might be expected to occur in real conversation:[8]

> *this person said **er now then** you're next*
>
> *I said **oh** I'm sorry*
>
> *so I said **well** before you take any more details*

So it is that, even in this short extract, we can see a variety of strategies being adopted, even though only one verb is predominantly chosen to launch the speech reports (*say*). We have also, in passing, observed how *shout* has been used in natural conversational contexts. It now behoves us to look wider and seek to account for whatever other strategies and usages we can find in our conversational corpus.

8.3 Reports with *-ing* form reporting verbs

We have noted that *shout* occurs in the *-ing* form in a number of examples of speech reporting. If we look for further examples of reports with the *-ing* form, we find a surprising number – surprising, that is, given the fact that almost all grammars, language-learning textbooks and research articles dealing with speech reporting seem blissfully to ignore the phenomenon. In just over one million words of CANCODE data, for example, *was/were saying* occurs 136 times in speech reports, always framing indirect reports. Examples include:

(8.5)

[Speaker is commenting on a reference to the death of British Labour Party Leader John Smith in 1994, an event which caused great sadness among Labour Party supporters.]

<S 01> Caroline **was saying** she still feels like shedding a tear when she thinks of that.

(8.6)

[Speaker is commenting on the way her water-lily flower opens and closes regularly.]

<S 01> **I was saying** to Kevin they're a very unusual flower, they must have some kind of time-clock.

(8.7)

[Speaker is passing on a bit of village news to a neighbour.]

<S 01> Brian **was saying** the village hall nearly caught fire last night.

The same occurs (13 times) with *tell*, as in (8.8) and (8.9):

(8.8)

[Woman commenting on the problem of tick infestation in dogs: the 'border women' is a reference to two women who own border terriers, an English breed.]

<S 05> Those border women, I should know their names, she **was telling** Colin one of them had a tick it was like a bluebottle.

(8.9)

[Speaker is commenting on the way firms respond to job applications.]

<S 01> Er my son is with the Electricity Board
<S 02> Yes.
<S 01> And he **was telling** me that they have this sort of procedure as well
<S 02> Mm.
<S 01> They have to reply er initially within, well I can't remember the number of days.
<S 02> So two or three working days.
<S 01> That's right that sort of thing.

A similar pattern is found in (8.10) with *read* and *suggest*:

(8.10)

[Speakers are discussing French politics.]

<S 01> Yeah I mean I think it would be true to say as Steve's indicated there is er a hell of a battle still going on because it has been the domain of the President although what the President's up to er I **was reading** in the paper yesterday that
<S 02>   ⌊Lame duck President.
<S 01> Well it wasn't so much lame duck it was close to that but they **were suggesting** that if people looked at Mitterand's private life er you know the the sort of thing that's been published in the British press lately'd be pretty tame.

What do these speakers mean by using the -ing form in their reporting verbs, and why should it be that linguists and language pedagogues have mostly ignored this uncontroversial, very natural-sounding usage?[9] It seems that our speakers are de-focusing from the actual words uttered by the original speakers and focusing instead on the content, in terms of its newsworthiness or topical relevance; the speech report may simply be there to introduce a new topic or argument. (I am grateful to Jeff Stranks for some illuminating insights here; personal communication) This may help us understand why the types of written texts often chosen for research on speech reporting are unlikely to exhibit such functions. Firstly, one thing that needs to be considered is the differences in the exigencies of speech reporting in different contexts. Waugh (1995) has made the point that journalistic speech reporting focuses on 'conveying information and [is] concerned with issues of referentiality, truth, reliability and accountability'. It is thus not surprising that a major study of reporting such as Thompson (1994), which uses a good many journalistic examples, does not include past -ing reports, since the past -ing takes the focus off 'reliability' and 'accountability'. Some spoken speech reporting is pre-occupied with the same demands as journalistic reporting, for example, the courtroom data in Philips (1985), which, although the data contains indirect reports, have none in past -ing form. Also, the vividness and 'real-time' staging of speech reports in oral narratives (especially during narrative 'peaks' or climaxes· see Larson 1978: 68–76; Coulmas 1986), may push storytellers towards reinforcing the fiction that they are reporting faithfully their protagonists' words. This may explain the fact that, in the narrative texts in the CANCODE corpus, speech reports are overwhelmingly direct speech, and with reporting verbs in past simple (said, told) or historical present says. But a great deal of spoken language is not concerned with faithful reproduction of speech, or even creating the illusion of it. Speech is often reported indirectly in casual conversation either as a topic-opener (8.7), or simply in support of some point being discussed or made (8.9), where the demands of veracity and the faithful reproduction of words spoken is of secondary importance. For that reason our Irishman in the anecdote at the beginning of this chapter greets all news with 'So Mary was saying': he wants to impress his audience that he has already heard the news, not the words. The past -ing form reports in the CANCODE corpus are genre-restricted, and seem to belong to more general, non-narrative, casual conversational contexts where they serve to signal topic management in the ways illustrated in extracts (8.5) to (8.10), and contrast with the 'focus-on-words-uttered' function of the past simple reports. It is unlikely that a corpus biased towards journalistic or legalistic texts will yield the kinds of *-ing* form indirect reports illustrated in any significant number.[10] It is even more unlikely that speech reporting approached as a phenomenon of the *sentence* (as it is in the works of many researchers) will be considered in this essentially interactive way. Much of the work done on speech reporting has preoccupied itself with the syntactic principle of 'backshift', i.e. how speech displaced from its original time of utterance is normally reported in the past (or how it is understood: see Boogaart 1996), such that direct quotations like 'I'm going home' tend to be backshifted to '(s)he *said* (s)he *was* going home'. Classic studies such as Coulmas (1985b), Comrie (1986), Goodell (1987) and Huddleston (1989), all concern themselves with backshift and pay no attention to the possibility of past tense *-ing* reporting verbs. From a pedagogical point of view, there would seem to be no justification for excluding the *-ing* form reports, especially since the same phenomenon occurs in other languages (e.g. French, Spanish). From a broader theoretical viewpoint, the lesson of this section is that discourse grammars should not be just an account of the above-sentence behaviour of conventionally described structures, but must also be prepared to encounter and explain structures not previously observed or discussed within the canon of grammar for any particular language.

8.4 Other reporting verbs

So far we have concentrated mainly on *say*, and some additional examples with *tell, read, shout* and *suggest*. Apart from *say* and *tell*, another frequent reporting verb in the corpus is *ask* (which appeared in an embedded report in extract (8.2), and it is worth considering it in some detail, for it tells us a lot about conversational speech reporting in general. There are more than 700 reports of various kinds with *ask* in the corpus. Only four of them are direct speech reports;[11] all the rest are indirect or narrated. By far the most frequent category (just over 200) is the speaker reporting his/her own acts of asking. The most frequent structural collocations following *asked/asking* are *for, to, if* and *about*, in descending order of frequency. Some examples are of the typical kinds of patterns practised in language classrooms, especially those with *wh-* and *if* reported clauses, where word order can be a difficulty for the learner:[12]

(8.11)

<S 01> I phoned up the hospital and **asked who I should address the letter to**.

(8.12)

<S 01> Then I saw Mark Porter and **asked if he'd seen you** he says yeah he's been playing snooker with me all afternoon.

(8.13)

[Speaker is talking about the arrangements for a funeral.]

<S 01> So I says em, well you don't interfere do you I mean so **I asked him what the arrangements were** oh there's a chapel of rest in the village em he says and I want to get him moved to the church, I said but aren't people going from the house ... all the wreaths came to the house but there was no hearse.

Extract (8.13) makes the point once again that questions do not have to be reported with *ask*: the speaker's second question about the funeral party going from the house is introduced by *said*, just as we saw in extract (8.2).[13] The other very frequent types of reports with *ask*, illustrated in the following examples, are of types that may well suffer from a lack of attention in the language class or else not be considered as significant aspects of speech reporting:

(8.14)

Feature(s): *ask (sb) for sth*

[Speaker is recounting a conversation with the doctor.]

<S 01> And **I've asked him for water retention tablets**.
<S 02> Mm mm.
<S 01> But they wouldn't give 'em me, erm I had an operation my stomach just kept going up and down didn't it bloating up and then going down.

(8.15)

Feature(s): (a) *ask sb to do* (b) passive voice

[Speaker talking about working in the health service.]

<S 01> And erm I'd heard one or two bad things about it all about these on-calls and things and you got really tired and and er I sort of was, the next thing **I was asked to do this job** and I didn't have any choice in the matter.

(8.16)

Feature(s): (a) *ask about sth* (b) unrealised (*irrealis*) speech reports

<S 01> You know, if you go to the doctor's er for something and then [<S 02> mm mm] you come out and **you haven't asked about it** [laughs] **you put off asking** don't you.

As well as the varied patterns of complementation in examples (8.11) to (8.16), the occurrence of passive and of potential, non-realised or irrealis speech reports has been mentioned. 31 passives or pseudo-passives with *ask* occur in the corpus, and the most consistent pattern is *I (be/get) ask to (do)*, as represented in these concordance lines:

Initially the r= one of the main reasons that I	[[was asked]]	to sit on the group was em ev everybody
one of my objectives one of the things that I	[[was asked]]	to achieve within the first year was to estab
Normally a manager does it but you know I	[[was asked]]	to do it. And em it's only comparatively rec
<\$=> and er I sort of was the next thing I	[[was asked]]	to do this job and I didn't have <\$O48> a
<\$=> Em <\$=> <\$?> Oh you know I've	[[been asked]]	to do some G C S E English <\$H> next te
a university+ <\$2> Ah yes. <\$1> +and I've	[[been asked]]	to do this study. <\$2> Mm. <\$1> So my
<\$1> +<\$O4> because what <\$O4> I've	[[been asked]]	to do is to talk to people who've had so
<\$1> <\$O3> Yeah. <\$O3> <\$2> And I	[[got asked]]	to do it cos they wanted er you know a go

Figure 1: Concordance lines for *I (be/get) ask to (do)*:

With this glance at *ask*, and with the other verbs reviewed, it is now becoming clear that the range of speech reporting in conversation is both syntactically and pragmatically richer than our initial spoken extract (8.2) might have suggested. As well as conventionally treated direct and indirect reports we have seen reports with *-ing*, passive voice reports, reports of speech events not actually realised, variation in positioning of reporting verbs, and so on.

Another reporting verb that occurs, in direct reports only, is *go*. Some examples follow:

(8.17)
[Young women talking about shaving their legs.]

<S 01> I didn't shave mine for a week when I went to Crete cos I thought
I'd get browner if I had hairy legs ... and my sister told everybody
when we went out at night that I hadn't shaved.
[3 turns later]
<S 01> Cos I was embarrassed and when we were out and I had a dress
she went look at her legs she's got hairy legs.

(8.18)
<S 01> I can remember getting to the customs in America and **this guy
went where are you staying,** when, **I went with with my friend
she went**
<S 02> ⌐How much money have you got.
<S 01> ⌐**Are you going out with him.**
<S 03> Yeah yeah.
<S 01> And **I went no**, are you sleeping with him I thought would be the
next question and **she went, no she said are you planning to get
married I went no** she said oh you're definitely leaving after the end
of the year.

(8.19)
[Speaker is recounting an incident in a bookshop when her friend only
vaguely knew what she was looking for.]

<S 01> And erm there's a new map out or something accompanies this
book Sue was going in like we went in and it was just art books and
we said oh d'you do sort of fantasy books or something Sue said and
I was going oh God like you know and **he was going oh what what
books did you want** and it was kind of like bit embarrassing really
he was going oh what is it a medical book or something you know
like no no

All the speech reports with *go* in the corpus are by young speakers under
30 years of age,[14] and all seem to be in contexts where the maximum
amount of dramatic/graphic representation is attempted, often with
mimicry in voice quality or other paralinguistic features. Tannen (1988)
reports that in her spoken narrative data, *go* was the most frequent
speech reporter (reporting verb) after *say*.

8.5 Tense and the reporting verb

Although *say* is by far the most frequent reporting verb in the corpus and although its simple past form *said* (with just under 2,000 occurrences) is by far the most frequent form, other tenses and forms also occur frequently. There are 113 cases of the (grammatically anomalous) historical present form *I says*, characteristically occurring in narrative reports. Typical of these are the following, one of which is extract (8.12):

(8.20)
[Speaker has contracted shingles and is recounting her interview with the doctor.]

<S 01> I asked I said is it contagious? **she says no she says no you know it's children's stuff she says** you know the chicken pox
<S 02>   ⌐Yeah
    chicken pox.
<S 01> **I says well I haven't been anywhere where there's been any children I don't know how I've got it.**

(8.21)
<S 01> Then I saw Mark Porter and asked if he'd seen you **he says yeah he's been playing snooker with me all afternoon** I was so mad these chips went up this wall and the language was
<S 02> [laughs]

(8.22)
<S 01> Bumped into his mum coming out **did you find him she says I says no I didn't** [laughs] and she went barmy then cos you used to didn't you.

Johnstone (1987) suggests such switches to the historical present on the reporting verb may not be random and may coincide with quotations of authoritative speakers' words, making them stand out from others' words. It certainly seems that historical present signals the foregrounding of the quoted speech in a way that (unmarked) past simple does not; it is thus an extremely useful discourse strategy in narratives where speech reporting is frequent, especially where there is rapid interchange of speakers' words which includes the narrator's reports of his/her own words.

Present tense *say(s)* also occurs frequently when reporting speakers' words that relate to permanent facts or truths, as well as to things speakers have said which are still relevant or important:[15]

(8.23)
[Speakers are assembling a portable cot borrowed from a friend. <S 02> has been given verbal instructions by the friend ('she').]

<S 01> It's not as difficult as it first seemed.
<S 02> **She says you've got to twist these round and it makes them solid** or something.

In (8.23) there is no implication that the instructions were given more than once, simply that what the friend said is relevant to what the speakers are now doing. Similarly in (8.24), the woman's reported words are still (and permanently) relevant:

(8.24)
[Speakers are discussing someone who wants to try out archery just once; the difficulty is that normally one has to sign up for a whole course.]

<S 01> That was what I was trying to get over to her on, it's something that you can't do one-off ... although **this woman at Marksman Bows says they will do an hour's individual tuition for a one-off visitor to give them a taste of it**

8.6 Discoursal functions of *as I/you say* reports

I have argued that forms such as the past continuous, historical present and present simple represent discourse strategies whereby speakers exercise control over entities such as topic, foregrounding and relevance. The expression *as I/you say* is also an important way of using speech reports to manage the discourse. In the one million word CANCODE corpus sample, *as I say* occurs 170 times, and *as you say* 29 times. The expression uses present simple tense to refer to recent speech, either (mostly) by the speaker or by his/her interlocutor(s). Usually, the discourse function is to summarise a topic, using the reiteration of key content, as in the following:

(8.25)

[<S 01> has been talking about how he and his wife built their own garden pond.]

<S 01> Then you put your concrete on top of that.
<S 02>   ⌊Concrete on top of that ... but a thin
      layer just for flooring.
<S 01> We put about four inches on.
<S 02> Yeah.
<S 01> Three to four inches.
<S 02> Oh right ... oh that's interesting.
<S 01> But **as I say we did it ourselves**.

(8.26)

[<S 01> and <S 02> are telling <S 03> about a building that they feel should be conserved but which is to be demolished and replaced by a petrol station, despite the fact that there is already a disused, boarded-up petrol station in the same road.]

<S 01> And it should've been a listed building but nobody listed it ...
      well the council have sold it to a garage company and it's going to be
      knocked down and a petrol station
<S 02>   ⌊Petrol station
<S 01>   ⌊was going to be put there
      so.
<S 02> It seems we've got one five hundred yards down the road
      that's been
<S 01>   ⌊That's empty
<S 02>   ⌊boarded up cos it doesn't make no money.
<S 03> Mm.
<S 02> We don't see the point in having it at the bottom of the street.
<S 01> But em the museum were very dischuffed that the council didn't
      let them know because I think if they had they could have had it
      listed and nobody would have been able to touch it ... so that caused
      a lot of trouble didn't it I mean.
<S 02>   ⌊Yeah.
<S 01>   ⌊with the petition and everything and
      it went to the council but the council still passed it.
<S 02> Well they said it was too late didn't they.
<S 01> Yeah so it's been passed and

<S 02> Just waiting for it to be knocked down and built.

<S 03> But **as you say the garage on the main road has been boarded up for some time.**

<S 02> It's been boarded up now for nearly seventeen months.

Support for the interpretation of *as I/you say* as having a discourse-marking function comes from the added presence of *but* in these two examples. *But* is the single most frequent preceding collocate of *as I say* (occurring 30 times), and is widespread in conversation generally as a marker of topic-summarising or topic-shift.[16] *As I/you say* differs from similar expressions *with I/you was/were saying*, which tend to take the conversation back to an earlier point in order to (re)develop a topic entity or add to it, rather than summarise or close it, for example:

(8.27)
[Speakers are discussing the closure of railway lines in Britain and the nostalgia for the age of steam railways.]

<S 01> There's a, there's a hell of a big following of steam trains.

<S 02>   └Yes oh imagine yes oh yes oh yes what did I say just now, I, yeah but some of that's nostalgia cos they've gone away.

<S 01> Yes.

<S 03> Yeah yeah.

<S 02> But **I was saying em earlier on** do you remember [<S 01> mhm] **that em it's a criminal waste what they've done** *the destruction is it's criminal you know.*

<S 03>   └Yeah yeah yeah yeah yeah.

<S 02> It's theft really.

<S 03> Yeah.

(8.28)
[Speakers are discussing the desirability of learning foreign languages.]

<S 01> Mm well yeah because they're going to be at a disadvantage aren't they in terms of the business world and er you know for, so from that point of view I think it'd be a good idea that that people did learn another language.

<S 02> Do you think it should be do you think they should
<S 01>   ⌐Language.
<S 02> **Back to what I was saying before** a bit although I'm I'm trying
not wanting to force that idea but would it be an idea if all
Europeans learned one second European language do you think, not
necessarily English.
<S 01> Well you can you can never tell what the circumstances are going
to be can you erm [sighs] yeah erm in, French and German seems to
be the the two languages that spring to mind as being used most
widely in Europe so I guess French if you can speak French German
and English maybe.

Close observation of real data can bring out the rich variety of discoursal
functioning of speech reporting strategies, and there are undoubtedly
many more which could be observed; the limits of this book mean that
we can only discuss the most frequent and salient types here. We shall
conclude this section with some examples which are presented simply
for observation. Extract (8.29) is taken from a conversation between two
young women who are checking and confirming arrangements made
with a third party for a social visit. The discourse strategy in focus here is
that of checking; what is of note is the variety of syntax and complementation which may not occur in formal written texts. Extracts (8.30) and
(8.31) reiterate the point (see also note 11) that canonical or unmarked
word-order (in this case that of indirect speech) may be disturbed in real-
time speech without any disturbance to communication:

(8.29)
<S 01> What we could try and do is ring Ali again try and ring her again.
<S 02> Yeah we will.
<S 01> When we're in Tunny Wells cos the thing is erm **did you say to
her what time.**
<S 02> No I never mentioned what time.
<S 01> **So you** said well
<S 02>   ⌐[Inaudible]
<S 01> **What did you say, we'll be up in the evening?**
<S 02> Yeah I think she thinks we're gonna be up in the evening.
[later]
<S 02> Yeah I think she thinks we're gonna be up in the evening.
<S 01> **Cos did you say to her about dinner or**
<S 02> Yes.

(8.30)

<S 01> Yeah this woman also told me on Monday this chap came in and he was hanging around for ages and he started asking me how you got into tourism. You know what qualifications [laughs] you needed.

<S 02> [laughs] **He was in the middle of an enforced career change he said.**

(8.31)

<S 01> Do you know how many students they're expecting in July.

<S 02> Yeah thirty-something though we're likely next term to have sixty-four students a lot of them may be six months and a lot of them will be Japanese here in August from what I've heard, about seventeen of them.

<S 01> Yeah.

<S 02> **And Liz is going to join them she tells me.**

8.7 Drawing the arguments together

We can now review the kinds of insights that might change our approach to the teaching of speech reporting. The following points, I suggest, would be important for a pedagogical model arising out of the observation of authentic spoken data:

1 The graphic speech introducers found in traditional literary reporting styles (including contemporary popular fiction) may occur only rarely in conversation, or not at all. Nonetheless, there is variety in the verbs used in conversational reporting.

2 All our examples so far have indicated that the kinds of adverbial phrases that specify the context of reporting verbs (as in the *Ivanhoe* text) do not occur with any significance in conversation.

3 Past simple is not the only tense found on reporting verbs, even though it may be the most frequent in some genres. Past continuous for topic management in casual conversation and historical present in narration occur with a frequency that cannot be ignored.

4 Although the position of *say* in direct reports varies between initial, medial and final in relation to the words reported, no other speech introducer displays this mobility and all other direct-report verbs are initial. However, word-order may vary from what is conventionally considered to be correct or canonical in indirect reports (e.g. verb-final

'ndirect reports, retention of interrogative word-order in reported
⁓estions).

common literary device of inversion of reporting verb and subject
The Black Knight,' *answered Rebecca*) does not occur in the spoken

6 There is great syntactic variety in spoken reports with *ask*, including
passive voice and different complementation patterns.

7 Unrealised speech is reported, as well as actual speech.

8 In the most general sense, it is clear that speech reports are best
observed in their real contexts of utterance. It is there that we see their
roles in the discourse, realising functions such as foregrounding,
dramatisation (Mayes 1990; Baynham 1996), the creation of relationships (Álvarez-Cáccamo 1996) and the general management of the
interaction.

What these points mean for teaching may be translated into a set of
principles:

1 Teaching speech reporting should not be over-obsessed with backshift
and sequence of tenses with indirect speech at the expense of the rich
variety of tense and aspect forms that real data throw up.

2 Word-order (e.g. in reports of questions) should be seen as more flexible
than traditional prescriptions might suggest, and some word-orders
frequently marked as errors (e.g. 'she asked me what *was* I doing')
should not be considered erroneous since they regularly appear in
native-speaker speech.

3 Once again, the principle of language awareness seems important
here: *exposure* to real data (without the necessary implication that it
has to be reproduced by the learner), will enable the learner to become
aware of forms such as *go* and the historical present which they are
likely to hear in the speech of native speakers, both in real-life
encounters and on the increasingly global media of films and television in English.

4 Frequent but tricky forms such as passive-voice reports (e.g. *I was asked
to take part in a survey*) may need a good deal of practice, and contrastive
exercises bringing out the different contexts of past simple and past
continuous reports may need to be designed to supplement what is
found in textbooks.

5 Although conversational speech reporting differs from literary speech
reporting, literary texts and conversational transcripts could be used

together, both in the teaching of literature and in teaching the spoken language, their potential for contrast being a useful means of promoting language- and literary-awareness.

As is the case with so many aspects of language surveyed in this book, the willingness to confront spoken data wherever possible, and not simply to rest on the assumption that what written texts tell us is sufficient for pedagogy, is likely to pay dividends in terms of authenticity of material in teaching and in a much better preparation for the learner for encounters with users of the target language in its spoken forms outside the classroom.

This book has come to its end. Over the eight chapters I have attempted to trace out a landscape illuminated here and there by glimmers of insight which the access to a spoken corpus has given me. A book such as this can only exemplify from a relatively small amount of the language that surrounds us each day, and can only base its conclusions on a limited number of language features. But some things emerge time and time again, whichever words or structures we look at, and these are that face-to-face interaction brings the people who use language slap-bang into the centre of investigation; it is simply impossible to idealise the data away from who said it, to whom, at what point, with what apparent goals and purposes, in the context of what relationship, and under what circumstances. Equally present have been concerns such as the mutual protection of face, the desire to converge socially, the joint construction of meanings and of generic activity, and the active roles of listeners. Thus the status I am advocating for the spoken language within applied linguistics, whether pedagogical applied linguistics or the many other branches of our profession that apply linguistic insights, is a fundamentally humanistic one; it is also one that respects language learners' status as human interactants themselves, both in their L1 and in their target language(s). Everyone is a 'native speaker' of something, and everyone knows what interaction is like, when it is successful, when it is frustrating or when it fails. Every learner I have ever taught wants to succeed in interaction. That does not necessarily mean they want to *sound* like L2 native speakers. It is rather to say that they want to *do* what L2 native speakers do and what they themselves do in their L1, and to learn the *ways of doing* in the target language, from which they can make their own choices. The more we know about how interaction is *done* in the language(s) we teach and/or learn, and the more we can clear our minds of presuppositions that the spoken language is just like the written but a bit sloppier and more prone to 'mistakes', the better it will be for all of us.

Notes

1 I owe this information to Barry O'Sullivan, a native of Tipperary, and at the time of writing a lecturer in English at Okayama University, Japan.

2 Lucy (1993: 18) observes that direct speech reports typically foreground 'the original *form* of the utterance' [his emphasis] as well as conveying 'its substantive message as well'.

3 Clark and Gerrig (1990) argue that speech reports are 'selective depictions' of original utterances.

4 Reyes (1984: 65) makes the point that quoting others' words in no way releases the reporter from the normal responsibilities of communication; the reportee's and reporter's voice are heard together:

> Citar ... no exime de la responsabilidad de la intención comunicativa; suscitar otra voz no es perder la propia, repetir es *decir*, en la medida que sea. [her italics]

5 Bauman's (1986: 66) data confirms the overwhelming preference for *say* as the reporting verb.

6 In the original data extract, reproduced here, <S 01> is telling <S 02> about a recently received teaching job offer:

> <S 01> She's left me two days to decide.
> <S 02> As in to do or not to do.
> <S 01> That is the question.
> <S 02> That's a good line yes.
> <S 01> Yeah [laughs].
> <S 02> Yes yes it's
> <S 01>   ⌊I thought of it first [laughs].
> <S 02> It was Match of the Day nineteen sixty seven I think isn't it **as uttered by Jimmy Hill** when when commenting on Brentford against Halifax in the er in the F A Cup

7 Person (1996) makes some interesting observations on the literary device of 'restarts' in direct speech reports. These are not dissimilar to the medial-placement of the reporting verb in spoken reports.

8 Bauman's (1986: 67) data once again confirms the frequency of this phenomenon as a speech-reporting strategy. See also Aijmer (1987) on *oh* and *ah* in natural conversation.

9 There are two exceptions to the neglect of the *-ing* form reporting verb that I have been able to find. Leech (1987: 31) gives *-ing* form examples of indirect reports with *read*, *tell* and *say* but is rather dismissive of them as colloquial 'exceptions' to the general rules of progressive aspect, and as representing a

stage of instability in the language. Eastwood (1994: 353–4) has examples of *ask* (in past and present continuous) and *wonder* (in present continuous) in the section on reported speech in his pedagogic grammar, but lets them pass without commenting on the tense/aspect choice. Ely *et al*'s (1995) data includes an occurrence of *was telling*, but it passes without comment.

10 Polanyi (1982) makes an interesting distinction between stories and reports; the latter, considered as neutral reconstructions of verbal events, do not have to justify their tellability.

11 For example:

> <S 01> So I actually stood there, to the doctor and I says well no I'm not happy you see cos, **he asked me you know sort of are you happy with the result** and I says well no I says I don't feel as if they've improved or whatever I says they're still aching and I've still got veins there

All four direct reports with *ask* have initial-position reporting verb.

12 Though it must be noted that native speakers do not always observe the 'rules' of word-order in indirect reports, for example in this extract, interrogative word-order is retained in an indirect report:

[Speaker is talking of an experience while staying in hospital.]

> <S 01> You know the sweetener, erm **I asked one of the cleaners could she get me something** because it was on a very bad day and she had to ring down for permission for somebody else to get one and then when she brought it we all had it sort of shared at the top end of the ward so that everybody could use it

13 Indeed, in one example, the speaker uses *ask* and then changes to *say* before quoting; this may be a reaction of the non-preference for direct reports with *ask*:

[Speaker is recounting the meal arrangements on a package tour holiday].

> <S 01> And then on Friday night **we asked the rep, I said by the way are we getting a meal tonight** she says no you don't have a meal.

14 Another direct-speech report-marker used by the younger generation in the corpus is *like*, which can occur without any reporting verb. For a full discussion see Romaine and Lange (1991).

15 Leech (1987: 25) accounts for such usages as referring more to the *result* of the communication rather than the communication itself.

16 See Schiffrin's (1987:61) remarks on *but* as a discourse marker.

Glossary

→ = see separate heading for that item

Adjacency pairs

Adjacency pairs consist of two utterances that go together in an anticipated way. A greeting (*Hello!*) anticipates a reply (e.g. another *Hello*). A question anticipates an answer; an offer anticipates an acceptance or a rejection. Adjacency pairs consist of two parts, a first pair-part and a second pair-part:

(First pair-part)   A: Want a coffee?

$\left.\begin{array}{l}\\\\\end{array}\right\}$ - adjacency pair

(Second pair-part)   B: Er yes please.

Back-channel

This refers to noises (which are not full words) and short verbal responses made by listeners which acknowledge the incoming talk and react to it, without wishing to take over the speaking **turn** (→). Typical back-channels in English are *mm, uhum, yeah, no, right, oh*, etc. In the transcripts in this book they are shown as occurring during the speaker's turn, though sometimes it is difficult to distinguish between back-channels and full speaking turns, and the decision to transcribe one way or the other is ultimately subjective. Here is an example with back-channels from speaker <S 01>, shown within square brackets [ ]:

<S 02> *Oh yes, yes, yes mind you my parents were really quite well-off when we lived in Ireland but the education in England was very expensive* [<S 01> **mm**] *and I can remember my mother had jewellery and silver and she used to keep selling it* [<S 01> **really**] *to pay for our extra music lessons and tuition in this and that* [<S 01> **mm**] *and er I it was, must have been difficult.*

Cleft structures

Cleft structures occur when the **clause** (→) is 'split' and becomes two separate

176

clauses but still only containing one message. Cleft structures can occur with *it* and with *wh*-words:

> Jeremy ate the cake. → It was Jeremy who ate the cake. (*It*-cleft)
> We need more money. → What we need is more money. (*Wh*-cleft)

Clause

A clause is a unit of language based around a verb. All clauses, except imperatives and clauses with subject **ellipsis** (➡), have a subject, and many have objects and adverbials too. Clauses may be 'finite' (i.e. with a verb that changes for tense, person, number), or 'non-finite' (i.e. with a verb that ends in an *-ing* form, or with a past participle, or with the infinitive form). Examples of clauses:

She loves nursery school.
(finite: subject-verb-direct object)

He never laughs.
(finite: subject-verb)

I knew the answer, but didn't tell her.
(two clauses: finite: subject-verb-object-linking adverbial + finite: subject-verb-indirect object)

Listening to that music, I forgot all my troubles.
(two clauses: non-finite: *-ing* form of verb-adverbial + finite: subject-verb-direct object)

To get there by six, you'll need to leave here at about 5.30.
(two clauses: non-finite: infinitive verb-adverbial-adverbial + finite: subject-verb-verb-adverbial-adverbial)

Clauses are the building blocks of sentences in written language. In all language, they are the most basic **unit** (➡) of communication.

Convergence

As conversations progress, speakers' contributions either converge with or diverge from one another. There may, for example, be temporary disagreement or misunderstanding, and so the speakers' **turns** (➡) will diverge. When the misunderstanding is resolved, the turns converge again. Or one speaker may be temporarily pursuing a different goal from another speaker. Convergence is an ideal state where speakers' minds mesh, where they are on the same wavelength, pursuing the same goals, and each participant sees the same need to co-operate and get to the desired outcome.

Deixis / deictic words

This term describes what may be termed the orientational features of language; deixis involves words which point backwards and forwards in a text as well as outside the text to a wider 'out-of-text' context. For example, words like *these/that/this/those* locate an utterance in relation to space and to the speaker's sense of closeness or involvement with something; words like *now* and *then* relate to the current moment of utterance; and words like *we/you/they/him/I* relate to who is speaking, who is present, included, excluded, etc. Thus, *I'd like to pop in to that little shop over there before we leave* contains deictics which orientate a listener interpersonally, temporally and spatially in relation to the proposition of the sentence. Certain contexts of language, such as language used to do things like packing, cooking, moving furniture, etc. involve a lot of deictics because the objects and other phenomena being dealt with are normally immediately visible to all speakers and thus forms of language such as *Could we just move that into this corner here?* are relatively commonplace.

Discourse markers

Discourse markers are words or phrases which are normally used to mark boundaries in conversation between one topic or bit of business and the next. For example, words and phrases such as *right, okay, I see, I mean*, help speakers to negotiate their way through talk indicating whether they want to open or close a topic or to continue it, whether they share a common view of the state of affairs, what their reaction is to something, etc. For example, in telephone and other conversations the discourse marker *anyway* usually serves to indicate that the speaker wishes either the current stretch of talk or the whole exchange itself to be brought to a conclusion, or to resume an interrupted topic. Similarly, *right* often serves to indicate that participants are ready to move on to the next phase of business.

Ellipsis

Ellipsis is pervasive in spoken discourse. It occurs in writing where it usually functions *textually* to avoid repetition where structures would otherwise be redundant. For example, in the sentence *We ran for the bus but missed it*, it is clear that *we* remains the subject of both clauses; or in the sentence *The chair was broken and the table too*, where it is clearly unnecessary to repeat the verb *was broken*. Ellipsis in spoken English is mainly *situational* (i.e. affecting people and things in the immediate situation), and frequently involves the omission of personal subjects, where it is obvious that the speaker will remain unambiguous. This feature is especially common with verbs of mental process: for example, *(I) think so, (I) wonder if they'll be coming to the party*. Such ellipsis also occurs with main or auxiliary verbs where meaning can be relatively easily reconstructed from the context.

Fronting (or front-placing)

Fronting refers to the movement of an element from its 'canonical' position and its relocation as the first element in a construction. Taking the sentence *I dedicated my life to that man and his music*, we can front the indirect object as follows: *To that man and his music I dedicated my life*. The process allows a focus or emphasis to fall on the fronted element (➔ **topics**).

Information staging

When speakers and writers create their message, they have choices as to how to stage the information. Staging choices include whether to bring an item to the front of the clause (➔ **fronting**), such as an object (e.g. *The second part we can leave till next week*), or whether to use a tense that backgrounds an event rather than foregrounding it (e.g. past perfect is a backgrounding tense, as is past continuous, while past simple forgrounds events). Staging the information means that the final message is not like a flat landscape, but has some elements that are more appparent/important than others.

Interactional

➔ relational

Relational/Interactional

Relational or **interactional** language is language which is primarily personal and social in orientation. Its effective use normally allows social and interpersonal relations to be maintained. In some contexts such as service encounters or even sometimes in formal interviews it is combined with **transactional** (➔) language to soften and make less forbidding the business of getting certain tasks done.

Speech acts

Speech acts refer to the communicative intention of what is said or written. In speech-act theory, all language is seen as *doing* things. Examples of speech acts are apologies, requests, denials, offers. Speech acts may be indirect, and often it is not easy for the analyst to decide what 'act' is being performed by a stretch of talk. Listeners decide in context what speech act is being performed, for example, *You mustn't worry* will probably be heard by the listener(s) as a comfort/reassurance, whereas *You mustn't come in here* might be heard as a prohibition.

Tails

The term 'tail' (sometimes called 'right-dislocated' item) describes the slot available at the end of a **clause** (➜) in which a speaker can insert grammatical patterns which amplify, extend or reinforce what (s)he is saying or has said. Examples of tails (in italics) include:

> **She**'s a really good actress, *Clare*.
> **Singapore**'s far too hot for me *it is*.
> **He**'s quite a comic *the fellow*, you know.
> **It**'s not actually very good is it *that wine*?

We may note also the extent to which tails cluster with different kinds of tags, hedges and modal expressions and how they often serve to express some kind of affective response, personal attitude or evaluative stance towards the proposition or topic of the clause.

Topics

Topics (sometimes called 'heads', or 'left-dislocated items') perform a basically orienting and focusing function, identifying key information for listeners and establishing a shared frame of reference for what is important in a conversational exchange. Topics are a subcategory of **fronting** (➜) and involve, most typically, placement at the front of a **clause** (➜) of a noun(s) or noun phrase(s) that anticipates a structure which then forms the main subject/object of the clause. Topics are in italics in the following examples:

> *The women in the audience*, **they** all shouted in protest.
> *That bloke in the green*, I can't stand **him**.
> This friend of ours, *Carol, her daughter*, **she** decided to buy one.

Topics are almost exclusive to informal spoken English. They parallel **tails** (➜), although tails generally serve a much more affective/evaluative purpose.

Transactional

Transactional language is language used in the process of conducting business and generally getting things done. It contrasts with **relational/interactional** (→) language.

Turns

A turn is a stretch of spoken language uttered by one speaker, before another speaker takes over. In this extract there are three turns, one of which is interrupted:

Turn 1 (interrupted) <S 01>Yeah it's ready for erm er
Turn 2   <S 02>   ⌐Thanks ever so much.
Turn 1 (completed) <S 01>   ⌐for
                    action ah it's all right.
Turn 3   <S 03> Afraid I forgot the cheese.

Units

All language is analysed in units. Units are stretches of language which may be classified in various ways. A word is a lexical unit. A clause is a grammatical unit. A sentence is a unit common in written text, but not so common in spoken language. In spoken language analysis, one of the most difficult questions is to define what is the basic unit of communication. Possible units for analysing spoken language include intonational tone-units (i.e. a stretch of language with one main rising or falling stress), speech **turns** (→), and **clauses** (→).

Vague language

Vague expressions are more extensive in all language use than is commonly thought and they are especially prevalent in spoken discourse. When we interact with others there are times where it is necessary to give exact and precise information (for example, concerning departure times for trains); but there are occasions where it would not be appropriate to be precise as it can sound unduly authoritative and assertive. In most informal contexts most speakers prefer to convey information which is softened in some way by vague language, although such vagueness is often wrongly taken as a sign of careless thinking or sloppy expression. Examples of vague language include phrases such as *or something, or anything, or whatever*, all usually in final position:

> Can you get me a sandwich or something?
> Have they got mineral water or anything like that?

CANCODE bibliography (1994–98)

CANCODE stands for Cambridge and Nottingham Corpus of Discourse in English. Cancode is a corpus-based project established in the Department of English Studies, University of Nottingham and at Cambridge University Press, Cambridge. All data collected by the project are the property of Cambridge University Press. The bibliography is of recent work published in whole or in part in connection with the project.

Carter, R. A. (1997) *Investigating English Discourse: language, literacy and literature.* London: Routledge.

Carter, R. A. (1998) Orders of reality: CANCODE, communication and culture. *ELT Journal* 52, 1.

Carter, R. A. and McCarthy, M. J. (1995a) Discourse and creativity: bridging the gap between language and literature. In Cook, G. and Seidlhofer, B. (eds) *Principle and Practice in Applied Linguistics.* Oxford University Press, 303–321.

Carter, R. A. and McCarthy, M. J. (1995b) Grammar and the spoken language. *Applied Linguistics* 16, 2, 141–158.

Carter, R. A. and McCarthy, M. J. (1997a) *Exploring Spoken English.* Cambridge University Press.

Carter, R. A. and McCarthy, M. J. (1997b) The English get-passive in spoken discourse: description and implications for an interpersonal grammar. Mimeo: University of Nottingham, Department of English Studies (submitted to *Journal of English Language and Linguistics*).

Carter, R. A., Hughes, R. and M. J. (1998) Telling tails: grammar, the spoken language and materials development. In Tomlinson, B. (ed) *Materials Development in L2 Teaching.* Cambridge University Press.

Hughes, R., Carter, R. A. and McCarthy, M. J. (1995) Discourse context as a predictor of grammatical choice. In Graddol, D. and Thomas, S. (eds) *Language in a Changing Europe.* Clevedon: BAAL/Multilingual Matters, 47–54.

Hughes, R. and McCarthy, M. J. (1998) From sentence to discourse: discourse grammar and English language teaching. *TESOL Quarterly*, 32, 2: 263–287.

McCarthy, M. J. Conversation and literature: tense and aspect. In Payne, J. (ed) *Linguistic Approaches to Literature*. Birmingham/University of Birmingham: English Language Research, 58–73.

McCarthy, M. J. and Carter, R. A. (1994) *Language as Discourse: Perspectives for Language Teaching*. Harlow: Longman.

McCarthy, M. J. and Carter, R. A. (1995) Spoken Grammar: what is it and how do we teach it? *ETL Journal* 49, 3: 207–218.

McCarthy, M. J. and Carter, R. A. (1997a) Written and Spoken Vocabulary. In Schmitt, N. and McCarthy, M. J. (eds) *Vocabulary: Description, Acquisition, Pedagogy*. Cambridge University Press, 20–39.

McCarthy, M. J. and Carter, R. A. (1997b) Grammar, tails and affect: constructing expressive choices in discourse. *Text* 17, 3: 405–29.

Stanfield, C. (1996) English as she is spoke (conversation with CANCODE researcher Jean Hudson). *Cambridge Language Reference News* 2, 2.

Tao, H. and McCarthy, M. J. (1998) Understanding non-restrictive relative clauses, which is not an easy thing. Mimeo: Cornell University, Department of Modern Languages.

References

Aijmer, K. (1984a) *Go to* and *will* in spoken English. In Ringbom, H. and Rissanen, M. (eds) *Proceedings from the Second Nordic Conference for English Studies*. Åbo: Åbo Akademi, 141–57.

Aijmer, K. (1984b) *Sort of* and *kind of* in English conversation. *Studia Linguistica* 38: 118–28.

Aijmer, K. (1985) Just. In Backman, S. and Kjellmer, G. (eds) *Papers on Language and Literature*. Gothenburg: Acta Universitatis Gothoburgensis, 1–10.

Aijmer, K. (1987) Oh and Ah in English conversation. In Meijs, W. (ed) *Corpus Linguistics and Beyond*. Amsterdam: Rodopi, 61–86.

Aijmer, K. (1988) 'Now may we have a word on this': The use of 'now' as a discourse particle. In Kyto, M., Ihalainen, O. and Rissanen, M. (eds) *Corpus Linguistics, Hard and Soft*. Amsterdam: Rodopi, 15–34.

Aijmer, K. (1989) Themes and tails: the discourse function of dislocated elements. *Nordic Journal of Linguistics* 12, 2: 137–54.

Aisenstadt, E. (1981) Restricted collocations in English lexicology and lexicography. *ITL Review of Applied Linguistics* 53: 53–61.

Alexander, L. G. (1988) *Longman English Grammar*. London: Longman.

Álvarez-Cáccamo, C. (1996) The power of reflexive language(s): code displacement in reported speech. *Journal of Pragmatics* 25 (1): 33–59.

Antaki C., Díaz, F. and Collins, A. (1996) Keeping your footing: conversational completion in three-part sequences. *Journal of Pragmatics* 25 (2): 151–71.

Ashby, W. (1988) The syntax, pragmatics, and sociolinguistics of left- and right-dislocations in French. *Lingua* 75: 203–29.

Ashby, W. (1994) An acoustic profile of right-dislocations in French. *French Language Studies*, 4 (2): 127–45.

Aston, G. (ed) (1988a) *Negotiating Service: Studies in the Discourse of Bookshop Encounters*. Bologna: Editrice CLUEB.

Aston, G. (1988b) *Learning Comity*. Bologna: Editrice CLUEB.

Aston, G. (1995) Say 'thank you': some pragmatic constraints in conversational closings. *Applied Linguistics* 16 (1): 57–86.

Atkins S., Clear, J. and Ostler, N. (1992) Corpus design criteria. *Literary and Linguistic Computing* 7 (1): 1–16.

Atkinson, J. and Heritage, J. (eds) (1984) *Structures of Social Action*. Cambridge University Press.

Bailey, C.-J. (1985) *Irrealis* modalities and the misnamed 'present simple tense' in English. *Language and Communication* 5 (4): 297–314.

Baker, E. (1924) Causes for the demand for spoken language. *English Journal* 13: 595–7.

Bakhtin, M. (1986) *Speech Genres and Other Late Essays*. In Emerson, C. and Holquist, M. (eds). Austin: University of Texas Press.

Banfield, A. (1982) *Unspeakable Sentences: Narration and Representation in the Language of Fiction*. Boston: Routledge and Kegan Paul.

Bargiela-Chiappini, F. and Harris, S. (1995) Towards a generic structure of meetings in British and Italian managements. *Text* 15 (4): 531–60.

Bauhr, G. (1992) Sobre el futuro cantaré y la forma compuesta voy a cantar en español moderno. *Moderna Språk* 86 (1): 69–79.

Bauman, R. (1986) *Story, Performance, Event: Contextual Studies of Oral Narrative*. Cambridge University Press.

Baynham, M. (1991) Speech reporting as discourse strategy: some issues of acquisition and use. *Australian Review of Applied Linguistics* 14 (2): 87–114.

Baynham, M. (1996) Direct speech: what's it doing in non-narrative discourse? *Journal of Pragmatics* 25 (1): 61–81.

Beaugrande, R. de (1997) Theory and Practice in Applied Linguistics: Disconnection, Conflict, or Dialectic? *Applied Linguistics* 18 (3): 279–313.

Beier E., Starkweather, J. and Miller, D. (1967) Analysis of word frequencies in spoken language of children. *Language and Speech* 10: 217–27.

Benwell, B. (1996) The Discourse of University Tutorials: An Investigation into the Structure and Pedagogy of Small-group Teaching across a Range of Academic Disciplines. Unpublished PhD thesis, University of Nottingham UK.

Bergstrom, K. (1979) Idioms exercises and speech activities to develop fluency. *Collected Reviews* Summer: 21–2.

Biber, D. (1988) *Variation Across Speech and Writing*. Cambridge University Press.

Biber, D. (1990) Methodological issues regarding corpus-based analysis of linguistic variation. *Literary and Linguistic Computing* 5 (4): 257–69.

Biber, D. (1993) Representativeness in corpus design. *Literary and Linguistic Computing* 8 (4): 243–57.

Biber, D. (1995) *Dimensions of Register Variation*. Cambridge University Press.

Biber, D. and Finegan, E. (1989) Styles of stance in English: lexical and grammatical marking of evidentiality and affect. *Text* 9 (1): 93–124.

Biber, D. and Finegan, E. (1991) On the exploitation of computerized corpora in variation studies. In Aijmer, K. and Altenberg, B. (eds) *English Corpus Linguistics*. London: Longman, 204–20.

Binnick, R. (1991) *Time and the Verb: A Guide to Tense and Aspect*. New York: Oxford University Press.

Birdsong, D. (1995) Iconicity, markedness, and processing constraints in frozen locutions. In Landsberg, M. (ed) *Syntactic Iconicity and Linguistic Freezes: The Human Dimension*. Berlin: Mouton de Gruyter, 31–45.

Blanche-Benveniste, C. (1982) Examen de la notion de subordination. *Recherche sur le Français Parlé* 4: 71–115.

Blanche-Benveniste, C. (1993) Repetitions de lexique et glissement vers la gauche. *Recherches sur le Français Parlé* 12: 9–34.

Blanche-Benveniste, C. (1995) De la rareté de certains phénomènes syntaxiques en français parlé. *French Language Studies* 5 (1): 17–29.

Blasco, M. (1995) Dislocation et thématisation en français parlé. *Recherche sur le Français Parlé* 13: 45–65.

Blommaert, J. (1991) How much culture is there in intercultural communication? In Blommaert, J. and Verschueren, J. (eds) *The Pragmatics of International and Intercultural Communication*. Amsterdam: John Benjamins, 13–31.

Boden, D. and Zimmerman, D. H. (eds) (1991) *Talk and Social Structure: Studies in Ethnomethodology and Conversation Analysis*. Cambridge: Polity Press.

Bolinger, D. (1976) Meaning and memory. *Forum Linguisticum* 1 (1): 1–14.

Boogaart, R. (1996) Tense and temporal ordering in English and Dutch indirect speech. In Janssen, T. and Van der Wurff, W. (eds) *Reported Speech: Forms and Functions of the Verb*. Amsterdam: John Benjamins, 213–35.

Boyer, A. (1694) *The Compleat French-Master for Ladies and Gentlemen*. London: Tho. Salisbury.

Bradford, B. (1988) *Intonation in Context* (student's and teacher's book). Cambridge University Press.

Brazil, D. (1985) *The Communicative Value of Intonation in English*. Birmingham: English Language Research, University of Birmingham.

Brazil, D. (1995) *A Grammar of Speech*. Oxford University Press.

Bressan, D. (1979) Idioms and second language teaching. *Teanga* 1: 31–40.

Brinton, L. (1987) The aspectual nature of states and habits. *Folia Linguistica* XXI (2–4): 195–214.

Brown, P. and Levinson, S. (1987) *Politeness: Some Universals in Language Usage*. Cambridge University Press.

Bublitz, W. (1988) *Supportive Fellow-Speakers and Cooperative Conversations*. Amsterdam: John Benjamins.

Bublitz, W. (1989) Repetition in spoken discourse. In Mullenbrock, H.-J. and Noll-Wieman, R. (eds) *Anglistentag (1988) Göttingen: Vortrage.* Tübingen: Niemeyer, 352–68.

Cambridge International Dictionary of Idioms (1998) Cambridge University Press.

Carter, R. A., Hughes, R. and McCarthy, M. J. (1995) Discourse context as a predictor of grammatical choice. In Graddol, D. and Thomas, S. (eds) *Language in a Changing Europe.* Clevedon: BAAL/Mutilingual Matters, 47–54.

Carter, R. A. and McCarthy, M. J. (1995a) Discourse and creativity: bridging the gap between language and literature. In Cook, G. and Seidlhofer, B. *Principle and Practice in Applied Linguistics. Studies in Honour of H. G. Widdowson.* Oxford University Press, 303–21.

Carter, R. A. and McCarthy, M. J. (1995b) Grammar and the spoken language. *Applied Linguistics* 16 (2): 141–58.

Carter, R. A. and McCarthy, M. J. (1997) *Exploring Spoken English.* Cambridge University Press.

Carterette, E. and Jones, M. H. (1974) *Informal Speech.* Berkeley and Los Angeles: University of California Press.

Celce-Murcia, M. (1991) Discourse Analysis and Grammar Instruction. *Annual Review of Applied Linguistics* 11 [1990] 135–51.

Černák, F. (1994) Idiomatics. In Luelsdorff, P. A. (ed) *The Prague School of Structural and Functional Linguistics: a Short Introduction.* Amsterdam: John Benjamins, 185–95.

Chadwyck-Healcy, (1994) *The Nineteenth Century on CD-ROM. Bibliographic Records.*

Chafe, W. (1982) Integration and involvement in speaking, writing, and oral literature. In Tannen, D. (ed) *Spoken and Written Language: Exploring Orality and Literacy.* Norwood, New Jersey: Ablex Publishing Corporation, 35–53.

Chafe, W. (1992) The importance of corpus linguistics to understanding the nature of language. In Svartvik, J. (ed) *Directions in Corpus Linguistics.* Berlin: Mouton de Gruyter, 79–97.

Chafe, W., Du Bois, J. and Thompson, S. (1991) Towards a new corpus of spoken American English. In Aijmer, K. and Altenberg, B. (eds) *English Corpus Linguistics.* London: Longman, 64–82.

Channell, J. (1994) *Vague Language.* Oxford University Press.

Chappell, H. (1980) Is the *get-passive* adversative? *Papers in Linguistics* 13 (3): 411–52.

Choul, J.-C. (1982) Si muove, ma non troppo: an inquiry into the non-metaphorical status of idioms and phrases. In Herzfeld, M. and Lenhart, M. (eds) *Semiotics.* New York: Plenum, 89–98.

Christie, F. (1986) Writing in schools: generic structures as ways of meaning. In Couture, B. (ed) *Functional Approaches to Writing Research Perspectives*. London: Frances Pinter, 221–39.

Clark, A. (1946) *Spoken English*. Edinburgh: Oliver and Boyd.

Clark, H. and Gerrig, R. (1990) Quotations as demonstrations. *Language* 66: 764–805.

COBUILD (1995) *Collins Cobuild English Language Dictionary*. London: Collins.

Cohen, A. (1996) Developing the ability to perform speech acts. *Studies in Second Language Acquisition* 18: 253–67.

Collins, P. (1996) *Get*-passives in English. *World Englishes* 15 (1): 43–56.

Collins, P. and Peters, P. (1988) The Australian corpus project. In Kyto M., Ihalainen, O. and Rissanen, M. (eds) *Corpus Linguistics, Hard and Soft*. Amsterdam: Rodopi, 103–20.

Compton, J. (ed) (1941) *Spoken English*. London: Methuen and Co. Ltd.

Comrie, B. (1986) Tense in indirect speech, *Folia Linguistica* 20 (3–4): 265–296.

Coningham, C. G. (1894) *Practical Business Conversation*. Yokohama: Kelly & Walsh Ltd.

Cook, G. (1989) *Discourse*. Oxford University Press.

Cook, G. (1990) Transcribing infinity: problems of context presentation. *Journal of Pragmatics* 14: 1–24.

Coulmas, F. (1979) On the sociolinguistic relevance of routine formulae. *Journal of Pragmatics* 3: 239–66.

Coulmas, F. (ed) (1981a) *Conversational Routine*. The Hague: Mouton.

Coulmas, F. (1981b) Idiomaticity as a problem of pragmatics. In Parret, H., Sbisà, M. and Verschueren, J. (eds) *Possibilities and Limitations of Pragmatics*. Amsterdam: John Benjamins, 139–51.

Coulmas, F. (1985a) Direct and indirect speech: general problems and problems of Japanese. *Journal of Pragmatics* 9 (1): 41–63.

Coulmas, F. (1985b) Nobody dies in Shangri-la: direct and indirect speech across languages. *Georgetown University Round Table on Languages and Linguistics*: 140–53.

Coulmas, F. (1986) Reported speech: some general issues. In Coulmas, F. (ed) *Direct and Indirect Speech*. Berlin: Mouton de Gruyter, 1–28.

Coupland, N. (1983) Patterns of encounter management: further arguments for discourse variables. *Language in Society* 12: 459–76.

Cowie, A. P. (1988) Stable and creative aspects of vocabulary use. In Carter, R. A. and McCarthy, M. J. (eds) *Vocabulary and Language Teaching*. London: Longman, 126–39.

Cowie, A. P. and Mackin, R. (1975) *Oxford Dictionary of Current Idiomatic English*. Volume 1 Oxford University Press.

Crowdy, S. (1993) Spoken corpus design. *Literary and Linguistic Computing* 8 (2): 259–265.

Crowdy, S. (1994) Spoken corpus transcription. *Literary and Linguistic Computing* 9 (1): 25–8.

Crymes, R. (1968) *Some Systems of Substitution Correlations in Modern American English*. The Hague: Mouton.

Crystal, D. (1995) Refining stylistic discourse categories. In Melchers, G. and Warren, B. (eds) *Studies in Anglistics*. Stockholm: Almqvist and Wiksell, 35–46.

Diaz, O. (1986) 'Partir du bon pneu': L'expression idiomatique à travers l'expression publicitaire. *Glottodidactica* 18: 75–82.

Dolz, J. and Schneuwly, B. (1996) Genres et progression en expression orale et écrite. Éléments de réflexions à propos d'une expérience romande. *Enjeux* 37/38: 49–75.

Downing, A. and Locke, P. (1992) *A University Course in English Grammar*. London: Prentice Hall.

Drew, P. and Holt, E. (1988) Complainable matters: the use of idiomatic expressions in making complaints. *Social Problems* 35 (4): 398–417.

Drew, P. and Holt, E. (1995) Idiomatic expressions and their role in the organisation of topic transition in conversation. In Everaert, M., van der Linden, E.-J., Schenk A. and Schreuder, R. (eds) *Idioms: Structural and Psychological Perspectives*. Hillsdale NJ: Lawrence Erlbaum Associates, 117–32.

Duranti, A. (1983) Samoan speechmaking across social events: one genre in and out of a 'fono'. *Language in Society* 12: 1–22.

Duranti, A. (1991) Four properties of speech-in-interaction. In Verschueren, J. (ed) *Pragmatics at Issue*. Amsterdam: John Benjamins, 133–50.

Duranti, A. and Ochs, E. (1979) Left dislocation in Italian conversation. In Givón, T. (ed) *Syntax and Semantics, Volume 12: Discourse and Syntax*. New York: Academic Press.

Dykema, K. (1949) The grammar of spoken English: Its relation to what is called English grammar. *American Speech* XXIV (1): 43–8.

Eastwood, J. (1994) *Oxford Guide to English Grammar*. Oxford University Press.

Edmondson, W., House J., Kasper, G. and Stemmer, B. (1984) Learning the pragmatics of discourse: a project report. *Applied Linguistics* 5 (2): 113–27.

Edwards, J. (1992) Design principles in the transcription of spoken discourse. In Svartvik, J. (ed) *Directions in Corpus Linguistics*. Berlin: Mouton de Gruyter, 129–44.

Eggins, S. and Slade, D. (1997) *Analysing Casual Conversation*. London: Cassell.

Ehlich, K. (1989) Deictic expressions and the connexity of text. In Conte,

M.-E., Petöfi, J. and Sözer, E. *Text and Discourse Connectedness*. Amsterdam: John Benjamins, 33–52.

Ely, R., Gleason, J., Narasimhan, B. and McCabe, A. (1995) Family talk about talk: mothers lead the way. *Discourse Processes* 19 (2): 201–18.

Emerson, C. (1983) The outer word and inner speech: Bakhtin, Vygotsky and the internalization of language. *Critical Inquiry* 10 (2): 245–64.

Engels, L. (1988) The effect of spoken and written-to-be-spoken English on word frequency counts of written English. In Klegraf, J. and Nehls, D. (eds) *Essays on the English Language and Applied Linguistics on the Occasion of Gerhard Nickel's 60th Birthday*. Heidelberg: Julius Groos Verlag, 407–25.

Ernst, T. (1980) Grist for the linguistic mill: idioms and 'extra' adjectives. *Journal of Linguistic Research* 1 (13): 51–68.

Esser, J. (1981) On the analysis of complex sentences: a study in the cohesion of spoken English. In Esser, J. and Hubler, A. (eds) *Forms and Functions*. Tübingen: Gunter Narr Verlag, 163–74.

Fairclough, N. (1995) *Critical Discourse Analysis*. London: Longman.

Fang, A. C. (1995) Distribution of infinitives in contemporary British English: a study based on the British ICE corpus. *Literary and Linguistic Computing* 10 (4): 247–57.

Fenk-Oczlon, G. (1989) Word frequency and word order in freezes. *Linguistics* 27: 517–56.

Fernando, C. (1996) *Idioms and Idiomaticity*. Oxford University Press.

Fernando, C. and Flavell, R. (1981) On idiom: critical views and perspectives. University of Exeter.

Fischer, K. and Drescher, M. (1996) Methods for the description of discourse particles: contrastive analysis. *Language Sciences* 18 (3–4): 853–61.

Fleischman, S. (1983) From pragmatics to grammar: diachronic reflections on complex pasts and futures in Romance. *Lingua* 60: 183–214.

Fleischman, S. (1990) *Tense and Narrativity*. London: Routledge.

Fleming, D. (1995) The search for an integrational account of language: Roy Harris and conversation analysis. *Language Sciences* 17 (1): 73–98.

Ford, C. (1994) Dialogic aspects of talk and writing: *because* on the interactive-edited continuum. *Text* 14 (4): 531–54.

Fox, B. and Thompson, S. (1990) A discourse explanation of the grammar of relative clauses in English conversation. *Language* 66 (2): 297–316.

Fraser, B. (1990) An approach to discourse markers. *Journal of Pragmatics* 14: 383–95.

Fraser, B. and Malamud-Makowski, M. (1996) English and Spanish contrastive discourse markers. *Language Sciences* 18 (3–4): 863–81.

Fretheim, T. (1995) Why Norwegian right-dislocated phrases are not afterthoughts. *Nordic Journal of Linguistics* 18 (1): 31–54.

Fronek, J. (1982) *Thing* as a function word. *Linguistics* 20: 633–54.

Gardner, R. (1987) The identification and role of topic in spoken interaction. *Semiotica* 65 (1/2): 129–41.

Geluykens, R. (1989) The syntactization of interactional processes: some typological evidence. *Belgian Journal of Linguistics* 4: 91–103.

Geluykens, R. (1992) *From Discourse Process to Grammatical Construction: on Left-dislocation in English*. Amsterdam: John Benjamins.

Genette, G. (1988) *Narrative Discourse Revisited*. Translated by J. E. Lewin. Ithaca NY: Cornell University.

Gibbon, D. (1981) Idiomaticity and functional variation: a case study of international amateur radio talk. *Language in Society* 10 (1): 21–42.

Giles H, Coupland, J. and Coupland, N. (1991) Accommodation theory: communication, context and consequences. In Giles, H., Coupland, J. and Coupland, N. (eds) *Contexts of Accommodation Developments in Applied Sociolinguistics*. Cambridge University Press, 1–68.

Givón, T. and Yang, L. (1994) The rise of the English *get-passive*. In Fox, B. and Hopper, P. J. (eds) *Voice: Form and Function*. Amsterdam: Benjamins, 119–49.

Gnutzmann, C. (1991) Linguistic and pedagogical aspects of English passive constructions. *Teanga* 11: 48–65.

Goodell, E. W. (1987) The treatment of tense in indirect speech. *TESOL Quarterly* 21 (2): 305–325.

Goodwin, C. (1984) Notes on story structure and the organisation of participation. In Atkinson, J. and Heritage, J. (eds) *Structures of Social Action: Studies in Conversation Analysis*. Cambridge University Press, 225–46.

Gottlieb, H. (1992) Idioms into Danish. In Nielsen, J. E. (ed) *Words that Teem with Meaning: Copenhagen Views on Lexicography*. Copenhagen: Museum Tusculanum Press, University of Copenhagen, 56–80.

Granger, S. (1983) *The Be + Past Participle Construction in Spoken English*. Amsterdam: North Holland.

Guitart, J. M. (1989) On Spanish cleft sentences. In Kirschner, C. and Decesaris, J. (eds) *Studies in Romance Linguistics*. Amsterdam: John Benjamins.

Gustafsson, M. (1975) *Binomial Expressions in Present-day English*. University of Turku.

Haegeman, L. (1983a) *The Semantics of **Will** in Present-day British English: A Unified Account*. Brussels: Koninklijke Academie.

Haegeman, L. (1983b) Be going to, gaan, and aller: some observations on the expression of future time. *International Review of Applied Linguistics in Language Teaching* XXI (2): 155–7.

Haegeman, L. (1989) Be going to and will: a pragmatic account. *Journal of Linguistics* 25 (2): 291–317.

Haiman, J. (1978) Conditionals are topics. *Language* 54 (3): 564–89.

Hale, E. E. (1903) Ideas on rhetoric in the 16th century. *PMLA* 18: 424–44.

Halliday, M. A. K. (1978) *Language as Social Semiotic.* London: Edward Arnold.

Halliday, M. A. K. and Hasan, R. (1976) *Cohesion in English.* London: Longman.

Harder, P. (1980) Discourse as self-expression: on the reduced personality of the second language learner. *Applied Linguistics* 1 (3): 262–70.

Harris, R. (1990) On redefining linguistics. In Davis, H. and Taylor, T. (eds) *Redefining Linguistics.* London: Routledge, 18–52.

Hasan, R. (1984) Coherence and cohesive harmony. In Flood, J. (ed) *Understanding Reading Comprehension.* Newark, Delaware: International Reading Association, 181–219.

Hasan, R. (1985) The structure of a text. In Halliday, M. A. K. and Hasan, R. *Language, Context and Text: Aspects of Language in a Social-semiotic Perspective.* Oxford University Press, 52–69.

Hasan, R. (1992) Speech genre, semiotic mediation and the development of higher mental functions. *Language Sciences* 14 (4): 489–528.

Hatcher, A. G. (1949) To get/be invited. *Modern Language Notes* 64: 433–46.

Heilenman, L. K. and McDonald, J. L. (1993) Dislocated sequences and word order in French: a processing approach. *Journal of French Language Studies* 3 (2): 165–90.

Heritage, J. and Watson, D. (1979) Formulations as conversational objects. In Psathas, G. (ed) *Everyday Language.* New York: Irvington Press, 123–62.

Herries, J. (1773) *The Elements of Speech.* London: E & C Dilly.

Higdon, D. L. and Bender, T. K. (1983) *A concordance to Conrad's* Under Western Eyes. New York: Garland Publishing.

Hockett, C. (1986) Grammar for the hearer. In McGregor, G. (ed) *Language for Hearers.* Oxford: Pergamon Press, 49–68.

Hoey, M. P. (1983) *On the Surface of Discourse.* London: Allen and Unwin.

Hoey, M. P. (1991a) *Patterns of Lexis in Text.* Oxford University Press.

Hoey, M. P. (1991b) Some properties of spoken discourse. In Bowers, R. and Brumfit, C. (eds) *Applied Linguistics and English Language Teaching.* Basingstoke: Macmillan/MEP.

Hoffmann, L. (1989) Towards a pragmatically founded grammar. In Graustein, G. and Leitner, G. (eds) *Reference Grammars and Modern Linguistic Theory.* Tübingen: Max Niemeyer, 111–32.

Holmes, J. (1738) *The Art of Rhetoric Made Easy, or the Elements of Oratory, etc.* London (no publisher).

Horman, W. (1519) *Vulgaria.* London (no publisher).

Hong, B. (1985) Politeness in Chinese: impersonal pronouns and personal greetings. *Anthropological Linguistics* 27 (2): 204–13.

Hopper, P. J. (1979) Aspect and foregrounding in discourse. In Givón, T. (ed) *Syntax and Semantics* Volume 12: *Discourse and Syntax*. New York: Academic Press, 213–41.

Hopper, P. J. and Thompson, S. (1993) Language universals, discourse pragmatics, and semantics. *Language Sciences* 15 (4): 357–76.

Hopper R., Knapp, M. L. and Scott, L. (1981) Couples' personal idioms: exploring intimate talk. *Journal of Communication* 31 (1): 23–33.

House, J. (1985) Contrastive discourse analysis and universals in language usage. *Papers and Studies in Contrastive Linguistics* 20: 5–14.

Houtkoop, H. and Mazeland, H. (1985) Turns and discourse units in everyday conversation. *Journal of Pragmatics* 9: 595–619.

Houtkoop-Steenstra, H. (1991) Opening sequences in Dutch telephone conversations. In Boden, D. and Zimmerman, D. (eds) *Talk and Social Structure*. Oxford: Polity Press.

Howes, D. H. (1966) A word count of spoken English. *Journal of Verbal Learning and Verbal Behaviour* 5: 572–606.

Huddleston, R. (1989) The treatment of tense in indirect speech. *Folia Linguistica* 23 (3–4): 335–340.

Hughes, R. (1996) *English in Speech and Writing*. London: Routledge.

Hughes, R. and McCarthy, M. J. (1998) From sentence to discourse: discourse grammar and English Language Teaching. *TESOL Quarterly* 32 (2): 263–287.

Hymes, D. (1972) Models of the interaction of language and social life. In Gumperz, J. and Hymes, D. (eds) *Directions in Sociolinguistics: The Ethnography of Communication*. New York: Rinehart and Winston Inc, 35–71.

Iacobucci, C. (1990) Accounts, formulations and goal attainment strategies in service encounters. In Tracy, K. and Coupland, N. (eds) *Multiple Goals in Discourse*. Clevedon: Multilingual Matters Ltd, 85–99.

Jackson, H. (1990) OCP and the computer analysis of texts: The Birmingham Polytechnic experience. *Literary and Linguistic Computing* 5 (1): 86–8.

Jaszczolt, K. and Turner, K. (eds) (1996) *Contrastive Semantics and Pragmatics* Volume II: *Discourse Strategies*. Oxford: Elsevier Science Ltd.

Jaworski, A. (1990) The acquisition and perception of formulaic language and foreign language teaching. *Multilingua* 9 (4): 397–411.

Jefferson, G. (1978) Sequential aspects of storytelling in conversation. In Schenkein, J. (ed) *Studies in the Organisation of Conversational Interaction*. New York: Academic Press, 219–48.

Johnstone, B. (1987) 'He says … so I said': verb tense alternation and narrative depictions of authority in American English. *Linguistics* 25 (1): 33–52.

Joos, M. (1964) *The English Verb: Form and Meanings*. Madison: University of Wisconsin Press.

Källgren, G. and Prince, E. F. (1989) Swedish VP-topicalisation and Yiddish verb-topicalisation. *Nordic Journal of Linguistics* 12: 47–58.

Kehe, D. and Kehe, P. D. (1989) Maintaining teacher control during pair/ group work. *Múinteoir Teanga* 2 (2): 35–9.

Kelly Hall, J. (1995). (Re)creating our worlds with words: a sociohistorical perspective of face-to-face interaction. *Applied Linguistics* 16 (2): 206–32.

Kirk, J. (1992) The Northern Ireland transcribed corpus of speech. In Leitner, G. (ed) *New Directions in English Language Corpora*. Berlin: Mouton de Gruyter, 65–73.

Knowles, G. (1990) The use of spoken and written corpora in the teaching of language and linguistics. *Literary and Linguistic Computing* 5 (1): 45–8.

Kooij, J. (1968) Compounds and idioms. *Lingua* 21: 250–68.

Komter, M. (1991) *Conflict and Cooperation in Job Interviews: A Study of Talk, Tasks and Ideas*. Amsterdam: John Benjamins.

Labov, W. (1972) *Language in the Inner City*. Oxford: Basil Blackwell.

Lakoff, R. (1970) Tense and its relation to participants. *Language* 46: 838–49.

Lakoff, R. (1971) Passive resistance. *Papers from the Seventh Regional Meeting. Chicago Linguistic Society* 149–62.

Lambrecht, K. (1988) Presentational cleft constructions in spoken French. In Haiman, J. and Thompson, S. (eds) *Clause Combining in Grammar and Discourse*. Amsterdam: John Benjamins.

Larson, M. (1978) *The Functions of Reported Speech in Discourse*. Dallas: The Summer Institute of Linguistics and the University of Texas at Arlington.

Lattey, E. (1986) Pragmatic classification of idioms as an aid for the language learner. *International Review of Applied Linguistics* XXIV (3): 217–33.

Lebra, T. S. (1987) The cultural significance of silence in Japanese. *Multilingua* 6 (4): 343–57.

Leech, G. (1987) *Meaning and the English Verb*. 2nd edition. London: Longman.

Lewis, M. (1993) *The Lexical Approach: The State of ELT and a Way Forward*. Hove UK: LTP.

Lindenfeld, J. (1990) *Speech and Sociability at French Urban Market Places*. Amsterdam: John Benjamins.

Longman Dictionary of English Idioms. (1979) London: Longman.

Loveday, L. (1982) *The Sociolinguistics of Learning and Using a Non-native Language*. Oxford: Pergamon.

Louw, B. (1993) Irony in the text or insincerity in the writer? The diagnostic potential of semantic prosodies. In Baker M., Francis, G. and Tognini-Bonelli, E. (eds) *Text and Technology: In Honour of John Sinclair*. Philadelphia: Benjamins, 157–76.

Low, G. D. (1988) On teaching metaphor. *Applied Linguistics* 9 (2): 125–47.

Low, G. (1995) Intensifiers and hedges in questionnaire items and the lexical invisibility hypothesis. *Applied Linguistics* 16 (4): 505–41.

Lucy, J. (ed) (1993) *Reflexive Language*. Cambridge University Press.

Mair, C. (1992) Problems in the compilation of a corpus of standard Caribbean English: A pilot study. In Leitner, G. (ed) *New Directions in English Language Corpora*. Berlin: Mouton de Gruyter, 75–96.

Makkai, A. (1978) Idiomaticity as a language universal. In Greenberg, J. H. (ed) *Universals of Human Language, Volume 3: Word Structure*. Stanford CA: Stanford University Press, 401–48.

Malkiel, Y. (1959) Studies in irreversible binomials. *Lingua* 8: 113–60.

Martin, J. (1992) *English Text: System and Structure*. Amsterdam: John Benjamins.

Martin, W. (1988) Variation in lexical frequency. In Van Reenen, P. and Van Reenen-Stein, K. (eds) *Distributions spatiales et temporelles, constellations des manuscrits*. Amsterdam: John Benjamins, 139–52.

Mathis, T. and Yule, G. (1994) Zero quotatives. *Discourse Processes* 18: 63–76.

Mayes, P. (1990) Quotation in spoken English. *Studies in Language* 14 (2): 325–63.

McCarthy, M. J. (1984) A new look at vocabulary in EFL. *Applied Linguistics* 5 (1): 12–22.

McCarthy, M. J. (1988) Some vocabulary patterns in conversation. In Carter, R. A. and McCarthy, M. J. *Vocabulary and Language Teaching*. London: Longman, 181–200.

McCarthy, M. J. (1991) *Discourse Analysis for Language Teachers*. Cambridge University Press.

McCarthy, M. J. (1992a) Interactive lexis: prominence and paradigms. In Coulthard, R. M. (ed) *Advances in Spoken Discourse Analysis*. London: Routledge, 197–208.

McCarthy, M. J. (1992b) English idioms in use. *Revista Canaria de Estudios Ingleses* 25: 55–65.

McCarthy, M. J. (1994) *It, this and that*. In Coulthard, M. (ed) *Advances in Written Text Analysis*. London: Routledge, 266–75.

McCarthy, M. J. and Carter, R. A. (1994) *Language as Discourse: Perspectives for Language Teaching*. London: Longman.

McCarthy, M. J. and Carter, R. A. (1997a) Written and spoken vocabulary. In Schmitt, N. and McCarthy, M. J. (eds) *Second Language Vocabulary: Description, Acquisition and Pedagogy*. Cambridge University Press, 20–39.

McCarthy, M. J. and Carter, R. A. (1997b) Grammar, tails and affect: constructing expressive choices in discourse. *Text* 17 (3): 405–29.

McCarthy, M. J. and O'Dell, F. (1994) *English Vocabulary in Use: upper-intermediate and advanced*. Cambridge University Press.

McGlone, M. S., Glucksberg, S. and Cacciari, C. (1994) Semantic productivity and idiom comprehension. *Discourse Processes* 17: 167–90.

McGregor, G. and White, R. (1990) *Reception and Response: Hearer Creativity and the Analysis of Spoken and Written Texts*. London: Routledge.

McTear, M. (1980) The pragmatics of *because*. In McCormack, W. and Izzo, H. (eds) *The Sixth LACUS Forum 1979*. Columbia SC: Hornbeam, 455–63.

Merritt, M. (1976) On questions following questions in service encounters. *Language in Society* 5: 315–57.

Miller, J. (1995) Does spoken language have sentences? In Palmer, F. R. (ed) *Grammar and Meaning*. Cambridge University Press, 116–35.

Mitchell, A. G. (1957) *Spoken English*. London: Macmillan and Co. Ltd.

Mitchell, T. F. (1957) The language of buying and selling in Cyrenaica: a situational statement. *Hespéris* XLIV: 31–71.

Moeran, B. (1984) Advertising sounds as cultural discourse. *Language and Communication* 4 (2): 147–58.

Moon, R. (1992) Textual aspects of fixed expressions in learners' dictionaries. In Arnaud, P. J. and Béjoint, H. (eds) *Vocabulary and Applied Linguistics*. Basingstoke: Macmillan, 13–27.

Moon, R. (1997) Vocabulary connections: multi-word items in English. In Schmitt, N. and McCarthy, M. J. (eds). (1997) *Second Language Vocabulary: Description, Acquisition and Pedagogy*. Cambridge University Press, 40–63.

Mutsu, H. 1894 *A Japanese Conversation Course*. Tokio [sic]: Z. P. Maruya & Co.

Nash, W. (1990) *Language in Popular Fiction*. London: Routledge.

Nattinger, J. R. and DeCarrico, J. S. (1992) *Lexical Phrases and Language Teaching*. Oxford University Press.

Nelson, F. (1992) Language corpora B.C. In Svartvik, J. (ed) *Directions in Corpus Linguistics*. Berlin: Mouton de Gruyter, 17–32.

Nelson, G. (1996) The design of the corpus. In Greenbaum, S. (ed) *Comparing English Worldwide: the International Corpus of English*. Oxford University Press, 27–35.

Noguchi, R. R. (1987) The dynamics of rule conflict in English and Japanese conversation. *International Review of Applied Linguistics* 25 (1): 15–24.

Norrick, N. (1986) Stock similes. *Journal of Literary Semantics* XV (1): 39–52.

Norrick, N. (1988) Binomial meaning in texts. *Journal of English Linguistics* 21 (1): 72–87.

Nyyssönen, H. (1992) Lexis in discourse. In Lindeberg, A.-C., Enkvist, N. E. and

Wikberg, K. (eds) *Nordic Research on text and Discourse*. Åbo Akademis Förlag, 73–80.

Ochs E., Schegloff, E. and Thompson, S. (eds) (1996) *Interaction and Grammar*. Cambridge University Press.

Ono, T. and Suzuki, R. (1992) Word order variability in Japanese conversation: motivations and grammaticization. *Text* 12 (3): 429–45.

Oostdijk, N. (1990) The language of dialogue in fiction. *Literary and Linguistic Computing* 5 (3): 235–41.

Owen, C. (1996) Do concordances require to be consulted? *ELT Journal* 50 (3): 219–24.

Page, N. (1973) *Speech in the English Novel*. London: Macmillan.

Palacas, A. (1993) Attribution semantics: linguistic worlds and point of view. *Discourse Processes* 16: 239–77.

Palmer, H. E., Blandford, F. G. (1924) *A Grammar of Spoken English*. First edition. Third edition 1969, revised and rewritten by R. Kingdon. Cambridge: Heffer.

Peacham, H. (1577) *The Garden of Eloquence etc.* London: H. Jackson.

Person, R. (1996) Restarts in conversation and literature. *Language and Communication* 16 (1): 61–70.

Persson, G. (1974) *Repetition in English: Part I, Sequential Repetition*. Uppsala: Acta Universitatis Upsaliensi.

Peterson, P. (1982) Anaphoric reference to facts, propositions and events. *Linguistics and Philosophy* 5 (2): 235–76.

Philips, S. (1985) Reported Speech as Evidence in an American Trial. *Georgetown University Round Table on Languages and Linguistics*: 154–70.

Polanyi, L. (1981) Telling the same story twice. *Text* 1 (4): 315–36.

Polanyi, L. (1982) Linguistic and social constraints on storytelling. *Journal of Pragmatics* 6 (5/6): 509–24.

Pomerantz, A. (1984) Agreeing and disagreeing with assessments: some features of preferred/dispreferred turn shapes. In Atkinson, J. and Heritage, J. (eds) (1984) *Structures of Social Action*. Cambridge University Press, 57–101.

Powell, M. J. (1992) Semantic/pragmatic regularities in informal lexis: British speakers in spontaneous conversational settings. *Text* 12 (1): 19–58.

Prodromou, L. (1997) Global English and its struggle against the octopus. *IATEFL Newsletter* 135: 12–14.

Psathas, G. (ed) (1979) *Everyday Language: Studies in Ethnomethodology*. New York: Irvington Publications, Inc.

Psathas, G. (1995) *Conversation Analysis: The Study of Talk-in-Interaction*. London: Sage Publications.

Quirk, R., Greenbaum, S., Leech, G. and Svartvik, J. (1985) *A Comprehensive Grammar of the English Language*. London: Longman.

Reagan, R. (1987) The syntax of English idioms: can the dog be put on? *Journal of Psycholinguistic Research* 16 (5): 417–41.

Reid, I. (ed) (1987) *The Place of Genre in Learning: Current Debates*. Victoria: Deakin University Press.

Reyes, G. (1984) *Polifonía textual: la citación en el relato literario*. Madrid: Gredos.

Rivero, M. (1980) On left-dislocation and topicalisation in Spanish. *Linguistic Inquiry* 11 (2): 363–93.

Robinson, R. (1617) *The Art of Pronunciation*. London (no publisher).

Romaine, S. and Lange, D. (1991) The use of Like as a marker of reported speech and thought: a case of grammaticalisation in process. *American Speech* 66 (3): 227–79.

Rosaldo, M. (1982) The things we do with words: Ilongot speech act and speech act theory in philosophy. *Language in Society* 11: 203–37.

Rundell, M. (1995a) The BNC: A spoken corpus. *Modern English Teacher* 4 (2): 13–15.

Rundell, M. (1995b) The word on the street. *English Today* 11 (3): 29–35.

Sacks H., Schegloff, E. A. and Jefferson, G. (1974) A simplest systematics for the organisation of turn-taking for conversation. *Language* 50 (4): 696–735.

Scarcella, R. (1983) Developmental trends in the acquisition of conversational competence by adult second language learners. In Wolfson, N. and Judd, E. (eds) *Sociolinguistics and Language Acquisition*. Rowley MA Newbury House.

Scarcella, R. and Brunak, J. (1981) On speaking politely in a second language. *International Journal of the Sociology of Language*: 59–75.

Schegloff, E. A. and Sacks, H. (1973) Opening up closings. *Semiotica* 8 (4): 289–327.

Schenkein, J. (1980) A taxonomy for repeating action sequences in natural conversation. In Butterworth, B. (ed) *Language Production:* Volume 1: *Speech and Talk*. London: Academic Press, 21–47.

Schiffrin, D. (1994) *Approaches to Discourse*. Oxford: Basil Blackwell.

Schiffrin, D. (1987) *Discourse Markers*. Cambridge University Press.

Schleppegrell, M. (1992) Subordination and linguistic complexity. *Discourse Processes* 15 (1): 117–31.

Schmitt, N. and McCarthy, M. J. (eds) (1997) *Second Language Vocabulary: Description, Acquisition and Pedagogy*. Cambridge University Press.

Schonell, F., Meddleton, I., Shaw, B., Routh, M., Popham, D., Gill, G., Mackrell, G. and Stephens, C. (1956) *A Study of the Oral Vocabulary of Adults*. Brisbane and London: University of Queensland Press/University of London Press.

Scotton, C. (1985) What the heck, sir: Style shifting and lexical colouring as features of powerful language. In Street, R., Capella, J. and Giles, H. (eds) *Sequence and Patterning in Communicative Behaviour*. London: Edward Arnold, 103–19.

Sherry, R. (1550) *A Treatise of Schemes and Tropes . . . Gathered out of the Best Grammarians and Oratours*. London: John Day.

Sifianou, M. (1989) On the telephone again. Differences in telephone behaviour: England versus Greece. *Language in Society* 18 (4): 527–44.

Sinclair, J. McH. (1995) Corpus typology – a framework for classification. In Melchers, G. and Warren, B. (eds) *Studies in Anglistics*. Stockholm: Almqvist and Wiksell, 17–33.

Sinclair, J. McH. and Coulthard, R. M. (1975) *Towards an Analysis of Discourse*. Oxford University Press.

Skehan, P. (1996) A framework for the implementation of task-based instruction. *Applied Linguistics* 17 (1): 38–62.

Stein, G. (1979) *Studies in the Function of the Passive*. Tübingen: Gunter Narr Verlag.

Stenström, A.-B. (1990) Lexical items peculiar to spoken discourse. In Svartvik, J. (ed) *The London-Lund Corpus of Spoken English*. Lund: Lund University Press, 137–75.

Stenström, A.-B. (1994) *An Introduction to Spoken Interaction*. London: Longman.

Stern, K. (1997) The Longman Spoken American Corpus: Providing an in-depth analysis of everyday English. *Longman Language Review* 3: 14–17.

Strässler, J. (1982) *Idioms in English: a Pragmatic Analysis*. Tübingen: Gunter Narr Verlag.

Stubbe, M. and Holmes, J. (1995) *You know, eh* and other 'exasperating expressions': an analysis of social and stylistic variation in the use of pragmatic devices in a sample of New Zealand English. *Language and Communication* 15 (1): 63–88.

Stubbs, M. (1986) Lexical density: a computational technique and some findings. In Coulthard, R. M. (ed) *Talking About Text*. Birmingham: English Language Research, 27–42.

Stubbs, M. (1996) *Text and Corpus Analysis*. Oxford: Blackwell.

Sussex, R. (1982) A note on the get-passive construction. *Australian Journal of Linguistics* 2: 83–95.

Svartvik, J. (1966) *On Voice in the English Verb*. The Hague: Mouton.

Svartvik, J. (ed) (1990) *The London-Lund Corpus of Spoken English: Description and Research*. Lund University Press.

Svartvik, J. and Quirk, R. (1980) *A Corpus of English Conversation*. Lund: Liberläromedel.

Swales, J. (1990) *Genre Analysis*. Cambridge University Press.

Swan, M. (1980/1995) *Practical English Usage*. Oxford University Press.

Tamony, P. (1982) 'Like Kelly's nuts' and related expressions. *Comments on Etymology* 11 (9–10): 8–10.

Tannen, D. (1986) Introducing constructed dialogue in Greek and American conversational and literary narrative. In Coulmas, F. (ed) *Direct and Indirect Speech*. Berlin: Mouton de Gruyter, 311–32.

Tannen, D. (1988) Hearing voices in conversation, fiction and mixed genres. In Tannen, D. (ed) *Linguistics in Context: Connecting Observation and Understanding*. Norwood, NJ: Ablex, 89–113.

Tannen, D. (1989) *Talking Voices*. Cambridge University Press.

Testa, R. (1988) Interruptive strategies in English and Italian conversation: smooth versus contrastive linguistic preferences. *Multilingua* 7 (3): 285–312.

Thomas, J. (1984) Cross-cultural discourse as 'unequal encounter': towards a pragmatic analysis. *Applied Linguistics* 5 (3): 226–35.

Thompson, G. (1994) *Reporting*. Collins-Cobuild English Guides no. 5 London: HarperCollins.

Thomspon, G. (1996) Voices in the text: discourse perspectives on language reports. *Applied Linguistics*. 17 (4): 501–30.

Thompson, S. E. (1997) Presenting Research: A Study of Interaction in Academic Monologue. Unpublished PhD Dissertation. University of Liverpool.

Tognini-Bonelli, E. (1996) *Corpus: Theory and Practice*. Birmingham: TWC (also forthcoming, to be published by Benjamins, Amsterdam).

Tottie, G. (1983) The missing link? or, why is there twice as much negation in spoken English as in written English? In Jacobson, S. (ed) *Papers from the Second Scandinavian Symposium on Syntactic Variation 1983*. Stockholm: Almqvist and Wiksell International, 67–74.

Tracy, K. and Coupland, N. (1990) (eds) *Multiple Goals in Discourse*. Clevedon: Multilingual Matters.

Trevise, A. (1986) Is it transferable, topicalisation? In Kellerman, E. and Sharwood-Smith, M. (eds) *Crosslinguistic Influence in Second Language Acquisition*. New York: Pergamon, 186–206.

Trueblood, T. (1933) Spoken English. *Quarterly Journal of Speech* 19: 513.

Tyler, A. E., Jeffries, A. A. and Davies, C. E. (1988) The effect of discourse structuring devices on listener perceptions of coherence in non-native university teachers' spoken discourse. *World Englishes* 7 (2): 101–10.

Ure, J. (1971) Lexical density and register differentiation. In Perren, G. E. and Trim, J. L. M. (eds) *Applications of Linguistics: Selected Papers of the Second International Congress of Applied Linguistics, Cambridge, 1969*. Cambridge University Press, 443–52.

Vakar, P. (1966) *A Word-Count of Spoken Russian*. Columbus, Ohio: OSU Press.

Valiouli, M. (1991) Right-dislocated anaphorically functioning nominals, concord and referential/attitudinal perspective. In *Proceedings: 5th Symposium on the Description and/or Comparison of English and Greek*. Thessaloniki: Aristotle University, 159–70.

Van Dijk, T. A. (1982) Episodes as units of discourse analysis. In Tannen, D. (ed) *Analyzing Discourse: Text and Talk*. Washington DC: Georgetown University Press, 177–95.

Vanrespaille, M. (1991) A semantic analysis of the English get-passive. *Interface* 5 (2): 95–112.

Ventola, E. (1987) *The Structure of Social Interaction: A Systemic Approach to the Semiotics of Service Encounters*. London: Frances Pinter.

Vorlat, E. (1985) 'Your marriage is going through a rocky patch': on idioms in the Lonely Hearts column. In Debusscher, G. and Van Noppen, J. (eds) *Communiquer et traduire: Hommages a Jean Dierick*. Brussels: Editions de l'Université de Bruxelles, 103–8.

Wald, B. (1983) Referents and topics within and across discourse units: observations from current vernacular English. In Klein-Andreu, F. (ed) *Discourse Perspectives on Syntax*. New York: Academic Press, 91–116.

Wales, M. L. (1983) The semantic distribution of aller + infinitive and the future tense in spoken French. *General Linguistics* 23 (1): 19–28.

Walter, B. (1988) *The Jury Summation as Speech Genre*. Amsterdam: John Benjamins.

Watts, I. (1740) *The Art of Reading and Writing English*. London: R. Hett and J. Bracstone.

Watts, R. J. (1989) Taking the pitcher to the 'well': native speakers' perception of their use of discourse markers in conversation. *Journal of Pragmatics* 13: 203–37.

Waugh, L. (1995) Reported speech in journalistic discourse: the relation of function and text. *Text* 15 (1): 129–73.

Wertsch, J. (1985) The semiotic mediation of mental life: L. S. Vygotsky and M. M. Bakhtin. In Mertz, E. and Parmentier, R. (eds) *Semiotic Mediation: Sociocultural and Psychological Perspectives*. London: Academic Press, 49–71.

White, B. (ed) (1932) *The Vulgaria of John Stanbridge and the Vulgaria of Robert Whittinton*. London: Kegan Paul, Trench, Trubner and Co. Ltd.

Wikberg, K. (1992) Discourse category and text type classification: procedural discourse in the Brown and the LOB corpora. In Leitner, G. (ed) *New Directions in English Language Corpora*. Berlin: Mouton de Gruyter, 247–61.

Widdowson, H. G. (1980) Models and fictions. *Applied Linguistics* 1 (2): 165–70.

Wilkins, D. A. (1976) *Notional Syllabuses*. Oxford University Press.

Williams, J. (1992) Planning, discourse marking and the comprehensibility of international teaching assistants. *TESOL Quarterly* 26 (4): 693–711.

Winter, E. O. (1982) *Towards a Contextual Grammar of English*. London: Allen & Unwin.

Ylänne-McEwen, V. (1997) Relational processes within a transactional setting: An investigation of travel agency discourse. Unpublished PhD dissertation. University of Wales, Cardiff.

Yngve, V. H. (1970) On getting a word in edgewise. *Papers from the 6th Regional Meeting, Chicago Linguistic Society*. Chicago: Chicago Linguistic Society.

Young, L. (1990) *Language as Behaviour, Language as Code: A Study of Academic English*. Amsterdam: John Benjamins.

Zelizer, B. (1989) 'Saying' as collective practice: quoting and differential address in the news. *Text* 9 (4): 369–88.

Zettersten, A. (1978) *A Word-Frequency List Based on American English Reportage*. København: Universitetsforlaget i København.

Zydatiss, W. (1986) Grammatical categories and their text functions – some implications for the content of reference grammars. In Leitner, G. (ed) *The English Reference Grammar: Language and Linguistics, Writers and Readers*. Tübingen: Max Niemeyer Verlag, 140–55.

Index